Incest

Also by Jean Renvoize

Children in Danger
Web of Violence

Jean Renvoize

Incest

A family pattern

Routledge & Kegan Paul
London and Henley

First published in 1982
by Routledge & Kegan Paul Ltd
39 Store Street, London WC1E 7DD and
Broadway House, Newtown Road,
Henley-on-Thames Oxon RG9 1EN
Set in 10/12pt Plantin by
Input Typesetting Ltd, London
and printed in Great Britain by
Billing & Sons Ltd Worcester
Reprinted 1983

British Library Cataloguing in Publication Data

Renvoize, Jean

   Incest: a family pattern.
   1. Incest
   I. Title
   306.7   HQ71

   ISBN 0–7100–9073–0

Contents

Acknowledgments

I am indebted to so many people for help given freely in the preparation of this book that it seems invidious to pick out individuals for special mention. There are, however, some whom it would be impossible not to thank publicly: in particular I want to express my gratitude to those who have talked openly and with insight about their personal experiences of incest.

In the United States I met with the hospitality for which Americans are famous. I owe especial gratitude to Hank Giarretto whose work in setting up the Child Sexual Abuse Treatment Program (CSATP) in Santa Clara County is extensively quoted, and to his wife, Anna Einfeld, and other colleagues including Eunice Peterson and Bee Brown. Joyce Moulton, counsellor and filmmaker, gave me unlimited help and introduced me to many people in the Seattle area. Among these I want particularly to thank Lucy Berliner and Doris Stevens of the Sexual Assault Center based at the Harborview Medical Center, Mavis Tsai of the University of Washington, psychologists Roger and Florence Wolfe, and Gary Wenet. I am also indebted to Mary Krentz Johnson, temporarily at San Francisco; Alvin Rosenfeld, Assistant Professor, Department of Psychiatry, Stanford University; Karin Meiselman, psychologist and author; Geri Hatcher of Los Angeles Social Services; Anne Topper of El Paso Social Services; Pat Wyka of the Victim Service Division of Colorado Springs Police; Bruce Gottlieb and Helen Alexander of the National Center for the Prevention and Treatment of Child Sexual Abuse and Neglect, Denver; Detective Mike Salvador, Aurora County, Colorado; Deborah Anderson, Hennepin County Attorney's Office; Caryl Bentley, Minneapolis; Allan Carlson, Hennepin County Child Protective Services Department; David Finkelhor, Department of Sociology and Anthropology, University of New Hampshire; Gene Abel of the New York Psychiatric Institute and members of the American Humane Association's Child Protection Division.

I also owe my especial thanks to Hugh de la Haye Davies, Principal Police Surgeon, Northamptonshire Police; Arnon Bentovim, Child Psychiatrist at the Great Ormond Street Hospital for Sick Children, and other fellow members of the BASPCAN Sub-Committee on Child Sexual Abuse; members of OPUS (Organization for Parents Under Stress), and Jean Moore, Senior Tutor, NSPCC.

Finally I owe a debt of gratitude to the Nuffield Foundation whose generous financial help enabled me to spend some time in the USA, without which stay this book would have been considerably poorer.

Introduction

The serious study of any social phenomenon goes through two phases. The first is the period of brainstorming, as new possible hypotheses about the causes of the phenomenon are added to the debate. The second is a period of refinement, when the wealth of theories challenges the scientist to find out which ones can really be empirically verified. Incest is still in its brainstorming phase, but pressure is building towards refinement. Perhaps soon we will have some systematic data about incest from which to begin the culling and weeding (Finkelhor 1978a).

Incest is no new social problem. Presumably there has never been a time when it was not happening. What is new is that it is now beginning to be discussed openly, studies are being set up, statistics collated and opinions formed. The last are frequently at odds with each other, but that is inevitable at this stage. There is not even universal agreement as to whether or not incest is a bad thing: in the United States quite a strong pro-incest lobby exists, although less complicated issues such as the increase in pornographic material (including films) which directly involve children recently raised such a furore that national protective legislation was passed at a speed that surprised even its proponents.

Articles on incest have appeared in nearly all the national magazines in Britain and America during the past few years, and radio and television have given time to a subject that a decade back would not have been considered suitable material for public exposure. This in itself causes concern among some: they fear that by making the subject over-familiar the abhorrence it arouses may disappear and be replaced by a tolerance they consider could only be harmful.

Is this a possibility? How inevitable is this abhorrence? Is it instinctive? Is it purely the product of a restrictive society? Since we know of no society which has ever allowed incest among all its members as a matter of course, and since – even in the few societies where it is allowed at all – it has always been restricted to certain members at certain times (Meiselman 1979), we may assume that a general prohibition on incest has always been considered necessary for the well-being of any sizeable group of people living together. Could this change?

Some suggest that the very strength of the taboo implies a universal desire to commit incestuous acts. But murder (other than that officially sanctioned by the state, such as in wars, capital punishment, etc.) is an action that also carries a powerful taboo. Few would suggest the strength of that taboo implies we all have murderous impulses which can only be controlled by such a taboo. There is, however, a difference in our feelings about incest and our feelings about murder. Could one reason for our weaker sense of abhorrence towards acts of murder be that we have become familiarized with it as a subject through 3,000 years of drama and literature? Although from Oedipus and Phaedra onwards incest has been used as a dramatic theme (currently there is an outburst of novels and films with incest as background or even foreground), it remains a comparative unknown, unthinkable and uncontemplated.

Perhaps the strength of such taboos owes more to the degree of social disruptiveness that would be caused if they did not exist than to any universal desire to act out the taboo? To what extent would widespread incest be socially disruptive – that is to say, how far would a breaking down of the incest taboo result in the decline of the family, the upsetting of morals and order? Extrapolating from contemporary statistics it seems, in fact, very likely that the frequency of incest has always been considerably higher than has ever been generally acknowledged, and yet the family has survived. One reason for this may be that childhood as we know it is a recent invention. Children as a group were not set apart as they are now: once you were old enough to work – and that could be as early as five or six years of age – you worked. After eight or nine you were a little adult, and were expected to behave as such. There was very little special indulgence towards children because of their tender age. Just as we have always known that child prostitution was rife in Victorian times, so we now know that incest was not the rarity even among the outwardly severe Victorian paterfamilias that it was generally supposed to be (Rush 1977). But always its occurrence was kept secret; the power structure of a family remained intact and society, at least, was unviolated.

But nowadays? Has not parental authority already so declined that an acceptance of incest, involving open sexuality and presumably equality between parent and child, would lead to the final demolition of the family structure as we know it? And perhaps thus to the breakdown of all authority? This argument which is sometimes used against opening up the subject of incest might have some validity if it bore any relation to the actual truth of what goes on in an incestuous family, in which in fact there is rarely any question of equality between the partners. Most fathers who have sex with their daughters are unusually authoritative within the family; they take what they want, however gently. The secret of incest tightens bonds rather than loosens them; the family becomes even more cemented together as a result of sexual abuse.

In America it was through the women's movement, together with the growing concern of the child protection lobby, that the prevalence of sexual abuse of children first came to light. Rape crisis centres and shelters for battered women found that unexpected numbers of young children who had been sexually abused by relatives were among their clients (an experience repeated in Britain when similar centres were set up). Feminists saw this as yet a further incidence of male power inflicting damage on females, and they supplied the main impetus toward the establishment of help and treatment for incest victims. But as knowledge has grown it has become evident that a large number of boys as well as girls are being abused, so the emphasis on the issue of male/female power has become less relevant.

Both the women's movement and the child protection lobby in the USA have sufficient political power and experience to ensure progress in bringing some of the issues before the public and in achieving a certain amount of legislation and financial aid. In Britain there is as much reluctance to take action on incest as there was over battered babies back in the early 1970's. In 1980 The British Association for the Study and Prevention of Child Abuse and Neglect (BASPCAN) set up a small working party on sexual abuse. Several other BASPCAN members, including myself, were coopted to help produce a pamphlet setting out basic information on incest. This was completed, approved by the Department of Health and Social Security and sent to various official agencies and voluntary bodies in the autumn of 1981. Requests are beginning to come in for seminars and lectures on incest, and it is hoped that gradually the same kind of cooperation that has been achieved in certain states in the US will eventually be attained here.

The need for publicity leading to increased understanding about why and how incest occurs, and what can be done about it, is clear. More knowledge, in spite of the reservations previously mentioned, can only result in a more healthy atmosphere; there is nothing healthy about a situation where perhaps as many as one in eight females and one in ten males suffer some kind of sexual abuse in their childhood, experiences they must forever keep silent about, which not only leave them with a strong sense of guilt but which frequently cause traumas that only intensive treatment can eradicate. It is this secrecy which until recently has ensured that almost nothing was known about incest. The general assumption has been that it only occurs among poor people living in cramped conditions or among isolated groups of peasants. Ancient jokes were told and then the subject dismissed, for it has been assumed that with a rising standard of living the practice of incest would disappear. Nothing could be further from the truth. Incest occurs in all classes, in all races, among people of both high and low intelligence. As long as it was thought to be confined to 'them' no one bothered much; now that it has been discovered to be among 'us' we sit up and take notice, even if we cannot quite bring ourselves to believe the statistics that are beginning to appear.

There is an understandable fear that interference might make matters worse, that exposure to legal processes can cause more trauma to the victim than the actual experience itself. On the surface this seems a highly plausible argument, but the experience of workers in the field suggests that usually the truth is otherwise. For one thing, most incest victims tell someone, usually their mothers, who commonly refuse to accept the truth of the story and take no action. The victim may not attempt to tell his or her story ever again, and this rejection and lack of concern for their suffering stays burned into them for the rest of their lives in addition to the distress caused by the incest itself. It seems that outside support and repeated assurances that they are not to blame is of the greatest importance to their eventual recovery, and victims who have never had this are likely to suffer more than children who have been through the drama of discovery.

Yet another argument against publicity is that it will interfere with a natural relationship between parents and children. Won't fathers feel they daren't touch their children without fear of being misunderstood? Worse, might they not worry that their normal desires to touch their children are perverse? Worst of all, could it even be that the psycho-analysts (wrapped up in their theories of oedipal anxieties) who thought that family nudity was too dangerous, too stimulating, will be listened to again? Won't – to sum up these fears – publicity about incest lead us straight back again to a Victorian-type repressive family life where sex is dirty, hidden, and never to be talked about? The simple answer is, it is ignorance not knowledge that leads to sexual repression. Openness about sex is essential to healthy family life, and part of that openness must include an understanding of the right kind of touching. Normal people know this without having to be told. It is the parent with problems who needs to be told to touch, and how to touch. It could be argued that a child who is never touched, is left to freeze emotionally and physically, is as badly off as a child who is touched inappropriately.

Many people still know amazingly little about the sheer mechanics of sex, and among families where incest has taken place this ignorance is particularly common. They know even less about emotions. The father or stepfather or whoever the perpetrator may be very often claims that 'no harm was done'. And underneath the public desire not to discuss incest there occasionally lies the same feeling, that when it comes down to it, what are we actually making a fuss about? Is it really so awful, after all, as long as there was no violence, no pain?

The answer is becoming increasingly clear – that yes, there nearly always is harm, nearly always is pain, even if it is emotional rather than physical.

> . . . sexual abuse robs the child and adolescent of their
> developmentally determined control over their own bodies, and
> they are further robbed of their own preference, with increasing
> maturity, for sexual partners on an equal basis. This is so
> regardless of whether the child has to deal with a single overt,
> and perhaps violent act . . . or with incestuous acts, often
> continued for many years, which may be . . . even tender,
> insidious, collusive and secretive (Kempe 1978).

We are all of us confused about sex, even the experts. Our ideas on how we should behave, what is morally OK, what leads to a good life, what to a bad – we none of us can be quite sure any longer. In particular we need to clarify how we feel about our children, how we should treat them, what we should teach them, for – the message is always the same – today's children are tomorrow's adults, tomorrow's future. To refuse to look squarely at the problem of incest is no longer possible: it is too common to ignore.

Chapter 1

Two stories: a daughter's and a father's

I picked these two stories to illustrate some of the realities of incest partly because for readers who know nothing about the subject they are fairly easy to take, and partly because they both have 'happy' endings. 'Happy' is in quotes only because the two protagonists have many years yet to live, and who can forecast what will become of anybody's life? I chose American subjects for the simple reason that at the time of writing the treatments which helped these two people are only available in the United States, but their experiences before treatment could have occurred anywhere in the Western world. For anyone who cannot see why fathers who have committed incest should be given sympathetic treatment, let them consider (leaving humanitarian reasons aside) the practical fact that imprisonment alone cannot cure such men: after receiving their punishment they are likely to commit the same offence all over again, and who does that help?

Debbie, the first subject, is a lively, intelligent woman of thirty-three, married to a successful businessman. Like many other incest victims I met she is so glad to feel free at last to discuss the secret she has hidden all her life that words pour out of her mouth. Her background was a middling one – her father was a lithographic draughtsman, and she and her family lived in a small flat in New York. Her aunt and uncle, who are important to the story, are more prosperous: one of their sons, to whom she is close, has become a psychologist and at a later stage in her life he was able to give her support when she needed it most. She is still very close to her past. Describing how she wanted her father to see her and to love her as his child, rather than as a woman with whom he was in love, her voice became very high, the sad bruised voice of a freshly wounded child. But at the end, talking of her new-found happiness with her husband, her voice showed real wonder at the joy of it, genuine happiness. There was no pretence – for her there has been a genuine

7

break-through. She also takes great pleasure in being able to help others by taking an active part in a newly set up national organization for incest victims.

In many ways her story is typical, and in others atypical. There was no intercourse – there often isn't; there was no force – there mostly isn't. Some suffer far greater degradation than she did, some less, but nearly all victims, girls or boys, are to a lesser or greater extent traumatised by their experiences.

John, the second subject, is a much quieter person. I first met him in the offices of the Juvenile Probation Department of Santa Clara County. He was one of four male workers in the department, all of a physical type I had come to associate with this kind of caring work – big, bearded men with gentle faces but a firm manner. John seemed slightly less at his ease than the others, but there was nothing specific – he could perfectly well have been preoccupied with whatever it was he was doing. I was therefore very surprised when later, at the offices of Parents United, Hank Giarretto (whose work will be described in later chapters) introduced him to me as an incestuous father who was prepared to tell me about himself. Unlike Debbie, he has told his story many times in public. He has done this primarily to help others, but no doubt the retelling has had a therapeutic effect for him. If the story has become slightly pat after so much repetition the pain behind it should not be ignored. He is not a man to express his emotions easily.

A daughter's story

The crazy thing is, my father was always very good to me. He was always very loving and he treated me differently to anyone else in the family. He could be really horrible to them, but not to me – I was someone special.

He couldn't let me alone. He was obsessed with me. I don't think he ever realized what he put me through. All the time he was coming up behind me – grabbing me, grabbing my wrist behind my back, and he'd push himself against me. My response was to kick and scream at him to let me alone, and mostly he would. But whenever there was no one in the house – which seemed like always – he'd expose himself, or walk out of a room naked with an erection. Even when my mother was around he'd wear a bath towel tied at his waist, and sit opposite me exposing himself to me.

She might say, 'Oh, don't sit like that.' But he wouldn't take any notice, and she never insisted he stop. She'd just say, 'Don't do that, it's really not right.'

I felt very angry with her. I always used to blame her for what he did because I thought it began when she started working. She was never at home. She was at work when I got home from school and she'd go out most evenings. She worked Saturdays too, so she wasn't very often there to protect me, even if she'd wanted to. For years I assumed it was because she wasn't available to him that he turned to me sexually.

We weren't a big family – just me and my brother who is four years older than me. Benny had a horrible childhood. It was as if my father didn't care for him at all. He didn't touch him sexually, but emotionally he really abused him. Benny must have been horrendously lonely, because I didn't have any kind of communication with him either, even though we shared a large room. When I was nine or ten they divided our room with a folding door, an accordian door. My mother and father slept on a pull-out bed in the living room. I was always uncomfortable about walking in there, knowing my parents were in bed together. You'd come out of the bedroom, and there was the living room, right there. In fact I needn't have worried, they'd not made love for years.

They never did touch each other much. My father treated my mother just awful. He was abusive to her – not physically but verbally. He was very bitter – talked down to her a great deal, treated her as though she were trash. She took it, and then I started treating her like that too. The worse I was, the more she took it. I used to think, I need a mother but she's not there, and she's taking all this because she's guilty. I felt that through my childhood, right from the earliest I can remember until a few weeks ago. I'm thirty-three now.

An important thing was, if I allowed my father to do what he wanted he was delightful around the house. Mostly he was really nasty to everyone except me, so arrogant, but when I was nice to him he was another man. It was like . . . ah! I was keeping peace; and I used that a lot, I know I did.

I suppose I was lucky. It wasn't like it was with some women I've met: he only once tried to force actual intercourse on me. He'd do things like . . . well, he'd ask me to lie down – fully dressed – in front of the television set and he'd watch me. I realize now he was masturbating but I'd no idea whatsoever then. Though I felt uncomfortable – I knew it wasn't right. Or he'd come over and say, 'I love you very much and I wouldn't do anything to hurt you, I just want to feel your body and do things like that. I promise I won't hurt you.' He used to perform oral sex on me – I remember lying on the bed, being really angry, just furious with him. He always went away when I wouldn't take any more. But I never knew for sure he'd go, I was always terrified he'd be forceful with me, rape me.

There was no privacy anywhere. He never stopped watching me, it was just a constant thing. He even drilled holes in the bathroom door. They were really minute holes, *minute*! and I'd stuff cotton wool into them with a tooth pick, but he'd pull it out again. I can't tell you how long I'd go without showering because of them. My mother swears she never saw them . . . maybe she didn't, but my cousin saw them and wondered what on earth they were.

My mother says now – yes, we've talked – that the only suspicious thing she can remember is once when he was standing by the accordian door in my bedroom – he'd drilled holes there too. She said, 'What the hell are you doing?', and he said, 'Oh, I'm just listening,' and she said, 'Get away from there, what do you think you're doing?' So he was at it even when she was in the house. I'd even undress under the covers. I'd know he was watching me, waiting for me to get undressed. At night he'd open my door and stand there, watching me. I'm sure now he was masturbating. I kept my eyes closed hoping he'd think I was asleep, but I knew he was there. No, I don't think he touched me when I was sleeping, though I may have blocked it out. Things are still coming back to me, like I always thought it started when I was about nine or ten, but now I know it was when I was five or six.

I lived in daily fear I was going to be molested. I never knew when I was going to walk out of my room and see my father there with an erection, when he was going to grab me, when he was going to approach me for sex. At night I slept in pyjamas, maybe two or three pairs, a dressing-gown and three blankets when it was baking hot. I covered right up to my nose, my mouth too if possible, leaving just enough space so I could breathe. It was horrible, sleeping like that, but I figured even if he was watching me he couldn't see anything.

As far as I can remember, and I really think it's true, he never made *me* perform oral sex on *him*. He'd ask me, sure; he'd want me to touch him and do all sorts of things, but I was too scared, I wouldn't, and he'd say, 'OK, if you don't want to you don't have to.'

You see, he really did care about me too. The only person he was nice to was me. He was never verbally abusive of me. He always tried to understand the things I was going through. Except we never talked about what he did to me, or the fact that I was terrified. As a child I survived because I'd think – my God, he loves me. This is my father, I trust him, he's all I've got. I had a mother I felt didn't love me – she was always trying to buy me off with clothes and things, but I was sure she didn't love me.

She was just an awful housekeeper, my mother – the house was always dirty and messy. She never asked me to do anything about it, but once in a while he'd get angry and say, 'C'mon, let's clean house, it's a disaster.' Then I'd help, but I'd never do it unless I was asked. She came home to cook dinner, then she'd go straight out again.

He used to pay me money for the sexual things I did. I remember the first time he offered to pay me I felt a mixture of anger, and disgust, and also – wow! he's going to pay for this! I think that's terrific! Part of me knew it was wrong, though I didn't know anything then about prostitution, but the other part thought, I can get things – that's really great. It was a big mixture, what I felt. He'd buy me presents, too, big presents. He'd say 'I know you'd really like a pair of roller skates', and he'd come home with them. He just adored me and everybody in the family knew it, so they didn't think anything special about the presents.

But I paid. Like when he kissed me it was always a wet kiss, and I was *repulsed* by it. If ever I went to kiss him, like a kid does, he'd turn his face so that the kiss would land on his mouth. He never missed an opportunity.

I desperately needed for people outside to think we were a happy family and everything was OK, because I felt if they saw me with-drawn or depressed, they'd know. I always had this fear people could just look at me and sense it. I was terrified of anybody knowing. I was sure it was only happening to me, it couldn't possibly be happening to anybody else. So to outsiders I was a happy, outgoing normal child. But back home it was a totally different image – I was miserable, depressed; I'd cry myself to sleep many nights.

When I got older I had a lot of boyfriends. That was all part of my facade, to show I was normal. Yet I thought sex itself was absolutely horrible. I'd hold hands, but . . .

Though, when I think about it, I suppose I wasn't really *that* turned off sex, because I remember the first french kiss, and I remember I wasn't repulsed by it, it was OK. And petting, that was OK. But no more.

(A long pause)

No, that's not true, either. I remember having a boyfriend when I was fifteen and he did touch my vagina, and that was OK too. Anything he would do was OK. I don't really remember if I enjoyed it though.

I think the point is I felt people could do anything they wanted to me, that it didn't matter what they did. I remember going upstairs in the apartment block and lying on the floor – it was cold marble – and him pulling my pants down and putting his fingers up me and that stuff and it was perfectly acceptable to me. I can't remember enjoying it, but I just know I wanted it done. He was seventeen and he wanted sex, but I would never go that far.

Yes, you're right. I wouldn't let him go any further than I did my father. Somehow I managed to stop them both at that point.

I never really thought about that.

You know, my father was a sad man. He didn't have any friends. When I was little there were one or two friends in the apartment block he'd go fishing with or old friends he grew up with, but eventually he lost even them. In the evenings he'd come home, and that was that. It was the same with the family. My mother'd say, 'Let's go visit some relatives for the day' and he'd say, 'I don't want to be with them, they're boring, I hate them.' He was very verbal about his feelings for his mother and father whom he hated. He'd had a terrible life. My grandfather was the most vicious, awful man anybody had ever met – many people have told me that. When he died people kind of sighed with relief. Everybody hated him, just despised him. He used to really beat my father up, badly. His brother wasn't beaten, but was verbally abused instead. Really vicious. As for his mother, as long as she didn't get hit she couldn't care less about any of them.

Things always went badly for him. He wanted to get into the war, and he couldn't because he had a back problem. He hated being with my uncle – his brother-in-law – who'd been a kind of war hero, and he'd walk out of the room if the subject of the war came up. Another thing. Once when he was young he saw a business opportunity. He asked his brother for the money and his brother said no. He asked his father and his father said, 'No, no way am I going to lend you money.' My mother's sister had just got married and it was she and her husband who lent him money. It was nearly their entire savings account. And the business failed. He was so humiliated – he couldn't look them in the face – but they said, forget it, it's over and done with. That's family. But he couldn't, of course. He was never able to pay them back. He was so humiliated.

It was always like that. I see a man with no self-esteem, no respect whatsoever for himself, and therefore seeing other people the same as he saw himself.

I don't blame my mother any more for wanting her own life, he treated her so badly. She had a good responsible job, working in a fuel oil place, managing it. I didn't know it then, but she had a lover, her boss. He was around the house a lot. He loved us, was there when I had my tonsils out, that sort of thing. My father was very suspicious of everyone she knew because she had a lot of men friends, but it was only when I was twelve or thirteen she took a lover. She told me the other day that when my father used to accuse her of sleeping with the other men she always denied it, and then when he confronted her about her lover she denied that too because she didn't want to hurt him by telling the truth. But my father tells me he felt dirtied by it all – he was always convinced that there were lots of lovers, he never believed her at all. So that was another thing knocking him down.

When I was about fourteen years old I finally said to my mother, 'I can't stand it any more, I'm really depressed and miserable.' I didn't tell her why I was so miserable. She thought it was because my brother was getting married – he was only eighteen but he'd got a girl pregnant. He didn't even know if he was the father. It's true I was very upset about it. My mother took me to a psychiatrist and he asked me, 'Would you like your mother to stay while we talk?' I said yes. Why did I say that? I suppose it was because I badly wanted for her to love me and I thought maybe that if I sent her away it would be such an awful rejection for her. I told him I was upset because of my brother. I just can't believe I did that. It was my perfect opportunity and I blew it. So he just told me, go home and you'll be fine. And that was that.

Shortly after that I went to stay with my uncle and aunt – my mother's sister. The second night I was there I fell apart and told them my father sexually abused me. That was all I said. I asked my aunt about it recently: I wanted to fill in the gaps. She says she held me and I cried a lot. I was really withdrawn and was just falling apart. They spoke to a psychiatrist friend of theirs and when they came back they said to me, everything will be OK, don't worry. They let me live with them for a couple of months because they didn't think I was ready to go home, but my parents came up for a visit. My father knew why I was there but my mother had no idea, just knew I was having problems. My aunt promised she'd talk to my father, but it turned out she never did.

During that visit my father molested me. I was terrified. I thought my aunt had spoken to him. I just couldn't believe it was happening. He threw me on the bed. He got on top of me, he was tugging at my clothes and he had his hand over my mouth and I was just kicking and screaming. I got him off me and I ran out of the room. Yes, I am sure he would have forced me if I hadn't struggled so. It was the only time he tried to rape me and I suppose I was so shocked it kind of gave me power. I can remember him being extremely heavy. I was just furious and I started pounding at him, kicking him. I remember him going at my clothes until I just threw him off.

After my parents left I stayed on, feeling terrible. My aunt hadn't said anything to my parents, so when I went back home it continued as before. Nothing had changed. I had about six months to go before finishing high school – I was about fifteen – and I meant to leave home then. I didn't care about my friends wondering why I was leaving because I knew they would think it was because I was pregnant – that was the big thing in those days.

Back home my dad was even worse than before, more persistent. He was always asking to have sex with me, always grabbing me, always looking at me. At school there was a counsellor I was crazy about who I talked to, but never about the real problem. All he knew was I was unhappy. There was another counsellor too, a woman, and sometimes I'd deliberately get into trouble. Then she'd say, 'I'm calling your mother to school', and I'd say, 'Good, do it.' But she never came. My mother says now she always came. Bullshit. I'm sorry, but she was never there. There were things going on at school when all the parents came, but not mine. They never came.

Somehow I survived, though. I guess you just do. My grandmother – my mother's mother – helped. She lived close by and when my dad molested me I'd run to her. She never asked me what the matter was, but I think she knew. She just used to hold me, and that made me feel good. My grandmother was my survival. She was really very important to me.

My husband was another help. I was sixteen, nearly seventeen, when we first started going out. I felt really comfortable with him, he was really nice. I never told him about my father though. One day I was running out of the building and I ran straight into David – he lived next door to my grandmother – and I was hysterical, sobbing, because that was always my reaction when my father grabbed me. I bumped right into him, and he said, 'What's the matter?' I said, 'Just let me go', and ran off to my grandmother's. He never mentioned anything about it and nothing was ever said.

With David there was just kissing and touching. I really liked that, and I wanted to go to bed with him, but he wouldn't – he didn't think it was right.

My father was still exposing himself to me, coming up behind and grabbing me. Always begging, 'please, please, I'm not going to hurt you.' When I'd say, 'leave me alone, you're crazy!' he'd look at me, like – I don't understand you, what's wrong? Yes, he went on paying me, and I know I liked getting that money. I'd got used to it, you see. He gave me quite a lot, and I took it.

It went on until I got engaged. Then at last he left me alone. I got engaged at nineteen and David was twenty, but I didn't leave home until I was twenty-one to get married. I often ask myself why I stayed, but in those days kids did, you just didn't leave until you got married. Dad was hell to live with then, though he was still very loving towards me. He didn't seem to resent my getting engaged – he adored David, he couldn't not, David was such a nice person, a really good person.

You know, I was very lucky with my husband, because I know the pattern is to fall for somebody who'd abuse me. I really think I was in love with David, he was such a terrific person. But I also know I needed to get out of the house, and he was my way out.

When we got married my father stayed pleasant to us, and he never again tried anything sexual. But he was awful at home. My mother was always making comments like, 'He's only happy when he's around you.' Or, 'You're the only one that can bring him out of his craziness.' Two years after we got married David and I moved right away, and my father went into a depression that lasted for years. He was withdrawn, cried constantly – my mother said he was unbearable to live with. For the first year I was away he wouldn't

even talk to me on the phone. Then when at last he did try to talk
he just broke down and cried. It was really awful.

Even though I was so many miles away I wasn't free of what he'd
done to me. It was devastating my whole life. From the time David
and I were married we had sexual problems that I knew were mine.
In the end, after about four years of marriage, I said to David – it
took me about five hours sobbing for me to get it out – 'My father
sexually abused me.' That was all, no details. I couldn't discuss it.
It was all right after that for a couple of months, then I came to
another stage when I was really down. I just couldn't function
sexually. I wouldn't want David to touch me, I'd want him to leave
me alone. I'd cry, and say I knew it was because of my father. That
helped and I'd get along for another couple of months. This went
on for twelve years. He didn't like it, but he accepted it. We
couldn't afford therapy. At one point I did go for counselling, and
the psychiatrist said, 'Debbie, in order to really help you I need to
see you two or three times a week at the minimum', but there was
no way I could afford it.

David was terrific, all through this he was very supportive of me.
It's been a good marriage, we communicate well, but I just couldn't
respond to him sexually. He's very demonstrative – I'd be in the
kitchen, say, and he'd come up behind and grab me, and my father
would come before me, and I'd just die. It's only now I've been
able to tell him that that was what my father did to me.

A year ago we moved again. I hadn't any friends and I became
very withdrawn. After a while I got desperate, but we were lucky,
I managed to find a therapist we could afford. She was marvellous,
she really understood. But it was absolute torture. I don't know
how my kids stood it. I'd lock myself in a room for days on end
and refuse to come out. My therapist said that's OK, if that's what
you have to do. I couldn't shop properly – I couldn't decide between
two brands of peaches in a supermarket, and I'd run out in tears.
Bringing up the past and dealing with it was the worst thing I've
ever done, but also the best.

It took four months to get through that period. I was seeing the
therapist once a week, and sometimes my husband had to drive me
there, I just couldn't do it on my own. Finally I got to a point in
my life when I woke up and said, dammit, I want to get on with
my life, I need to do things – I can't take this any more. I knew
then I had to confront my parents to clear it out of me.

I went back east alone – David said it all made him too angry and he couldn't have been properly supportive of me if he'd come. First I went to see my uncle and aunt, the ones I'd stayed with. One of their sons had become a psychologist, and he was great, he's always cared a great deal for me. We all talked together, and my uncle and aunt tried to persuade me not to speak to my parents. They said, 'Do you realize it will devastate their marriage, it'll destroy them.' I told them I'd spent my whole life worrying about how it was going to hurt somebody else, and I just couldn't do that any more.

The truth is, their own family was messed up too. They had four kids, and one of them they used to beat up. Even in front of me, when I was staying there, they'd beat him really hard. He'd come to me and I'd hold him. It was just awful. Apart from the one who's become a psychologist all the kids are in terrible shape, they have horrendous problems. I could see as I was talking to my uncle and aunt they were putting themselves in my parents' place and seeing me as their son they'd beat up and sent to hospital.

Yes, my aunt is my mother's sister, so I guess those two had had their problems as kids too, for both the families to turn out wrong. When I was confronting my aunt and uncle I knew it was opening up a can of worms for them. But finally they got to the point I thought they'd never get to, where they looked at me, and said, 'Do what you have to do.'

So I went to my parents. I said to my dad – it was horrible – I'd like to talk to you alone outside. We sat down and I said: 'Dad, I love you as a daughter loves a father, but when I was a little girl you started making sexual advances towards me and I was horrified and scared. I've got to tell you the *hell* you put me through for twenty-five years and how you've almost ruined my life and my marriage. I'm not here to blame you or to accuse you, but you need to know why I'm here now, and we've got to talk about the reality of the past and put it behind us.' I'd thought and thought about what I was going to say and I knew I just had to get it all out straight. I had to know whether I'd distorted any of it. I went through it all in detail, the sexual things he'd done to me, the holes in the doors, all that, and he just looked at me and admitted everything. That was incredible, because my therapist said he's going to deny it all, they nearly always do.

He explained a lot of things I didn't know, how he thought my mother had lovers, how he started with me younger than I'd realized. I could hardly believe that, but when I got out old photographs of me when I was five or six I could feel the fear I felt then, feel my stomach in knots. He was always taking pictures of me, making me pose for him, sexual pictures. Every time I turned round he was either there naked or he had a camera, and he'd take pictures of me from the back when I was turning round to run.

He said to me: 'I was so passionate about you I couldn't control myself. Every time I did something to you and you'd yell I'd walk away and know I was wrong, and I'd tell myself I mustn't do it any more. When you went to your aunt's I knew why you were there and that I mustn't touch you ever again. But when you came home I couldn't keep my hands off you.' Then he . . . broke down, and in the end I walked up to him and we held each other. He said to me, 'I'm in love with you as a woman. I don't love you as a daughter.' And he started sobbing and said, 'I never wanted to admit that to you. I look at you and see a woman I am in love with.'

But he can't have been in love with me as a woman when I was a child – I was a little girl then, not a woman. It was a lot for him to admit what he felt; I think he knew it was the end of our relationship. He said, 'I'm so glad you don't live close by. For years I couldn't stand being separated from you, but now I realize it would be hell to be close to you. I couldn't stand it.'

I had hoped to end up with a father/daughter relationship. I still haven't solved that. I know I'm going to have to face him again and say, 'Dad, can you love me as a daughter, can we have that sort of relationship?' I'm pretty sure he's going to say no, and then I'm going to have to mourn . . . for the father who is dead. I've already mourned for the little girl who lost her father. He's my father, but I'm not his daughter, and that's hard for me, very hard.

This is what it is, for a victim of incest. Here is this wonderful man who is the most important person in your life, whom you idolize and trust, and he's betraying your trust. Part of you is *angry*, but another part is saying, maybe it'll stop, maybe it'll go away. I'd keep thinking, this is going to be the last time, praying that it was and that he'd look at me and say 'You're my *baby*, I love you, let me hold you.' My mother never held me, never loved me – when my father wasn't being sexual he'd love me the way I wanted to be loved, hold me right, and I must remember that when I was little he did this. He was all I had! How could I help but hope somehow he'd miraculously change?

I talked with my mother after. We had a 24-hour marathon. I had already told her two years previously that my father had sexually abused me when I was a child and she was appalled. Then a year later I mentioned it to her again and she told me she didn't believe me. So this time I just moved right in and told her everything. *She was horrified.* She couldn't even hear. When I was telling her the sexual parts she said, 'I can't listen.'

This time she had to accept it was true. And we talked, we really talked. She told me about the men in her life, how my dad hated going out, hated being sexual – she said that! – so she went out with friends instead. We talked about my childhood, how I felt she was never there for me, and she said she'd loved me a lot, she'd done for me all she knew, what her mother had done for her. But she'd never had cuddling and loving and being physical herself – and she just didn't know how to do it. She said she'd never imagined anything between my father and me: she said, 'Who'd have thought it? In those days you never thought things like that.'

I was cold to her, she said, and it was true, I was really horrible to her. It was like – you did this to me, and you're going to pay. I was blaming her for everything as I felt it was because of her my father was treating me like that.

It was incredible, those twenty-four hours. She told me how much she loved me, and I really understood she meant it. I think the thing we were sorriest about was that we'd missed out on so many years. But she was devastated by what she'd learned. She still doesn't know how she's going to cope with it – she won't try therapy. I have to get across to her she's not unique, there are thousands in the same position as her. The same thing I had to learn.

They didn't talk to each other for weeks after that, my parents. Now they've fallen back into the old pattern of whatever's necessary for living. But they've not had sex in ten years.

For me, it's been incredible. In the therapy group for husbands and wives my husband found men going through the same thing he had, having the same feelings. We were all dealing with sexual problems, so it was a great help. The men have learned the necessity for sexual communication and the importance for a woman of feeling her body belongs to her. She has a right to say no. David and I are doing great. We're at a fabulous place right now. We really talk, it's so open and honest between us. I'm starting to enjoy myself sexually, to be in touch with my body – I feel like my life's just begun and it's incredible. I feel just wonderful about it, really wonderful.

And helping others, that's something I'm really looking forward to. To be part of a national organization – I can hardly believe that. That I'll be part of it, that there won't be any more need for anyone else to suffer in silence the way I did all those years. In a way, I think perhaps that's going to be the best thing of all.

A father's story

When I started having sexual feelings for my stepdaughter I couldn't understand what was going on. I thought, why do I have these feelings? There was nobody I could talk to about it. I couldn't talk to my wife, I couldn't tell *her* what was happening.

Karen was two and a half years old when her mother and I married – it was a second marriage for both of us. She had two children, Karen and an older son, but I had none, though later we had a daughter of our own. Before we married we got on really well. We had a lot in common with each other – we liked to do the same kind of things, be together. I was very much in love, and we had no problems with our sexual relationship – it was really good. But after we'd committed ourselves and got married all that changed. Everything changed. She was rejecting me sexually and emotionally, and I just couldn't understand it. I felt there must be something wrong with me but I could never ask her about it because I was afraid she'd confirm that there was.

We went on for a long time like that, getting more and more remote from each other until in the end we weren't communicating at all. She used to go away for quite long periods, and it was during these times that I began to turn to my stepdaughter. I wasn't looking for any special involvement, but she was the only one in the family who was close to me. She'd come over and hug me, or sit on my lap, and say, 'Daddy, can I get something for you, can I get you a beer?' when I came home from work. Or she'd go out and get the paper for me – you know, those kinds of things.

I was feeling really low about myself by then, and I badly needed to have somebody to love me and to be able to love somebody back. I began to depend on Karen for this kind of nurturing, and I felt she had the same needs herself because her mother was away such a lot of the time. I'm not giving any excuses for what I did. I was an adult and I should have known better, but when it started – just with touching at first – there was no one I could talk to, though I badly wanted to. I felt guilty as hell.

No, at the beginning she didn't at all mind what I did, she was quite willing. I don't mean she enticed me, she was just being a natural loving kid. You've got to understand she was only eight years old, and daddy could do no wrong, daddy's always loved me, daddy's always cared for me, so I'm sure to her it must have been OK. But gradually the sexual involvement became heavier and heavier to the point where when she was twelve or thirteen I was actually having intercourse with her. Of course the relationship changed, it had to. As she got into her teens I started becoming jealous, more dominant, not letting her go out with her peers because I was afraid she'd tell somebody and that she'd find out that her peers' fathers didn't do this, that it wasn't OK at all. We started having arguments and I felt completely lost. I didn't know what to do, I felt my whole family was coming apart at the seams. I knew I needed help but I didn't know how to go about getting it.

Was I in love with her? I don't know. I may have thought I was. It certainly became like an obsession to be with her, and I didn't know how to break through that. It was like being in a spider's web and not knowing how to escape — the more you struggle the more enmeshed you get.

It came out in the end because my wife got fed up with our arguments and said she was going off to her mother's. For once she took Karen with her, and Karen ended up telling her grandmother about it. I was arrested four days later.

No, I had no anger against my stepdaughter for doing that, nor for any members of my family. I was glad to be arrested, because I knew then I would no longer have to keep it a secret, that I'd get help. I wasn't angry at all, only thankful she'd had the courage to tell somebody.

I was arrested in an outlying town almost at gun-point by a beat policeman who hadn't had any of the special training we offer now. He was very angry — it had come through to him as rape. I can understand his anger — maybe he had a couple of children at home himself. He didn't beat me up or anything, but it was obvious he would have liked to. But when I was able to show that arresting officer what had happened, what I'd gone through, what my family had gone through, he became very sympathetic, very helpful. He ended up taking the handcuffs off me, and becoming supportive of me.

Going to court — I think that was one of the worst things I have ever had to go through, being handcuffed and shackled and having my wife and mother there in the courtroom – that was one of the hardest things I ever did. In court I took full responsibility for what I'd done, I didn't try to get out of anything. Why should I? I was only too glad it had come out into the open at last. After the court proceedings and I was bailed out, I was able to talk to my wife for about an hour.

I tried to explain it to her, show her how it had happened. It was very traumatic for her – she was very shocked, very hurt. She couldn't believe something like that had been going on in the house: she'd had no idea at all. She refused to stay nearby, took the kids away to friends while I was going through the court process. I must admit I found that very hard to understand because I thought she would at least listen to me and stay in the area so I could see her.

One night I tried to commit suicide. I was alone, back home on bail, with no support from my family or my friends. My wife had told them and they broke off all connections with me. I'd got to a point where nothing mattered any more. But then I called the Crisis Intervention Unit at one of the local hospitals to get help before it was too late.

They took me into hospital and a couple of days later I was put into one of the psychiatric wards. When I saw the psychiatrist there I asked him what he could do for me – I said I couldn't go on without support – and he said, 'I just don't know what I can do for you.' That helped, in fact, to know that there was a professional who didn't know what to do any more than I did.

At the hospital we had groups in the morning and afternoon, but they weren't much help as there was no one there who shared my experience. There was a woman with everyday problems she couldn't cope with, a girl of sixteen (my daughter was sixteen), and a homosexual who didn't know how to relate to women, no one at all with my kind of problem. I was able to say my wife had left me and that it was very traumatic for me, and that was as far as I could go.

When I came out of hospital I felt really low about myself again, and couldn't think about anything except suicide. Then I saw an article in a local paper about Hank Giarretto's programme. I called him and was put on to one of the fathers in the group who told me not to stay alone but to go over straight away. I did that and we talked for a while. It ended up with my being asked to go to a Parents United group and I agreed to, but at the back of my mind I more or less decided not to go because I'd already been in these hospital groups and didn't see why this one should be any different. I drove around for a while, not knowing what to do, but there wasn't much choice – so I changed my mind and went. I knew there wouldn't be any women there – because why would any women be any different from my wife? But from the time I walked into Parents United not only did I get support from the men but also from the women, even from women who'd been molested as children as well.

They stood by me all through the time I was going through the criminal justice system. I was given ninety days, forty-five suspended, and was put on a work furlough programme doing volunteer work through the Parents United programme. During that time my wife returned and she came to the group for about four months, but it wasn't any use, we couldn't get together. We're divorced now.

Karen came to the Daughters and Sons United group for about five months – as a matter of fact she's been back a couple of times since she left the programme – it really helped her. I see her twice a month, and we have a very good father/daughter relationship. We're able to talk about a lot of things – you know, boyfriends, general things. She's not on her own, and she'll be eighteen in a couple of days, so things are looking up for her. She's going to be all right.

Now I work full-time on the Crisis Intervention Scheme – this is my paid job. I'm in close contact with the criminal justice system, with police officers, other social workers. I co-facilitate a group, do a leadership group, and I'm heavily involved with Parents United as well.

It's been my family, Parents United, for two years now. I don't want to give it up. I put a lot of energy into it, and I get a lot of energy back. Through it I've learned more about myself than I ever did in the whole of the rest of my life. I feel very differently, I feel a kind of self-esteem I never had before. It makes the business of living another matter altogether.

Chapter 2

What is incest?

Legal definitions of incest are too narrow to be of much use to anyone concerned with the subject from a sociological point of view. English law defines incest as being sexual intercourse between a male and female whom the man knows to be his daughter, sister, half-sister, grand-daughter or mother. If the female is under thirteen years of age the crime carries a possible sentence of life; if she is over thirteen seven years is the maximum sentence. In fact the courts rarely award a sentence greater than two to five years. Attempted incest carries a maximum sentence of two years, and seven years if the victim is under thirteen. If a woman over sixteen has intercourse with her father, brother or half-brother, son or grandfather this is also legally defined as incest. The law in Scotland and in Northern Ireland differs in certain respects. In America the definition of incest varies from state to state, though sexual intercourse with a blood relative too close to marry is generally necessary for the term incest to be used. Punishment varies considerably.

But intercourse is only half the story. Anyone working in this field will soon discover that any number of acts may be committed which frequently are at least as traumatic to the victim as full intercourse. Neither does the offender have necessarily to be the father – anyone in a parental position, such as a stepfather, may cause exactly the same kind of damage to the victim as an actual father. Equally, 'he' may be a *she*. And the victim may be male, not female. The permutations of incestuous activity are as great as ingenuity and availability permits.

The only useful definition of incest for the purposes of this book therefore must be one which is broad enough to include a variety of sexual activity that would not in law be defined as incest but which is not so broad that there ceases to be any point in using the word 'incest' at all. Patricia Beezley Mrazek (1980) writes: 'The definition problems are perhaps best exemplified by the fact that although 42 of the American states include the element of sexual molestion in their child abuse reporting statutes, 34 of them do not even attempt to define it.' It has been suggested to me that I drop the word 'incest' and use only the term 'sexual abuse' to avoid this problem of definition. But sexual abuse can include many activities that are essentially different in nature to the experience that this book is about, namely, the experience of a younger, usually powerless, person who has been led into sexual activity by an older person whom they probably trust and love and who is part of their everyday home life. Before arriving at a working definition, then, let us look at what is known about incest – who does it to whom, how long for, what exactly they do, how old the victims are, and any other factor that seems relevant.

Although the word incest has always carried the automatic implication of a close blood relationship, there are cases where this expectation would have been waived by most observers. Let us imagine the following: a man deserts his wife and three-month-old daughter. A few months later the woman takes a lover who lives with her for the rest of her life as a common-law husband. The child grows up to know this man as her father, which he is in every sense except the one of consanguinity. He himself regards her and cares for her as though she were his actual daughter. Most people would consider that if this man had sexual relations with the child he was in essence committing an act of incest, even though there was no question of a blood tie. Certainly from the child's point of view there would be no effective difference: to her it is unquestionably her father who has committed this act.

Some will object that it is the very fact of close blood relationship that brings a special, unique horror to the act of incest: the chorus wailing at Oedipus is bemoaning that Jocasta was his mother – they do not care that Oedipus never knew his real parents and cannot possibly have had the kind of mother/son relationship with which we are concerned. True. And yet to modern psychologists the most important factor in the early life of a child is the relationship she has had with her parent figures, regardless of their actual physical link. In the imagined case above they would expect the child to be as affected by her experience as though the man had been her actual father. A later understanding of the difference as she grew up might affect her adult feelings about the childhood incidents, to a certain extent, but as a child these are unlikely to concern her. John, whose story we have just read, mostly referred to his stepdaughter as 'my daughter', and there is no doubt she saw him quite straightforwardly as her father and suffered accordingly.

Many people working in this field use the classification of overt 'sexual activity involving genital contact between people too closely related to marry' (Rosenfeld 1979) or some similar wording, and most people would assume stepfathers came under this classification. Yet, in English law, intercourse between a man and his stepdaughter is described not as incest, but as 'unlawful sexual intercourse' if the child is under sixteen. It is an offence because of her age rather than their special relationship. Indeed, once she has reached sixteen they may then behave as they like, whether the stepfather is still with her mother, or whether they have divorced, without any legal offence being committed. The only special prohibition in these cases is that the two may not marry. Thus a stepfather could have been having sex with his stepdaughter from her earliest childhood, could leave her mother and take up residence with his stepdaughter and live with her openly as though they were husband and wife, without suffering any penalty provided their early sexual relationship is kept secret, and provided they do not attempt to marry legally.

What specific act should be included in our definition of incest? Obviously intercourse is among them, but such cases are among the minority (Finkelhor 1978b; Berliner & Stevens 1979; Tsai 1980, personal communication). Leaving aside the rare and horrifying cases where tiny children, even babies, are raped, it seems that most incest starts gently, much as both Debbie and John described in Chapter 1. From two or three years of age children may be touched or fondled so unobtrusively they are not aware anything special is happening. This is likely to increase in intensity as time goes on, leading to exhibitionism, genital manipulation, cunnilingus, fellatio, mutual masturbation, manual penetration of the child's vagina or anus, anal intercourse and/or vaginal intercourse. The trauma inflicted on the victim is not necessarily related to the actual activity – six episodes of cunnilingus do not equal one act of intercourse. On the contrary, a child whose father does nothing more than continuously expose himself to her in a deliberately sexual manner all through her childhood may well be more damaged than an adolescent who experiences a brief period when unforced intercourse takes place between her and her father. The fact that Debbie never knew when she was going to come out of her room and find her father exposing himself to her seemed to affect her more than anything else he did to her.

It will come as a surprise to many readers to learn that a considerable number of child sexual abuse cases involved adolescent offenders and younger victims, many of whom are related. This will be looked at in greater detail in a later chapter, but it is relevant here to point out that in such cases most adolescents confine themselves to manipulation of the genitals of their younger victim or to having the victim manipulate them (Wenet 1980, personal communication). In a study of sibling incest Finkelhor found that among the younger children hardly any attempted intercourse: even among those thirteen years of age and older only 18 per cent attempted or achieved intercourse (Finkelhor 1980a).

The amount of overt force used seems to be more important than the choice of act. However, most incestuous activity occurs without the use of overt force, although many would claim that a child of three or four is unquestionably being forced to obey simply because of the powerful position of the father, even if he or she is quite unaware that anything untoward is happening. The Harborview Medical Center, Seattle, reporting on 593 children under sixteen who had been molested between October 1977 and August 1979, showed that 16 per cent of those children suffering intra-family abuse (over half the total) were made to submit by the use of physical force or by the showing of a weapon, 16 per cent were threatened with force, 63 per cent were coerced 'by adult authority', 3 per cent by a 'tangible enticement' and the remaining 2 per cent in unspecified ways. It may not occur to children who have been taught by their parents never to take sweets from strangers that the bar of chocolate being offered by daddy ought to be refused for exactly the same reason. At the age when incest commonly starts most children will have very little idea of their own anatomy, let alone of adult sexual behaviour.

Earlier studies seemed to suggest that incest usually started in early adolescence, but as we have seen this view is no longer held. In the Harborview report mentioned above (for this statistic family abuse was not separated from non-family abuse) 22 per cent of the children were between one and six years old, 40 per cent were between seven and twelve years, and 38 per cent between thirteen and sixteen years. Wenet (ibid.) found that most of the victims of the adolescents he was working with were six years old and younger (the adolescent perpetrators themselves were between twelve and eighteen). Yet another study reports that on average incest began at about the age of ten but was not reported for two years (Muldoon 1979). Frequently children either forget or blank out memories of early incidents from their minds, and if the incest is revealed when they are older it is the age they have reached that is most likely to be written down in the statistics, which probably explains why earlier researchers reported a later age of commencement.

Some fathers seem to wait for the children to reach a particular age before they begin to molest them. A policeman told me:

> The one in particular I'm thinking of is sixteen now and it started with her when she was nine. And the reason she came to me is because she's just found out that her father had been doing it to her sister [who's eleven now] for the last two years, so he started on her at nine too. The girl had always thought if she let her father go on doing it to her he'd leave her two younger sisters alone. Her real worry now is that the youngest sister is only eight and so far he's left her alone, but she's worried he'll begin on her as well when she gets to nine. I often see this sort of thing – it seems there's an age when a man thinks his daughter's ready, and that's when it begins. I don't know if there's any special age in general when it starts, though. I've had girls saying it's been happening ever since they can remember, or that dad plays with their little brother or sister who's only eight months old.

A further point necessary to a useful definition of incest is the duration of the molestation. It appears that once incestuous behaviour has begun it nearly always continues until a specific event stops it, such as it being discovered, or the now adolescent girl who objects to the curtailment of her freedom or to a younger sister being assaulted, tells someone what is happening, as in the case mentioned by the policeman. Finkelhor (1978a) writes that Maisch and Gebhard (1965) report the relationships last anywhere from six months to seven or eight years. The Harborview Sexual Assault Center found that only 17 per cent of their cases of intra-family abuse consisted of a single incident. Of the rest, all of which were active until discovered and brought for treatment, 22 per cent had been going on for less than six months, 23 per cent for between six months and a year, 29 per cent for between one year and five years, and the remaining 9 per cent for more than five years. It should be remembered that all these were cases that were found out – where an incestuous relationship only comes to light years later when a mature woman comes for therapy it is usual for her to tell of a sexual relationship that lasted for many years.

Mavis Tsai, talking to me about a sample of such women into whose childhood she had researched, said she had found the general pattern to be that the longer the relationship continued, and the more frequent the sexual episodes were, the worse the women were affected. The harm that incest does will be explored more deeply in a later chapter, but for the time being it is helpful if the reader bears in mind that for vast numbers of people incest has been a continuous background to their entire childhood – and 'vast' is no exaggeration, as will be seen when we come to look at the size of this problem.

Another factor only recently coming to light is that large numbers of boys are also victims: their silence has meant that incest has nearly always been thought of as a relationship between father and daughter. It has been suggested to me by various researchers – male as well as female – that this reticence is mainly due to males not liking to be caught out in a passive position. Few male incest victims ever report incest while it is actually happening, and are reluctant to reveal their past even if as adults they go into therapy for any reason. Usually the abuser of the male child is also male; although mother/son incest occurs it is far less frequent and less overt than the relationships between fathers and daughters.

Tsai and Wagner (1979), quoting other people's research into the sex of the victims, write:

> female victims outnumbered male victims by 10 to 1. Male victims were chiefly involved in homosexual activity. These statistics are suspect since women who sexually exploit young boys are rarely reported. In such situations, boys usually do not consider themselves to be victims. Due to the sexual socialization process in our society, young males are likely to view such contacts as sexual initiations while females view these encounters as sexual violation.

Of the Harborview offenders, 96 per cent were male, the remaining 4 per cent female. Research carried out by Cordelia Kent (1979) found that among groups of local elementary schoolchildren

> there were an equal amount of boys and girls who revealed personal accounts of sexual exploitation; though boys were much less likely than girls to report. Incest still appeared to

involve more female victims. Most of the offenders mentioned were males; however, both boys and girls related experiences involving female offenders.

When male perpetrators have incestuous sex with male victims it might be assumed there is a strong element of homosexuality present, but this is not necessarily the case. In general it seems that basically the perpetrators take what is available. Wenet (personal communication):

In two-thirds of our cases [of adolescent offenders] the boys molested children of the opposite sex and in one-third children of the same sex. However, even in the last cases, our feeling is that it doesn't have as much to do with homosexuality as with what children were accessible. The girls who mostly fondled the genitals of the younger child, both orally and manually, also did it to boys or girls, whatever was available.

Finkelhor in his survey on sex among siblings (1980a), writes:

Homosexuality made no difference [as to whether the sexual experience was positive or negative]. It would be plausible to think that the greater stigma of homosexuality would make homosexual sibling sex more problematic. But this was not the case.

That more than one child in a family is likely to be the object of the father's attention is borne out by Harborview's statistics, which show that 34 per cent of the siblings of the primary client were also abused. High as this figure is it should be remembered that many of these cases were picked up early, before progression to other family members was likely to have taken place.

I was told of a case that illustrates this omnivorous approach of some fathers:

The entire family had been molested by their father, including a 22-year-old boy who is now a physical instructor in the army and married. The next was a 20-year old girl, a very bright student at university, after her an 18-year-old boy, then a 14-year-old boy and three more daughters in the same sort of descending age. They'd all been sexually assaulted by dad – he did everything you can think of to them, though I think he only had anal sex with the oldest. The mother knew, they all knew, but everyone was terrified of him, really scared. When

they talked about him I had the impression of some great big
monster who'd rip my head off as soon as I approached him. It
had come out into the open because he'd fallen ill and had been
taken to hospital, so one of the kids had plucked up courage
and got help while he was out of the house.

I went to see him, this terrifying man. I was really nervous.
And in walked this tiny person, not more than 5 feet 2 inches,
shaking and nervous, a very slight man with no kind of
presence whatsoever. Yet they were all scared stiff of him! He
didn't even work. It was his wife who kept the family going, as
she had a good job in a factory. When he'd married her she had
quite a large family already, and only the two smallest children
were his. When the two older boys got old enough to say no
and push him off they did so, but neither of them had the
courage to defend the younger ones, though they knew exactly
what was going on.

Since the oldest boy, the physical instructor, was already married
at twenty-two his homosexual experience does not appear to have
alienated him from women, but it seems unlikely that, after an
upbringing like his, his home life can ever be entirely normal.

To sum up, then, for our purposes incest is a sexual relationship
that may continue for years or be expressed overtly by nothing more
than a single act, that takes place between a young person under
the age of consent and an older person who has a close family tie,
which is either a blood tie as with father/daughter/son, mother/
daughter/son, brother/sister, or is a substitute for such relationships,
as with step-parent or parent's lover where the substitute has effectively taken over the role of the missing parent. The sexual act/acts
can vary from exhibitionism to full intercourse: the only essential
is that they shall be perceived either contemporaneously or later by
the younger person to be of a sexual nature and of sufficient intensity
to cause disturbance in that younger person.

From a legal point of view this definition is obviously too open-
ended, but this book is primarily concerned with the subject as a
whole. The above definition, therefore, is the one that will be used
in the following pages, and I hope the reader will approve it as he
or she comes to understand the complexities of incestuous
relationships

I do not intend in this book to spend much time speculating on the history of incest. It is a fascinating exercise, searching through anthropological evidence and speculating on ancient customs, but we can never know for sure exactly what used to happen behind the bushes, in the tent or under the pile of skins. We don't know what is happening today, so how can we be certain of what happened some thousands of years ago?

We can be sure of a few facts. Certainly nearly every society we have ever known anything about has had a taboo against incest (Henderson 1972). A few societies have nevertheless allowed certain members to commit incest of specific types at certain times. The best known was in Egypt during the Pharaonic and Ptolemaic period when brother/sister marriages were allowed and occasionally, though very rarely, father/daughter marriages. But as far as we know such marriages were not permitted to ordinary citizens until after the Roman conquest of Egypt when brother/sister marriages were allowed in classes other than the ruling one (Meiselman 1979). Presumably the main motivation of these marriages was to preserve property intact and to avoid splitting it up between various family members. With the arrival of Christianity incestuous marriages were forbidden amongst all classes.

Other ruling families, such as those of Hawaii and of the Incas of Peru, were also permitted intra-family marriages and sometimes, as in Egypt and Persia, this habit spread for a limited period to commoners. From a religious viewpoint, since there are many legends of gods mating with their own offspring, it was perhaps not too difficult to stretch such behaviour to human royalty and beyond, providing a sufficiently good excuse could be found such as the retention of property or the unavailability of any other partner. Who could Adam's sons marry except their sisters? Mormons in Utah permitted incest to ensure that their children only married within the church, until a state law was passed banning this in 1892.

Occasionally primitive societies have allowed incestuous relations for specific activities such as magical ritual. Meiselman quotes instances such as the belief of certain African villagers that a hippopotamus hunter can be sure of a kill if he has sexual relations with his daughter before the hunt, on the grounds that by the act he will have killed something within himself, thus making him a murderer capable of the necessary courage to take on a hippopotamus. She also quotes Weinburg (1955) as reporting that he found a current belief in certain groups in the United States that incest with a prepubertal daugther could cure venereal disease, the rationale being that the man can 'catch' purity in the same manner that he origially caught the disease.

Many suggestions have been put forward as to the origins of the taboo on incest. There is the argument that a family is strengthened by social ties outside itself, expressed neatly by Mountain Arapesh tribesmen of New Guinea when Margaret Mead asked a gathering of old men why incest was forbidden within the tribe:

> What, you would like to marry your sister! What is the matter with you anyway? Don't you want a brother-in-law? Don't you realize that if you marry another man's sister and another man marries your sister, you will have at least two brothers-in-law, while if you marry your own sister you will have none? With whom you will hunt, with whom will you garden, whom will you go to visit? (Mead 1950).

Genetically incest is unwise: research (which will be looked at more closely in a later chapter) has shown that in children born of incestuous matings both mortality and physical and mental handicaps are significantly higher. But where recessive genes are not present and where both parents are healthy then the children will probably be healthy too. The counter-argument to the suggestion that genetics were behind the origins of the taboo against incest – that livestock is deliberately interbred in order to perpetuate *good* qualities – is not really valid, since such interbreeding has to be very carefully controlled. Dog owners, for example, are only too familiar with poorly-controlled inbreeding, where problems such as congenitally-malformed hips, ingrowing eyelashes, chronic respiratory ailments have become major complaints among certain breeds of dogs. Since in any case it seems unlikely that primitive man had much understanding of how a child was conceived in the first place, it has always seemed to me doubtful that genetic problems had much effect on forming the taboo. It would have been different if every such union resulted in deformed children, but clearly this would not have been the case.

Another argument, which we considered earlier, is that incest breaks up the natural construction of a family by bringing jealousy and strife into a relationship, by making control of rebellious children difficult and by changing the natural protective relationship between parents and children. But for early man everyday life would have been a continuous struggle, and the question of children's rights and their emotional needs cannot have been of importance.

The taboo against incest seems to be of immense antiquity and some deeper, not necessarily rational, objection has to be found to explain the horror with which nearly all societies have regarded incest. That biological or economic reasons do not alone account for the horror becomes clear when you consider how various types of incest are regarded. Brother and sister incest has never been as strongly condemned as father/daughter incest, while mother/son has been always considered the most dreadful of all. But if biological reasons were the main consideration surely mother/son incest is the least likely to be worrying, since by the time a boy is able to produce live sperm his mother will be past her peak of fertility. Whereas between post-pubertal siblings the greatest danger of all exists since fertility will be extremely high, yet brother/sister incest is the least condemned. Again, from the economic viewpoint of bringing in outside contacts, broadening the family base, etc., brother/sister incest is obviously more damaging than incest between parent/child since two members, not one, of the future generation are involved.

That it is 'natural' not to want to commit incest, and indeed to find the very idea of it repugnant, is highly doubtful, although this is a common, usually unconsidered, argument. I would have thought that if something were 'unnatural' and no one wanted to do it anyway, it would be quite unnecessary to invent such a powerful taboo against it. Children enjoy touching and being touched, holding and being held. Adults too are happy when communicating their feelings by touch. Differentiating between sensual touch and a purely paternal or maternal touch may not always be as easy as one might like to imagine. With warm uninhibited people one might easily overlap into the other without any harm being done, as long as the adult is aware of what is happening and is instantly able to change gear. The young child will not know his responses are turning sexual – he is quite unsophisticated in such matters at this age – and it is entirely up to the adult to draw the line, to take the responsibility for what is happening. The body has a limited number of responses. A breast-feeding mother who has not blocked out the truth of her own feelings knows there is a strong sexual element in the first few moments when a child sucks at a bursting breast. This strong erotic sensation lapses to a quieter sense of fulfilment and pleasure when the milk begins to be drawn off, but at what point the pleasure changes from sexual to maternal is impossible to calibrate.

Undesired sexual emotions are always difficult to handle, and one way is to refuse to admit they exist at all. Unfortunately, as we will see later, it is precisely in families where this sort of repression exists, where sexuality is not an open happy thing but is something to be denied and hushed up, that incest often occurs.

Conjectures about the psychological reasons for the incest taboo are perhaps the most fascinating of all, but there is not space here to explore them. The truth most probably is that it is not one but a whole constellation of factors which caused the extremely powerful feelings about incest which still exist today, although the modern approach to sexual mores has somewhat modified this horror for numbers of people.

Of even more interest than the origin of the incest taboo is the history of research into incest itself. It was Freud who first opened up the subject of childhood sexuality, to the dismay and shock of his Victorian peers. That Freud himself later denied some of his early findings is now becoming well known. Florence Rush (1977) writes at length on how he came to change his original views on the reality of incestuous relationships between father and daughter. Freud had many patients who suffered from hysteria, the clinical symptoms of which include among others a loss of voice, deafness and paralysis. At first he accepted as true the complaints by these women that they had been sexually molested by their fathers or their brothers, and concluded there was a connection between neurosis and sexual abuse.

In a letter to his friend Wilheim Fliess (Bonaparte, Freud & Kris 1954) Freud wrote: 'I have come to the opinion that anxiety is to be connected, not with a mental, but with a physical consequence of sexual abuse.' In 1896 Freud publicly presented his theory that hysteria had social rather than biological causes, and specifically identified childhood sexual abuse as causing the trauma which finally resulted in hysteria (Rush 1977). He quoted eighteen cases to support his theory, all stemming from sexual abuse in childhood. In a paper (Freud 1953), he wrote: 'It seems to me certain that our children are far oftener exposed to sexual aggression that we should suppose.'

Yet after that 1896 presentation he never again openly placed full responsibility on the male perpetrators. The repeated incrimination by the women of their fathers, most of them middle-class Viennese like himself, had made him deeply uneasy, and gradually he began to reject his earlier views. The details of how this happened and suggested reasons for this change of mind are elaborated in Florence Rush's article. As his work progressed and he explored his own unconscious motives more deeply he found in himself memories of desire for his mother, hostility towards his father and even discovered in his brother and sisters the 'existence of some hysterical features [suggesting] his father had been thus incriminated' (from an unpublished letter to Fliess 1897). He realized through a dream that he was feeling 'overly affectionate' towards his daughter Mathilda, and saw the dream as fulfilling 'my wish to pin down a father as the originator of neurosis and put an end to my persistent doubts.' From this, claims Rush:

> He presumed that all his patients had the same need and therefore came to suspect that their stories of fathers as seducers were 'defensive fictions' . . . he relegated his patients' testimony to fantasy, discarded his seduction theory and replaced it with the incipient Oedipal complex.

Eventually he was to write:

> Almost all my women patients told me that they had been seduced by their father. I was driven to recognize in the end that these reports were untrue and so came to understand that the hysterical symptoms are derived from phantasies and not from real occurrences' (Freud 1966).

However, something had to be causing the neurosis, and blame was shifted backwards to the pre-Oedipal period (before the age of three years) when the mother was the main object in the child's life. For 'it was really the mother who by her activities over the child's bodily hygiene inevitably stimulated and perhaps even aroused for the first time pleasurable sensations to her genitals.' It is true that in general psychiatric interest in Britain is currently centred mainly on this same pre-Oedipal age, but the situation is seen as being far more complex, involving the whole family, the backgrounds of both parents, outside pressure, and anything else bearing on the developing relationship between mother and child.

Freudian therapists and analysts, however, who are still convinced of the validity of Freud's theory of the Oedipus complex and of 'penis-envy' from which every female is supposed to suffer, will usually dismiss their patients' relations of their seduction by their fathers as fantasy, or, where incest indubitably has taken place, they will see the victim as the seducer, for the Oedipus theory postulates a strong impulse in every child for physical union with the parent of the opposite sex. Thus the desire of the little girl for her father and also for a penis which she herself can never possess results in fantasies and/or seductive behaviour. If this Oedipal situation is not satisfactorily worked out so that the child can move on to a more mature relationship with her parents, trouble must result. If this occurs it is the child, not the parent, who is seen as the originator of the trauma which she then suffers.

In whatever new theory this old idea is wrapped up, the image of the small girl as seductress is still common. That most small children will respond as desired to parental pressure, that the apparently adult sexual behaviour some children display has had to be learned and does not come naturally to a young child, that parents are the ones who have the power and the responsibility, remains unimportant for these theorists. Their adult clients, full of unresolved guilt and grief, are likely to have that guilt reinforced or to be 'driven out of therapy into psychosis because of the therapist's repeated denials of the reality of their experience (Rosenfeld 1979a). If the client can afford a full course of treatment he or she may nevertheless be 'cured', perhaps by the passing of time or by the presence of a sympathetic ear as much as by the therapist's theories, but many non-Freudian therapists have told of the relief of clients who previously had had their guilt reaffirmed by Freudian therapy when being told the simple truth that – whatever the daughter's behaviour – it is entirely the father's responsiblity to control any situation that might arise between him and his child.

Because of Freud's innovative work later researchers such as Kinsey were able to take the existence of sexual impulses in children for granted. Kinsey showed that some sort of childhood sexual experience was more or less universal, and also that the sexual abuse of children was far more common than had been previously realized. But he seemed not at all perturbed by this discovery, and little was made of it. David Finkelhor (1979b) suggests that the reason the work done by Kinsey and other researchers on incest was so slow to reach the public was that many people working in this field were politically motivated to

steer clear of association with the issue of child molesting. They were busy lobbying for sexual reform: greater availability of contraceptives, more and better sex education, more enlightened treatment of sex offenders, fewer restrictions on erotic literature, decriminalization of consensual sex acts, permissiveness toward childhood sex exploration and so forth. The liberal professional feared, with some justification, that the concern over child molestation was likely to scuttle their reform efforts. Child molestation was being used by conservatives to oppose sexual reform.

While in America in the 1940s and 1950s various sex crimes concerning children were being made much of in the press, as was the infamous 'Moors' case in Britain in the later 1960s, the liberal effort was concerned to play down child sex abuse in order not to put back the general reform of sexual mores. They claimed that such abuse was rather infrequent, and that child molesters were not the 'sex fiends' presented in the media:

> Thus, concern over child molesting bloomed [among the public] for a period, but in the face of concerted resistance from the professional and research community, people who are ironically now the most interested in the problem, interest waned and the problem went into eclipse for 20 years (Finkelhor 1979b).

The battle for sexual reform is now more or less over, though there is still much mopping up to be done. The women's movement, which in the United States has more power than in Britain, took up the cause of children, having seen them as too frequent clients in their newly-established rape clinics, as did also many concerned professionals. But no progress is ever straightforward. The liberal workers in this field are finding, in the United States at least, that their new opponents are not the conservatives who once used child molestation to prove general moral decay, but certain groups who have gone to the other extreme and demand sexual 'liberalization' for children. We shall look at the 'pro-incest lobby', as it is sometimes called in Chapter 7, but it is interesting to note how difficult it is for social reformers to achieve their aim without producing unwanted and unexpected side effects.

Finally, it is worth considering for a moment the importance of people's attitudes towards incest, as these affect every aspect of discovery, treatment and punishment. There are those who profess to declare that incest hardly exists. A police surgeon on hearing I was writing a book on the subject told me that he had never seen a case in all his fifteen years of medical practice, which included eight years of being a police surgeon, nor had he ever heard it discussed among his colleagues. So how, he asked me, could I write a book on something that was obviously so terribly rare? Neither for that matter had he ever personally seen a case of physical abuse of a child by its parents. Did I honestly expect him to think about the possibility of battering or incest when examining a child patient? he asked me, amazement in his voice – what sort of doctor would he be if he had thoughts like that! What indeed.

Fortunately, such blinkering is uncommon. The majority of people who work in any of the caring services are well aware of the existence of incest, though an understanding of the size of the problem is only just beginning to filter through. All the same, there is too frequently a resistance against acknowledging the existence of any particular case. Sometimes this is caused by straightforward embarrassment. A policeman commenting on new police recruits said:

> There he is, driving down the street looking at his reflection in the shop windows and hoping for something really exciting to happen like a robbery – not too big – when the radio comes on and it's an incest case. The first thing he thinks of is, Jesus, what the hell do I do? It's not easy to talk to people about this – to talk to a young girl and ask her personal questions – they're young men themselves, they don't know how to handle it.

Others see the fear of incest as being so deeply entrenched within us that even professionals may be incapacitated by it!

> Dread of incest is buried deeply in the human unconscious and evokes volatile and unpredictable emotions. Professional helpers are not free of the incest dread. Many react either evasively when a case is referred or irresponsibly by failing to ensure the victim's safety through conscientious treatment and follow-up. Criminal justice personnel cannot claim immunity from the panic induced by incest, since their effect on sexually abusive families usually adds up to either rejection of the child's plea for help, if the evidence is not court-proof, or severe punishment of the entire family if the offender confesses. Finally, social scientists must also be afflicted with the dread of incest. How else can we account for the paucity of studies on

incest which, with few exceptions, are superficial in conception and scope? (Giarretto 1978).

Of course, from a medical point of view unless somebody in the affected family talks about it openly incest is very difficult to diagnose. It took a long time for physicians to recognize baby battering for what it was and to overcome their initial repugnance sufficiently to allow them to accept that parents could abuse their own children. Now it is almost as though they have discovered a new disease, and one hopes there are few doctors remaining who do not have at least a working knowledge of what physical symptoms to look for. But physical trauma rarely occurs in the sexual abuse of children unless rape has taken place or a small child has been crudely penetrated or infected with venereal disease. There are few observable interesting symptoms to attract the attentions of a doctor who has a bent towards physical medicine; there can be no X-rays to show up the disease, no wondrous medicines to be discovered or prescribed. The only way of uncovering it, unless they are told, is to listen very carefully, to ask the right questions and to always bear in mind the possibility of incest. Not easy for a busy doctor with a hundred other things on his mind, nor particularly tempting for a doctor who is not very interested in psychology.

People's attitudes are also deeply affected by the way they perceive sexual politics. As we have seen, feminists at first saw incest as an example of men subjugating women. Another closely related example is the so-called 'victim/perpetrator model' (Rosenfeld 1979b). This is a tempting label as it gives us a 'goodie' on the one hand – the daughter, and a 'baddie' on the other – the father, and helps combat those who claim that children who suffer incest and women who get raped are seductive and have 'asked for it.' But the truth cannot be so simply expressed without blurring the actuality of the experience. A further aspect of the way women frequently were, and are, blamed for the occurrence of incest, is that it was often assumed women drove their husbands into their daughter's arms by being frigid, and also were blamed for refusing to listen to their daughter's pleas for help. Women in the feminist movement are understandably unhappy to accept any truth in these last two statements, and yet repeatedly we hear exactly these two accusations from male offenders and their daughters. The facts seem to be that very often the mother herself has been an incest victim, so that it is not surprising if she has sexual difficulties in her marriage (bearing in mind that the father also most probably had his own childhood problems) and is unwilling or unable to face the possibility that the same pattern may be happening to her own daughter.

As we saw earlier, the attitudes of therapists vary greatly. Even for those clients whose problem is acknowledged to be based on reality and not on fantasy, the treatment they receive will not necessarily meet their needs. A psychologist who feels strongly that the sexual problem of the offending father needs to be treated directly, said to me,

> We see people time after time who've been through standard psychotherapy and it's failed. They're told 'Don't lets talk about your current problem, let's talk about your toilet training, let's talk about your feelings for your mother.' The therapist doesn't want to deal directly with the incest, they feel uncomfortable in trying to deal with that, so they say – oh, that's just a symptom, let's get back to the roots of all this. I don't want to hear about molesting your daughter, I want to hear about . . ., etc. This approach can be of use, of course, but basically you have to focus on the sexual problem itself.

As for attitudes towards punishment, these range from the humanistic approach as exemplified by Giarretto's treatment programme, to the 'string em up' or 'cut off their balls' approach. What punishment, if any, a man gets will depend almost entirely on where he lives. There is little consistency of punishment, and the laws on incest badly need revising. Certain reforms are already being explored, but nothing is likely to happen very quickly. The well-being and the future of many thousands of people are at stake, as we shall see in the next chapter when we try to formulate some opinion of the size of the problem. Whether the legal process results in punishment or in treatment, there is no way of dealing with the offender without deeply affecting his family. For the families' sake there has to be a change in the attitudes of everybody concerned, from the neighbours next door, the police, the social workers, right through to the examining magistrate.

Chapter 3

Incidence of incest and how to discover it

How large a problem are we discussing? Until recently most of us thought incest was rare except among a few backward pockets of isolated or over-crowded people whose behaviour would alter with increased prosperity, education and social welfare. We now know this conception of incest as a class-related problem is far from the truth. Recent research has shown incest to be more widespread than anyone had previously considered possible.

The first difficulty in assessing the incidence is caused by the problem of definition, which means that the law cannot answer our question in any meaningful way. This applies both to Britain and to the United States. For 1977 the British Home Office reports 295 cases of incest (an act of *intercourse* taking place between a man and certain family females, remember – father/son, brother/sister intercourse, etc. being excluded) and 243 cases of 'unlawful sexual intercourse' (intercourse with a minor regardless of relationship) with children under thirteen years of age. In America national statistics specifically relating to the incidence of sexual abuse of children are not kept. Each state has its own legal requirements for reporting which vary considerably. Some will cover only caretakers, not including, for example, brother/sister, uncle/niece, grandfather/grand-daughter incest unless the offenders were adult and in charge of the child. Some local jurisdictions have no system at all for gathering such information. Others prosecute under a number of different statutes which may apply equally to adult victims, and children will not be separated out in the crime figures – these will include such acts as indecent exposure, indecent assault and battery, carnal abuse, sodomy, rape, etc. Yet others will keep separate figures for child abuse, but this will probably include every kind of abuse, physical as well as sexual. And even when sexual abuse is reported to the police it is likely to be of such a serious nature that the reporting could not be avoided, so that these cases are probably not truly representative of incest as a whole.

But even with serious sexual assault, such as rape, reporting is by no means invariable – a recent survey in the United States found that under half the rapes committed were actually reported. Abel *et al.* (1979) estimate the national figure for rape to be 'approximately 57 per 100,000 females at risk' – a true figure cannot be given because reporting varies from city to city. If we double this figure to include unreported rape and bear in mind that Wells (1958) found that 84 per cent of a large sample of rape victims studied were under sixteen years old and 58 per cent were under thirteen, we may agree with Abel that 'rape is a (comparatively) common crime that is usually committed against children.'

This reluctance to report extends to all fields of sexual abuse. In a random survey of eighteen female pyschiatric outpatients (seen for complaints other than incest) carried out by Alvin Rosenfeld (1979b) it turned out that one-third had a history of incest, and that none of these six had previously reported the molestation to anyone in authority. Indeed, either they had informed no one at all of their experience, or had told at the most one or two relatives. When therapy began only one of these patients spontaneously reported to Rosenfeld her history of incest. Two reported it during the evaluation of their cases, two further patients later admitted it when asked about it directly, and one (a young child) eventually told her grandmother, though while still in therapy. Rosenfeld points out that since half of these women only revealed their history late in therapy and not all the patients were seen for a lengthy period of time, this estimate of one in six is 'the lowest possible estimate for this sample' of eighteen women patients. He considers it very unlikely they had fabricated their story.

Why are victims of sexual abuse, children in particular, so reluctant to talk about what has happened to them? Embarrassment at discussing intimate sexual details deter many. Younger children feel that they themselves have done wrong and fear they will be punished if they tell. Prohibitions about 'sneaking' are strong among children, and a young child may not be able to differentiate between when one may honourably tell and when one may not. Many will be reluctant to bring trouble on the offender. Horror at the event combined with a strong desire to forget all about it or to pretend it never happened may be another reason for not reporting the event. A further and very important factor is that although some victims do overcome their reluctance to tell someone, very often the person told refuses to hear. We will see later, for example, how children frequently tell their mothers and are either ignored or told to hush, or perhaps are told they are lying or misunderstood what happened. This happens less often when a stranger is involved, but outside molestation is the exception rather than the rule – usually the offender is either within the family or well known to its members. Even social workers, doctors and others who ought to be able to cope with such information often in fact cannot. Too many adults, even professionals, will subtly discourage a child from talking about their experiences, or successfully ignore their own suspicions that sexual abuse might have occurred.

Another understandable reason why so little incest is reported is that in order to avoid neighbours and business associates learning what has happened, efforts will be made to deal with the matter privately. In addition there is a natural reluctance to expose child victims to the criminal justice system.

Partly in order to overcome the problem of under-reporting some researchers used retrospective studies, as in the one reported above by Rosenfeld. An earlier survey by Gagnon (1965) of 1,200 college-age females showed that of the 26 per cent who reported having a sexual experience with an adult prior to the age of thirteen, only 6 per cent had previously reported the incident to any authority. In 21 per cent of the incidents reported to Gagnon, the victim had never before told anyone at all about the offence.

It is clear then, that official figures on a national scale, in Britain as in the United States, do not begin to convey the size of the problem, partly because the real figures are not available due to lack of reporting, and partly because in any case sound statistics cannot be collected as long as there are no universal and adequate definitions of what exactly is wanted. However, in the United States there has been considerable increase over the last few years in the reporting of sexual abuse cases, mainly because of changed child abuse legislation and because of an increase in public awareness of the subject, and it is to be hoped that the same change will soon be seen in Britain.

Estimates of the incidence of incest have changed dramatically in size during the last few years as more and more facts have come to light. For example, in the past few people ever considered including sexually assaulted boys; yet it is beginning to appear that among young boys sexual abuse (not necessarily incestuous) may be nearly as great a problem as among young girls. During their 'Child Sexual Abuse Prevention Project' the Sexual Assault Services, Hennepin County (Kent 1979) found that in a study of approximately 800 elementary-aged schoolchildren, there were as many boys as girls who had been victims of some form of sexual exploitation. These were schoolchildren in an ordinary school setting, not children who had come to the attention of the authorities because of any obvious problems or delinquency. Boys notoriously dislike reporting any kind of sexual abuse, so that the actual numbers of boys suffering assault is particularly difficult to ascertain, but Deborah Anderson, director of the same Sexual Assault Services, told me that 16 per cent of the victims of sexual abuse passing through her office were male.

As we have seen, incest means so many different things to different people that estimates of incidence cannot be properly compared. Nevertheless I shall attempt to do just that, since there is no other material to work on. Many researchers avoid this problem by referring to 'sexual abuse' rather than 'incest', which can confuse rather than elucidate the problem, especially as sometimes the term seems to be used interchangeably. To help the reader in the following few pages I shall italicise the actual phrase or other relevant words used by the individual researchers, and remind him that not all people have the same definition, even when the word 'incest' is used.

We will start with Weinburg's estimate of approximately one case of incest per million *inhabitants* (Weinburg 1955). This figure, though frequently quoted, is now thought by most workers in the field to be a serious underestimate. Vincent De Francis, former director of the Children's Division of the American Humane Association, ran a study of *child molestation* in New York City from 1966 to 1969 (De Francis 1969). This study indicated over 3,000 reported cases for each of the three years concerned. From those figures De Francis estimated there would be a national annual referring rate of 100,000 cases. The population of the United States in 1970 was approximately 203,000,000 making an estimated figure of one child molestation in every 2,030 population. Mavis Tsai (Tsai and Wagner 1979), referring to De Francis' projection, writes 'considering the widespread reluctance to report this phenomenon, the unreported incidence may raise the estimate anywhere from 5 to 20 times greater than what is reported. Clearly the problem of sexual abuse is pervasive.'

The American National Center on Child Abuse and Neglect (Washington DC) estimates the annual national incidence of *child sexual abuse* to be between 60,000 and 100,000 cases a year, similar to De Francis' estimate. In Britain such studies are only just beginning to be carried out. After conducting a survey among professionals who had dealt with sexually abused children, Pat Beezley Mrazek, Margaret Lynch and Arnon Bentovim (1981) calculated from the figures given them that a minimum of 3 in every 1,000 children would be referred to professionals for some form of sexual abuse during their childhood. (Note that the previous figure relates to the number of sexually assaulted children per so many *inhabitants*. This last figure relates purely to the number of assaulted children per 1,000 *children*.)

Some people have attempted to arrive at a rough estimate by comparing sexual abuse with physical abuse. 'In terms of child oriented crimes, child sexual abuse and more particularly incest, may be as prevalent as child physical abuse' (E. Younger, Attorney General of California, 1976). Some professionals to whom I have spoken, both in Britain and the United States, consider it likely there is far more sexual abuse than physical abuse, though this was guesswork based on personal experience, not on statistics. De Francis himself is reported to believe the incidence of sexual abuse to be much greater than the incidence of physical abuse.

Let us turn from guesswork to the few facts as yet available. We have already glanced at Gagnon's retrospective study (1965) where he found that a quarter of 1,200 college-age females had reported a *sexual experience* with an adult prior to the age of thirteen, and at Rosenfeld's eighteen psychiatric outpatients, one-third of whom reported an *incestuous* history.

Incidentally Rosenfeld refers to several other studies of female psychiatric patients which revealed that approximately 4 per cent of the patients had had *incestuous* experiences: Lukianowicz (1972) found that 4 per cent of all the female psychiatric patients seen in County Antrim, Ireland, had a history of incest, while Browning and Boatman (1977) quote a figure of 3.8 per cent of child psychiatric patients in Oregon with a similar history. Rosenfeld also refers to other studies which made similar observations. Although in themselves these findings showed a considerably higher proportion than would have been expected from earlier estimates they are in themselves much lower than Rosenfeld's findings in the study just referred to, where one-third of his patients disclosed a history of *incest*. The difference between these sets of figures is clearly due to the fact that Rosenfeld made a deliberate attempt to find out whether or not incest had occurred. Introducing his own study Lukianowicz writes:

> The present study is concerned with the problem of father-daughter incest in County Antrim . . . come across . . . mostly accidentally. . . . The great majority of subjects were women referred . . . by their family doctors with various nervous complaints. Some of them, quite casually, reported incestuous experiences with their fathers in their childhood. Such statements were made rather unexpectedly and quite spontaneously, without any questioning or prompting on our part. We are aware of the fact that by adopting such a restrained attitude we have probably missed a great number of possible cases of incest. Yet even with this guarded and passive approach we have collected 26 cases of paternal incest (out of a total of 650 selected patients). We know of 9 further such cases (all of them sisters of our patients) but as they officially were not our patients we have not included them in the present survey.

I have quoted this introduction at length because Lukianowicz's figure of 4 per cent is very frequently repeated without an accompanying explanation of how he discovered his clients' incestuous background, and wrong conclusions are therefore often drawn, particularly in England where until very recently there have been few studies on this subject published in British medical journals. Bearing in mind that Lukianowicz (a) is referring only to father/daughter incest, (b) waited for patients to volunteer the information, and (c) did not (quite properly) include the nine sisters, we can understand why Rosenfeld's figure of 33 per cent was so much higher.

Working from De Francis' three-year study which revealed 3,000 victims annually of child molestation in New York, the American Humane Association (1972) estimated a total of 200,000 to 300,000 cases of *female child molestation* (including unreported cases) in the United States annually, at least 5,000 of which will be cases of *father/daughter incest*.

Geri Hatcher, project director of the Child Sexual Abuse Prevention Project, Los Angeles County Department of Public Social Services, (personal communication, 1980), found that in the two years the project has been running, out of a population of around one and a quarter million (her department deals with only a quarter of Los Angeles County), approximately 300 *families* with *incest* problems have been seen. In general, once a programme becomes known the number of cases presented increases, so we may assume that this average of 150 *families* a year out of one and a quarter million people is the minimum figure.

Mavis Tsai, again in a personal communication (1980), discussed a survey conducted among a thousand university students in Seattle attending a class called Psychology of Human Sexual Behaviour. She agreed that there might be a slight bias in that the students had chosen to attend these classes, but it is one of the most popular classes of all and is taken by students from every kind of discipline. The survey showed that one in eight had had some kind of *sexual experience* in their childhood, ranging from 'touching-up' to intercourse.

Another, more detailed, study was carried out by David Finkelhor (Finkelhor 1978b) among 795 college undergraduates at six New England colleges and universities. These students, who filled out questionnaires about their childhood sexual experiences, were mixed in terms of religious, social class, ethnic and urban rural background. All were attending various social science courses. Of the women students, 19 per cent reported some kind of *sexual victimization*; 11 per cent of these experiences had been with adults when they themselves were under twelve; 6 per cent with a child or adolescent at least five years older than themselves, and 4 per cent with adults at least ten years older when they themselves were aged between thirteen and sixteen (some had had multiple experiences). 44 per cent of these experiences were with family members – few were victimized by total outsiders unknown to the family. From his figures Finkelhor extrapolates that 9 per cent of all women are *sexually victimized by a relative*, and 1.5 per cent have sex with their *own fathers*.

Of the men, 9 per cent had been *sexually victimized*, which is an interesting figure considering how few males voluntarily report sexual abuse to the authorities, and bears out earlier speculations that sexual abuse among boys is nothing like as uncommon as has previously been supposed.

It is clear from the figures quoted in these last few pages that the incidence of incest has been grossly underestimated in the past. Even these numbers do not contain the entire truth – for example, Finkelhor's figures for his student population, as he himself admits, has to be an underestimate as 'the lower income strata of the population which tend to have the highest rates' is underrepresented. Also he considers it unlikely that every student was fully open about his or her past when answering the questionnaires.

A question that is sometimes asked is: has there been an actual increase in incest in recent years which might account for these higher figures? The obvious answer is that most of the increase may be accounted for by the growth of a new understanding among researchers that few people will voluntarily talk about their incestuous past – the right questions have to be asked in the right way if the truth is to be found out. Public opinion is also changing: just as the fear that they might batter their child is nowadays something a parent may admit, thereby obtaining help before serious damage is done, so gradually people are finding the courage to ring up Parents Anonymous groups and other agencies, asking for advice and help on incest problems. In Britain such approaches are still rare in comparison to the calls concerned with physical abuse but in the United States where more help is available (though not in every state by any means) the reporting rate is increasing rapidly.

In San José, where Dr Giarretto was behind the first-ever child sexual abuse programme, referral rates have increased at the amazing rate of thirty families in the first year (1971) to over 600 cases in 1978. Dr Giarretto puts this increase down to media publicity and a growing confidence in the way the programme that he and his colleagues have worked out assists the families. This type of increase is seen again and again whenever help becomes available. In Aurora County, Colorado, for example, where local police have set up a small child abuse unit, reports of crimes against children by the family, including incest, have increased from 134 in 1977 to 653 in 1979 (personal communication 1980). It is true that crime figures in general increased during this period, but not to the same extent. My informant, Detective Salvador of the child abuse unit, was unable to give me official figures of incest cases as these had not then been worked out, but he calculated that out of a recent 600 cases of *child abuse*, 55 were *incest* cases – this was over a period of ten months. He considers that when it becomes as acceptable to report incest as it is now acceptable to report physical abuse, the figures are bound to increase considerably.

Some people, however, think that not all of this increase is due to a changed climate of opinion and to researchers' growing vigilance. David Finkelhor, for example, who has done much excellent work in this field, first told me that compared with a century or two ago he thought that in general incest was probably decreasing: 'These things get discovered at the point when they are starting to decline – before that nobody would bother about child abuse, it was just accepted as a part of life.' But, he added,

It may be that sexual abuse has been increasing in the very short term, within, say, the last thirteen to twenty years. Family break-up has exposed children to men in positions of authority who don't have quite the same inhibitions their natural fathers may have. My research does indicate that stepfathers are much more likely to commit sexual abuse than natural fathers. But against that fact the high rate of divorce means that mothers can take their children out of homes where the fathers have been conducting themselves in a tyrannical and abusive way. Yes, it's true that many women then go and find themselves a similar kind of man, but the fact is that a large number of children are being raised today without any fathers at all. The statistics are that 30 to 40 per cent of all children born today in the United States will spend several years of their lives in a single-parent family, and nearly all of those are mother-headed households.

He pointed out that the emphasis on sex by the media in general, and in particular the new style – more common in America than in Britain at the moment – of using extremely young models for advertisement purposes, cannot help males who are attempting to control inappropriate sexual desires. However he doubts if this actual increase, if it exists at all, is anything more than a temporary phenomenon, and believes that certain kinds of abuse such as exhibitionism are actually decreasing. Comparing the latest figures with certain studies done a generation back, such as Kinsey's famous work on sexuality, he finds that altogether there seems to have been little change.

Karin Meiselman, author of the book *Incest* (1979), also considers that family break-up might be responsible for an actual increase in sexual abuse. In a personal interview she speculated that anything that breaks down family relations and increases peoples' inability to trust and talk openly to each other will increase the possibility of incest. She mentioned Weinburg who states that incest increases after wars, when children and fathers, separated by military service, no longer have the same relationship. Equally, divorced fathers who see their children only occasionally may lose some of the normal inhibitions. Alcoholism, also, which is frequently associated with incest, is becoming an increasing problem and Meiselman suggests this too may be another factor in a possible increase in incestuous behaviour.

Finally, then, it appears that though there might be a slight actual increase in incest, it is insignificant in comparison to the huge jump in reporting that is already happening in certain areas. In Minnesota, for example, the strengthened child abuse reporting laws, which among other changes require cases of incest to be included in the statistics of child abuse, have resulted in a considerable increase in reporting. Between 1974 and 1977 the number of child abuse cases in general reported to the Minnesota Department of Welfare increased more than fourfold. In Hennepin County alone the isolation of incest statistics resulted in 1972 (the first year these separate figures were required) in fourteen cases of incest being reported. As workers became accustomed to looking for incest, and as facilities to help incest families also became available, so the rate rapidly increased to the point where in 1977 200 cases were reported. There is no reason to suppose that similar increases would not be found in Britain if similar reporting laws became mandatory.

The last word on the subject of incidence may be left to David Finkelhor (personal communication 1980):

> My experience is that the vast majority of children never tell anybody and it never comes to light – I would say that 75% never gets discovered, even perhaps as high as 90% never gets discovered. I think it really needs a public health programme.

Certainly if the numbers really are as huge as some people suspect we shall need to rethink our entire approach to the problem.

We have already seen in Chapter 2 how influential was Freud's eventual conclusion that most of the incestuous experiences reported by his clients were nothing more than fantasies resulting from their own childhood sexual desires for their fathers. Although in general modern psychiatry has moved away from this theory, the myth that children commonly lie about sexual abuse remains active in many quarters, and has helped to keep alive the assumption that incest is a rare event.

As Erin Pizzey of Chiswick's Womens Aid says, 'Children rarely lie about this sort of thing. Why should they? If anyone doubts that there's much incest about, let them come here and talk to some of our families. They won't stay doubtful for long!'

It is very important that investigators especially bear the truth of this in mind, and do not assume they should necessarily accept the word of an adult before that of a possibly confused and inconsistent child. If children lie at all, it is more likely to be in the form of a denial that incest ever happened. Many researchers agree that this is so: Anderson (1979) for instance, reports that out of nearly 1,500 cases coming to the attention of the County Attorney's Office they never found any child who claimed that incest had occurred when it had not, but that a number of children had denied it when in fact it had occurred. This denial is particularly likely to happen in court when under pressure from the family, especially if the father denies the charge and the mother backs him.

Psychiatrists have told me they have found patients can be very adaptable on this point; while incest victims may have a strong desire to tell the truth and be absolved of the guilt they feel, they may also have an equally strong need to pretend it never happened at all, that their parents did not behave thus to them and that they had imagined the whole thing. If the psychiatrist tends to assume that most of his incest patients are fantasizing this attitude will be communicated to the patient even without anything being said overtly, and as often as not the patient will oblige and not insist that incest actually occurred. Although most psychiatrists are conscious of the possibility that direct questioning about incest might tempt a patient to fabricate a story if she thinks it could win her heightened interest, it appears this rarely happens. This is as true of adults as it is of children (Shengold 1963, Rosenfeld 1979b).

It may be argued that young children cannot always distinguish between truth and fantasy. Among small children this is true in so far as they may embellish their story or give various versions of it because what actually happened may not be at all clear in their minds; in their relation of the event they will not only be trying to make sense of what happened for themselves, but also they will be attempting to organize their story in a way they imagine will make sense to an adult. After all, how can a child of four, say, who has finally learned habits of personal hygiene, accept as a possible behaviour the fact that father has put his penis in her mouth? Part of her mind will blank it out as an impossible act, and equally she will not believe that any adult could possibly accept the truth of such a ludicrous story.

In a home where sex is considered suspect, dangerous, even dirty, a child unexpectedly seeing an adult in the nude may be deeply shocked, and even imagine the episode to be deliberate when it is not. Such misapprehensions do occur, but practised observers ought to be able to discover the true situation without too much difficulty. Equally, a small child may exaggerate her story in order to impress an apparently unbelieving listener, but experienced workers say it is always apparent when a child moves from fact to fiction.

Another problem with young children is that often they do not know the real meanings of words. When a study of children in nursery school was carried out it was found that a word like 'rape' could mean almost anything: the responses ranged from 'stripping off', 'murder', 'stealing' to the more sophisticated 'something you don't want to do before you get married' and 'it's when people come into your house and everyone takes off their clothes and someone does dirty things to you.' Even children a few years older are still very uncertain exactly what rape is; a study of children aged between five and eight showed that in the main they had the same kind of misconceptions, though violence was more likely to enter into their descriptions. Again, experienced workers will be aware of this kind of difficulty, and will bear in mind that few children will deliberately lie about important issues, even if they aren't too much concerned about fibs.

Between the ages of eight and twelve a child should be able to distinguish without much trouble between fact and fantasy and to understand properly events that happen to him, although he may still be unclear about the exact meaning of certain words. All the same, great care must be taken to find the truth of the matter, or dreadful damage may be done to a family, especially if the charge becomes known to the public via the press. Newspapers are happy to print scandalous stories but find acquittals or proofs of innocence of less interest and may not report them at all, with the consequence that a wrongly-accused man's name may never be fully cleared as far as his neighbourhood is concerned.

The general impression, then, among professionals working in this field appears to be that few children will lie deliberately in matters of this sort in order to 'get' somebody, and that it is fairly obvious when this happens. Such a child is likely to be angry, very ready to accuse, whereas most genuine victims, at least before they have had treatment, are withdrawn, quiet children who are obviously having difficulty in expressing what has happened to them.

If questioned patiently and with warmth, genuine victims will give details of a kind that show clearly enough they have experienced what they are talking about. As we have seen, it is not enough to take her word if a small child accuses her aggressor of rape, for example – because by rape she may merely mean he stole her purse and threatened to knock her down if she told anyone. But careful questioning that does not put any words into the victim's mouth will usually reveal exactly what happened.

I witnessed one such session – unusually the 'victim' turned out to be no victim at all, at least not of sexual abuse – which I will describe in detail because it was particularly interesting in that it showed how easily an unpractised investigator could come away with the wrong impression.

A young girl of eleven who had a history of problems had told her teacher that two foster-fathers had 'frenched' her, as she called it, apparently meaning they had both given her 'french' kisses. She also accused one of them of having 'gone to bed' with her sister, who was two years younger than herself and who had been previously raped (she claimed) by one of her mother's boyfriends. The teacher had informed the police, and a policewoman, very experienced with dealing with children, had been sent along to investigate. She was kind enough to let me go with her. We knew, before we met the older sister, that the younger child had neither denied or corroborated this story when she had been seen by the teacher, but had merely 'looked blank'.

The policewoman, whom I will call Anne, saw the teacher before the child was called, and asked a few questions. The teacher was a rather tense woman who combined boldness with nervousness, so that in her presence you had an uneasy feeling of some underlying explosion about to take place. She was, however, a bright woman, very interested in her job, with a determinedly cheerful manner which she obviously used in front of the children. She explained how the girl (whom I shall call Jill) often had problems at school, but this was not to be wondered at since her mother was virtually a prostitute who had lived with a series of abusive, hard-up boyfriends who regularly beat her up, and whose father had left her mother several years previously. Jill was not unintelligent, and when she tried she could work well, but sometimes she would not turn up at school or suddenly would behave destructively in a way that disturbed the other children. When, the previous day, this had happened, the teacher asked Jill to stay behind after class and had said to her (the voice in which the teacher reported this to us showed exactly how bright and cheerful she had been during this interview), 'well, what's your excuse this time? It had better be good!' Jill had replied promptly 'What about this, then? I was frenched! Is that good enough for you?'

I was expecting Anne to ask the teacher further questions, but it seemed she had now obtained from her all she needed. She already knew something about the child's background. Basically what the teacher had told her was true; in addition Anne knew something the teacher didn't know, that when some time previously Jill had finally been taken into care after having been picked up by the police wandering around on her own late at night waiting for her mother to reappear, she had been sent to carefully chosen foster-parents who had looked after children for the local authorities for many years with great success in a number of difficult cases, including several involving sexual abuse. Anne knew that not even foster-parents such as these are necessarily above suspicion, but in this particular instance she strongly doubted the man would have behaved as the girl claimed. She also knew the foster-parents in the reception home to which Jill had been taken, and had similar confidence in them.

By now a young social worker, who had helped place Jill in the foster-home, had arrived. She sat down quietly, and we all waited for Jill to be sent for. When she came she seemed quite at ease, not at all embarrassed and told her story without difficulty. It was much the same as she had told her teacher.

The doubts I had had about the story when I realized how provocative the teacher had been in her questioning were soon dispelled by the girl's calm, truthful manner. The teacher sat back, obviously pleased with her pupil's behaviour, pleased also with herself for being the observant kind of teacher she so clearly desired to be.

Anne said very little, but smiled a lot. Sometimes she would interrupt gently, saying, 'Slow down now, you're going much too fast for me.' Or, 'I'm missing what you're saying, I didn't quite catch that. What did you say happened?' Gradually she clarified all the points, without ever putting any words into the girl's mouth. Soon it became apparent that very little, if anything, had happened. It appeared that the foster-father in whose home she was now living (whom she called grandpa) expected her to kiss him goodnight, as is normal for foster-fathers who after all are meant to be father-substitutes. I was told later that in fact he had recently had a stroke and since then his tongue protrudes very slightly from his mouth. Whether or not Jill thought this was 'french' kissing or whether it merely gave her the idea I never found out. Certainly she had no clear picture of what 'french' kissing was – never once did she suggest that he, or the previous foster-father, had attempted to put their tongues right into her mouth. There was, incidentally, no apparent disgust with the kissing – she related it quite calmly with no suggestion of disturbance.

When questioned about the rape of her sister by one of her mother's boyfriends there was again no corroborating evidence, and when asked where she had learned about rape she giggled, and said, 'At the cinema'. Asked what it meant she said it was knocking someone around a bit, pushing you about. Since her mother's boyfriends were invariably abusive this last was only too likely to have happened. She claimed the event had happened when they were all on a trip to the country; that no, she hadn't actually seen it happen, but she knew that it had. The story about the same sister being in bed with the foster-father in the reception home was similarly vague – Jill alleged she had come into the bedroom and seen the two of them in bed under the covers. She immediately left the room and when she returned half an hour later the man was out of the bed, doing up his belt. Asked what she saw in the first instance she said as they were under the covers she hadn't been able to see anything, then changed this slightly, saying he was half-sitting up and leaning over her sister, but she couldn't see their faces.

During the recital of all this the girl showed virtually no emotion; several times she repeated that she was telling the truth and why did no one believe her: once she openly asked Anne if *she* believed her. Anne had not replied. At this point I felt very sorry for Jill, persuaded by her manner it was likely she was telling the truth, and thought the policewoman was being rather heartless in not giving her at least a partial assurance. But now Anne began to question her about her mother and her father, and another side of the girl began to be revealed. Her ease of manner disappeared, tears came to her eyes, and soon she was crying openly. The interview became very involved, but it soon appeared that what the girl actually wanted was to go home, and she had hoped to achieve this by pretending that the foster-homes she had been sent to were even less suitable than her mother's home.

At first she told Anne she wanted her mother, she couldn't bear not to be with her, but eventually she agreed that since her mother

knocked her about, rarely cooked any meals and was herself frequently incapacitated because of some beating-up, her mother's
home was not a good place for her and her sister to be. She then
finally admitted the real truth, which was that what she really
wanted most of all was to live with her father, but she was also very
anxious that someone should look after her mother whom she loved
in spite of everything, and who was clearly not capable of looking
after herself. Since both Anne and the social worker knew that Jill's
father was in fact dying of cancer – the child knew he was seriously
ill but discounted this – they had no choice but to keep the girls in
care. The basic facts had been told again and again to Jill (though
not that her father was actually dying, only that he was too unwell
to look after her), but she could not accept them. Now, in desper-
ation, she had told the stories of the rape and the sexual assault.

I saw how easily one could have taken the girl's story at its face
value – as indeed the teacher had – purely because she was so calm
and never deviated from her story. But the policewoman explained
it had been easy to see she was not telling the truth. Her manner
was not that of a girl who really had been assaulted; she gave none
of the details that a true victim would have, told us nothing that
she could not have observed any night of the week on television –
which was probably where she had obtained the few details she did
give. She had exaggerated certain innocent facts, added some more,
and used words to describe these acts that she knew were naughty,
even bad. She had intended no maliciousness to the foster-fathers,
was only attempting to achieve her own desires. It had soon become
obvious to Anne that something other than the alleged sexual
assaults was the real problem, and by carefully questioning, after
first satisfying herself there was no substance in Jill's claims, she
had drawn out from the girl what it was that had caused her to
make her accusation, and what she had hoped to achieve by it.

I have related this interview at such length because it does point
out various aspects discussed earlier and also because it brings some
reality into what until now has been a rather abstract chapter. It is
not difficult to absorb a number of facts and to imagine one knows
more than one does, but in dealing with people, and with children
in particular, there is no substitute for experience combined with
compassion and wisdom. The teacher had plenty of the first and
some of the second, but even so she had still drawn the wrong
conclusions, possibly because she was over-keen to be a really helpful, aware teacher.

Having considered the magnitude of the problem, it will be helpful to learn how to begin tracking down the many thousands of unreported cases of incest. Where do we start looking? What action can we take? The starting point is to remember that only a minority of victims volunteer information. The pattern of reporting varies from area to area, depending to a great extent on the facilities available. In a British survey conducted among various professional groups in the UK (Beezley Mrazek, Lynch and Bentovim 1981) it was found that almost no social workers were referring incest cases to the police, nor were social workers referring cases to family doctors, although they did send a few to paediatricians. On the other hand half of the referrals to child psychiatrists came from social workers, the rest being from family doctors, paediatricians, the family and schools. Over half the cases seen by family doctors came directly from the family, and one-third from the police. Half of the cases seen by paediatricians came from family doctors; others were from hospitals and various other sources. Of the 111 cases seen by police surgeons 97 per cent came directly from the police, but they themselves made virtually no referrals on to paediatricians or psychiatrists. The police had received three-quarters of their referrals directly from parents, primarily the mother. The remainder were from the victims (eleven) and relatives (four) and a further seven from professionals including police officers, teachers, the court and a social worker.

In America, Geri Hatcher of the Los Angeles Social Services told me that the majority of their information comes from the schools, who also have to contact the police at the same time. The police at Aurora County, Colorado, similarly found most of their reports came from the schools and the social services. Observant police may also occasionally suspect incest but in general are likely to desist from making inquiries unless they feel the evidence is likely to be sufficiently concrete to warrant bringing a charge. One English policeman told me confidentially that where he thought it was suitable and the case treatable he would unofficially inform the social services of his suspicions so that the family got aid rather than prosecution, though this is probably a rare attitude in the police force at present. He was clearly aware that many social workers do not pass on information to the police about incest if they can avoid it.

Other professionals whom one would think likely to report a fair number of cases do not seem to do so: both in Britain and in the

United States few doctors, detention centres, clergymen, youth centres pass on information, which probably indicates that victims and offenders alike will only talk to people they know extremely well or thoroughly trust not to report them. Children sometimes talk to their closest friends, and these friends may in turn talk to their own mothers who then inform the social services or the police. This last is a fairly common source of reporting. In the United States school counsellors are a more normal part of school life than in Britain at the moment, and as much of the reporting comes from these counsellors this is an aspect of prevention and discovery that could well be emulated in the UK.

Where telephone facilities exist, such as Parents Anonymous or the Samaritans, people unable to admit their problems personally to anyone can sometimes bring themselves to be more open with a sympathetic and anonymous listener. The problem of confidentiality arises here: it is an open question as to whether or not a listener who has been given the name and address of a person actively involved in incest (offender or victim) ought to inform the police of what he knows. The law is quite clear that he should, incest being a criminal offence. I was present at a Parents Anonymous group meeting in London when this point was being thrashed out, and while the majority felt that confidentiality was the cornerstone of such telephone services, one or two volunteers felt it was wrong under any circumstances to break the law. In the event the majority carried the day and the remaining dissenting member chose to cease membership. Each Parents Anonymous group in Britain is autonomous and there is no overall policy which each group is bound to follow, but when at regional meetings the problem has been discussed no attending group has been found to disagree with confidentiality in principle.

The Samaritans have the same attitude. They know they are breaking the law by withholding information, and have discussed the situation with the police, but it is their opinion that there is no way they can betray this confidentiality – whatever the crimes, whether it is incest, theft, or even murder – and still expect people to call them for help. They are aware there is a risk they could be prosecuted, but since there could be no possible long-term advantage to the police in doing this, it seems unlikely this could ever happen.

Henry Giarretto, director of the Child Sexual Abuse Treatment Program, (CSATP), who even if he wanted could not withhold information from the authorities as his programme is a part of the Santa Clara Juvenile Probation Department, told me,

> When someone calls us up on the phone we warn them not to give us their name as we should have to report them to the police. We advise them to talk to us, tell us their problem, but anonymously. Then we spell out the alternatives, explain we have discovered that families who don't report do not do as well as those who do. And we remind them there's no guarantee it won't be reported later on, anyway, when their child grows up and becomes more independent and maybe talks to a friend. Or a typical problem might arise – the daughter will run away and eventually report and then the family will be in much worse straits than if they came forward now and say to the police that they want to be helped.

Advice like this is obviously useful in areas such as Santa Clara and certain other American counties where treatment for the entire family is available. Where arrest, prosecution and jail is the inevitable outcome of a confession, such advice is unlikely to be given or taken.

As we have seen, sometimes incest is revealed during the course of a patient's treatment, but often it takes six months or more of contact before a victim is prepared to discuss what is still a painful issue for her. Even then there may need to be a fair amount of effort on the part of the therapist before it can be talked about. When a child is the patient and the whole family is investigated quite often it is discovered that the entire family is involved in incest, or at least the greater part of it, frequently without individual members having previously realized there were victims within the family other than themselves.

There are a few statistics available listing how sexual abuse is revealed and who reports it, but I have only come across one survey which relates purely to incest, that of the American Humane Association (Julian and Mohr 1979). They based the survey on a national study conducted in 1976 in which 99,579 'usable reports' of child abuse and neglect were received. Looking only for cases of incest between natural father and daughter, they whittled these figures down to a small number of cases (102) which met their extremely strict criteria. They gave the following sources of initial reports:

Medical personnel (inc. own doctors) 8.8 per cent
Teacher & other school persons   13.7
Public school agency   6.9
Private social agency   3.9
Court   6.9
Law enforcement   10.8
Victim   19.6
Relative   5.9
Sibling   6.9
Parent/parent substitute   11.8
Anonymous   0.0
Friend/neighbour   3.9
Other   .9
                                   _____
                                   100.0 per cent

The authors point out that from the table we may see that the victim (19.6 per cent) is the most frequent reporter, followed by school personnel (13.7 per cent) and parents or parent-substitutes (11.8 per cent). But perhaps a more pertinent way of looking at the figures is to say that only in one-fifth of the cases did the report come from the victim, and so we must look elsewhere for our initial source of information.

A revolutionary way of getting in touch with victims has been successfully explored by the Child Sexual Abuse Prevention Project organized by the Sexual Assault Services of Hennepin County, Minneapolis, who felt that the best way to tackle the sexual exploitation of children was through the schools. Before work could be commenced it was thought advisable to obtain permission of parents, and notices were sent advising them a project was about to be tried out in their children's schools. Meetings were held and the project explained. The first need for the researchers was to find out how much the pupils (from kindergarten age onwards) already knew about sexual abuse, how correct the knowledge was, and what, if any, their experiences were. The first school selected for the experiment was chosen partly because several of the Sexual Assault Service personnel had children actually attending the school, and they were already familiar with its routine and the staff. During the pilot programme time spent with each class varied. When mutual trust had been established and techniques of discussion were perfected a second session more specifically related to sexual abuse was organized, which involved a professional group of actors whose company is called the Illusion Theater.

It was this last which was the most revolutionary aspect of the programme, and for which it has become most known. The main function of the theatre group was to demonstrate different aspects of touching to the children through what they call the 'Touch Continuum.' These actors have always been involved in current issues and, in order to prepare themselves for this new work, with the help of the Sexual Assault Services they soaked themselves in everything they could find out about sexual assault, from sexual abuse itself through to the reporting laws, how the supporting services worked, etc. As they studied the background they themselves began to remember their own childhood experiences, which helped them in the development of their script. Eventually they evolved a simple piece called 'Touch', which sets out to present in a nonsensational way the differences between nurturing and exploitive touch. From this a poster was prepared which illustrates the main points the group are making, and which is used when the actors themselves are not available.

The pilot project was extended to four schools, in two of which the actors directly participated, while in the other two schools the posters were used. A total of 1,500 students were eventually exposed to the programme during the course of the two-year project, and much useful information was gathered as a result, some of which will be looked at more closely in other sections of this book. One in six of the elementary students reported some kind of sexual victimization; more than half of these children had never previously told anyone about their experiences. Most of the reporting came after the classes, when after thinking about the presentation the children would talk to a friend or a parent. But sometimes it would be revealed through carefully chosen leading questions during the discussions in the classroom, when an answer might betray intimate knowledge of a kind a child would not be expected to have, or through a child himself asking a suspiciously detailed question. Whenever it was thought there was sufficient reason to suspect a child might be being abused, reporting procedures were followed, involving both teachers and children.

Clues that gave away the possibility of sexual abuse were, for example: an exceptional need on the part of the pupil for the teacher's attention during the discussion or the presentation; the pupil becoming restless and growing increasingly agitated; the child avoiding eye contact, sinking down in his chair, pulling away from his fellows, clutching his stomach or complaining of a severe headache or dizziness. It is suggested that a child displaying one or more of these symptoms should be carefully observed. Unexpectedly specific answers were a useful guide: for example, to the question, 'What kind of person sexually assaults other people?' one answer was given which clearly showed personal experience – 'maybe some man asks little girls to help find a kitty named Fred and then makes them touch them down there.' Another girl persistently lifted her hand to ask questions during the discussion – to the teacher this was remarkable because normally the child never made herself noticeable at all. The researchers found that it did not necessarily follow that sexual abuse lay behind these symptoms, but usually some problem did, such as physical or emotional abuse.

There was no question of the theatre group portraying specific sexual actions, nor would such an approach be necessary. Too many people grabbing hold of someone without obvious loving care, or one person 'teasing' another rather brutally, amply illustrates the point at which fun ceases to be warm and becomes threatening. The discussion preceding or following the acting are of course adapted to suit the age of the child.

The programme was an undoubted success and is now being studied and copied elsewhere. The Illusion Theater, the members of which say they learned as much from the students as they taught them, are sharing their discoveries nationwide. Professionals such as teachers, lawyers, police, social workers, doctors, have seen presentations and discussed the material used. They reported they have found the experience invaluable. The programme is of course aimed at prevention through education as well as the discovery of actual victims. Since reporting will presumably increase rather than decrease in areas where such measures are taken we shall probably never know how effective from a preventative point of view such a programme is, but as there is such widespread ignorance about sexual abuse, especially about its existence within the family, it seems unlikely the programme will not achieve its original aim.

Finally, in this section on how and when incest is reported, it might be worth considering in more depth the fact that the most usual time for female victims themselves to report to the authorities is when girls arrive at pubescence and early adolescence. The American Humane Association, whose table of the source of initial reporting we have just read, writes: '58.2% of the reporting victims of incest were 14 or 15 years old.' This is typical of many studies, and is the age most often suggested to me during the course of personal conversations with doctors, social workers and researchers both in Britain and the United States.

The reasons for this are straightforward. In the first place the American Humane Association's survey was dealing only with father/daughter incest. This is the type of incest that was most frequently studied in earlier surveys, and is also what most people think of when they talk about incest. It is possible therefore that as reporting increases we may find different ages of reporting for other types of incest, such as sibling incest, father/son, mother/son/daughter. But as far as father/daughter incest is concerned the break-point often comes at pubescence which is the age at which family becomes secondary, and the normal desire for separation begins to be felt by the growing girl. A need to expand beyond the family environment is sensed, a desire to become a separate person in her own right. Perhaps she comes into contact with variations of the main message of the women's movement, which says: Be yourself, make your own life – you don't have to be a victim. At the same time she is beginning to feel intensely aware of her own developing sexual feelings, and to relate these to what has been happening between herself and her father.

This is the point when buried emotions are most likely to erupt. Few female adolescences are easy for parents or children to cope with, however healthy the relationship between them, and where jealousy and fear is added – as is inevitable in the case of the incestuous fathers – this period is likely to be especially traumatic. The father will be unwilling to lose what has become for him a vital part of his life, but as the child moves more fully into adolescence and has deepening relationships with her peers (or desires for such relationships – she may be too inhibited by her experience to achieve them) she will attempt to rebel against him, especially as she realizes perhaps for the first time just how condemned incest is by the world at large. It is now that she is likely to express her distress to her friends, or to turn to the authorities. A further precipitating cause at this age is that quite frequently the father begins to pester other children in the family as he senses his daughter's withdrawal, or as he considers they have now grown old enough to approach.

Barbara Myers, an incest victim who has become very active in working for incest victims, writes movingly of her own experiences with her peers at this age (Myers 1979). I have slightly abridged the following quotation:

> I never knew how to act, how to look, or what to wear in school. I always felt that everyone was laughing at me or talking about me behind my back. I felt that they somehow knew about my father, so I attributed most of these feelings to my looks. I couldn't bring myself to wear makeup or earrings like the rest of the girls; I didn't want to be sexy or look like a woman. Worst of all, I never really had any peers. They thought I was aloof, whereas I simply didn't know how to relate to them. How could I join in their conversations about boyfriends and first kisses when I was having sex with my father? I never felt like a part of that teenage world because I never was. I could only relate to older boys who were two or three grades ahead of me. The boys talked about sex a lot, and at least that was something to which I could relate. The other girls thought I was a slut because I only hung around with older boys, but none of those relationships was sexual. I never knew how to explain it to them, so I always felt left on the outside.
>
> I always skipped classes that required close contact or focused attention on me. I couldn't stand up in front of a class; I was afraid they would see something, or if I opened my mouth, everything about my father would come pouring out. I never asked any questions for the same reason and for fear of sounding stupid. Gym class was a great source of anxiety for me. I wouldn't undress in front of the others; I was afraid they would see something if they saw my body. To me it was always dirty and ugly and a source of shame. I felt fat, even though I was skinny; I thought I looked different, even though I didn't. I was good at individual sports that didn't require group participation, and I liked them. But I was inept at anything that required involvement with others. Maths and spelling were my best subjects, naturally, because I could do them alone. I failed both gym and home economics, because when we weren't doing activities that could be done individually, I didn't go to class. I think of school as an incredibly isolated experience which, like everything else, I survived because I had to.

Sexual abuse sometimes comes to light when a family is investigated because one or more children have been abused physically. It is very difficult to know how closely physical and sexual abuse go in hand as statistics vary greatly according to their source, but in general it seems most cases of sexual abuse are not accompanied by physical abuse.

Potter and Mohr (1977) write that in 65 per cent of reported sexual abuse cases physical abuse was not reported at the same time. De Francis (1969) found only 11 per cent of sexual abuse cases had involved physical abuse. Finkelhor (1979b) writes categorically that 'sexual abuse and physical abuse of chidren do *not* tend to occur simultaneously' (his italics). The Harborview Medical Center, Seattle, report that of nearly 600 sexually abused children coming to them for attention only 14 per cent had been asssaulted physically. In 10 per of the cases the mother was also abused. On the other hand the Minnesota programme for victims of sexual assault (Muldoon 1979) found in a survey that in 47 per cent of families where incest had taken place physical abuse of children had also occurred; in 39 per cent of these cases the wife had been assaulted. Johnston (1979) found that of her sample of ten sexually abused children six had also been physically abused at some time in their lives. In addition, in an unpublished paper she writes that the National Center for the Prevention and Treatmemt of Child Abuse and Neglect, Denver, had found that about 60 per cent of the sexually abused children coming to them had suffered physical abuse as well. In a newsletter called 'The Link' published in Minneapolis in 1978 a special study of eighty prostitutes was reported. It was found that thirty-three had been sexually abused by a family member, and that two-thirds of the women had been beaten by a family member – in roughly a third of each of the cases the beating was carried out by the mother, father or sibling respectively. Half of the beatings had begun between the age of ten and thirteen, and 40 per cent before the age of ten.

Although these last figures suggest there may be considerably more physical abuse connected with sexual abuse than is commonly supposed I suspect this may be partly due to the samples surveyed, as in talking to people working in the field and also in reading related papers this supposition does not seem to be confirmed. However, it is obvious an open mind needs to be kept on this subject.

Feelings about the two types of abuse are highly contrasted. The 'spare the rod, spoil the child' attitude to child upbringing has softened considerably this century, but one still hears of styles of discipline in some areas that would be considered physically abusive in others. Overtly cruel behaviour would certainly be unacceptable, and yet one constantly reads in newspapers of cases of severe physical abuse in which neighbours must have been aware of what was happening, though no one reported it. But if sexual abuse were known about neighbours would soon gossip and almost certainly some action would rapidly be taken. The same difference may be seen in the treatment of families which come to official notice. In sexual abuse cases almost invariably either the child or the perpetrator is removed from the family setting while investigations are carried out. In cases of physical abuse this is much less likely to happen. I have no comparative figures for Britain but in child abuse in general the pattern is much the same for Britain and the United States, where (Julian and Mohr 1979) it was found from an examination of the national study figures that in 41.7 per cent of cases of physical abuse no further action was taken after the initial investigation, contrasted with the incest cases of which only 17.6 per cent received no further attention. Of the incest victims 32.4 per cent went into foster care and 19.6 per cent were taken temporarily into some form of shelter, while the equivalent figures for physically abused victims were 9.6 per cent and 4.6 per cent respectively.

One interesting fact that emerged from the last mentioned survey was that in the incest cases 93 per cent of the families were a two-parent family with both mother and father being present, whereas in the physically abusive family this was only true of three-quarters of the families. Perhaps not unexpectedly there were twice as many incestuous families where only a father or a father substitute was present (7 per cent) as there were abusive families. (It should be remembered that only cases of father/daughter incest were being considered in this review.)

Noticeable differences in the sizes of households was another factor that emerged. Over 36 per cent of incestuous families had four or more children as against nearly 17 per cent of abusive families. The national figure for the general population was just over 6 per cent. These figures are borne out by other international studies. Family discord was noticeably higher in incest families – nearly 66 per cent as against 42 per cent, although it seems little actual fighting takes place in these households. More surprisingly the survey showed that over 32 per cent of the incest families revealed alcohol dependence as against 14 per cent of the abusive families, although alcohol is known to be closely linked with physical abuse. Finally this survey showed noticeable differences in mental health problems and mental retardation, from which over 37 per cent of the incestuous families suffered as against nearly 20 per cent of the physically abusive families.

There are of course some cases where sexual abuse is simply a part of deliberate maltreatment also involving physical abuse. Men who act out their hatred for and fear of women by terrorizing their household may use sex as a punishment and an instrument of humiliation, brutalizing their daughters as well as their wives. But this pattern is unusual; it is more common for feelings towards the daughters to be generally benevolent, even loving, although severely self-centred. Presumably there is a desire for sexual gratification whenever sexual abuse takes place but, apart from the type of case just mentioned, usually there is also a conflicting desire not to hurt the child. This pattern may be seen again and again, and is clearly exemplified in both the histories of Debbie and John in Chapter 1.

In the opinion of some therapists this fact has an important bearing in the prognosis for the future of abused children. A physically abused child is sometimes the scapegoat of the entire family, picked on by other siblings as well as her parents, but even when she is not scapegoated she can hardly feel loved or wanted while actually being shaken, bitten or battered by a parent who at the moment of abuse clearly wants to cause her pain. The sexually abused child, on the other hand, mostly has at least one parent who is specially attentive to her, who buys her presents and puts her in a privileged position. She may be terrified of him when he is in his sexual mood, but usually this does not seem to detract from her feelings for him as a father who needs love and affection. I heard the kind of comment that Debbie made from many other victims as well – if only he could always be just daddy, if only he wouldn't be this other man but would just hold me and love me like a normal father.

As a result of the loving attention the sexually abused child often receives she is likely to feel less bad about herself than a child who has been physically hurt by an abusing parent, however much that same parent may later grieve and hate himself/herself for what has been done. Reinforcing this difference is the fact that incest victims come more frequently from two-parent homes which means that their lives are likely to be more stable, more comfortable, more normal than the physical abuse victim. People working with both types of children have told me they feel far more hopeful about the future of incest victims, *provided they receive help*, than they do about the other children. But without help, their future is unpredictable.

Chapter 4

The fathers

Incestuous fathers are as adept at rationalizing their behaviour as the rest of us. A common rationalization is that they no longer are turned on by their wives, or that their wives are not interested in sex, so they are therefore forced to turn to their children. Pointing out that while many men cease for various reasons to have sex with their wives most of them do not use their children will only bring forth further excuses. This might be on the lines that keeping it in the family is better than risking breaking up the home by committing adultery and perhaps falling in love with another woman. Or the risk of venereal diseases if prostitutes are employed might be brought up, or an expressed dislike and shame at having to turn to such a source. An unexpected finding is that a number of incestuous families are extremely religious; and to some incest is thought to be preferable to adultery.

Yet other fathers claim they have a greater need for sex than most men, and that they can think of little else. But several female therapists and group leaders have told me that when working with offenders they themselves have felt no sexual rapport towards the men and had no sense of the men seeing them or other females in the group as sexual beings. If anything, the situation is usually quite the opposite, with the men being rather shy, unconfident and having very little idea of how to make themselves attractive to a woman. Although this observation is based on the personal feelings of a few women professionals and is obviously not conclusive it fits in very well with other findings about incestuous males.

Another rationalization sometimes given is that they want their children to have a proper introduction to sexuality and that first experiences with a loving father will be beneficial. Many insist that no harm was caused to the child and there is nothing to blame themselves for. Or they might say that although they would be willing to stop they cannot break the habit, even though they are no longer enjoying it. Giarretto tells of fathers who are convinced they are driven into incest by irresistible evil forces, or that they have a strange mental disease they cannot control. Sometimes it is claimed the incestuous relationship reduces stress, and helps keep the family stable and together. It may be true in some circumstances incestuous activity relieves stress temporarily, but inevitably further stress is caused by the consequences of the action itself.

Lastly there is the occasionally used rationalization which comes from people whose beliefs and ideas about sexuality are so contorted by neurosis, religious bigotry or upbringing that they are incapable of seeing how painfully absurd their excuse is. Basically this is that the girl is a whore at heart and sex at home keeps her off the streets. These fathers make comments such as 'She's a tramp; she asked for it.' By the time the incest is actually revealed there may well be some truth in these comments regarding the girl's promiscuity; that the father has probably been molesting the girl ever since she was small and is himself the primary cause of her behaviour is something he is unlikely to confess to.

Roland Summit (Summit and Kryso 1978), while discussing the kind of man who sees women either in terms of sanctified virgin or shameless whore, tells of one man who first physically abused his daughter when she was small, then over-protected her. When at the age of eight she was raped on the street he was distraught, crying out that his little virgin had been taken from him. He then persuaded his wife that it would help his daughter to come to terms with what had happened if she watched them make love. The wife, herself an incest victim, submitted, although afterwards she was convinced he had used this demonstration as a preliminary to beginning a sexual relationship with the girl. It was not until a couple of years later when the husband punished his wife by committing fellatio with his daughter in front of her on two separate occasions that she at last found the strength to call in the police and bring the affair to an end.

Why are these men as they are? Can their behaviour pattern be changed? Earlier research (Weinburg 1955) placed incestuous fathers into three main types: (1) promiscuous males whose incestuous behaviour is part of their sexual psychopathology; (2) paedophiles and (3) the male in what he called the 'endogamic' family where the family unit appears unremarkable to outsiders but where incest is part of the family dynamics. Certain new research which I will look at shortly suggests that these last two cannot always be so easily separated, but for most professionals (2) and (3) are seen as being quite different. For Weinburg the 'promiscuous' family (1) is one which is so totally disorganized that incest is merely part of the general chaos and probably passes unnoticed in most cases. Alcoholism, violence, neglect, promiscuity, criminal and other anti-social behaviour characterizes this type of family, and even where incest is discovered there is rarely much attempt to isolate the reasons for it. We do not know how frequent it is in comparison with 'endogamic' incest, about which far more research has been undertaken, and which inevitably forms the basis of most of this book. Certainly the type of incest coming before most of the professionals I have dealt with has been mainly of the endogamic type and since most of the fathers in these families are men whose sole social deviancy is their sexual behaviour it would seem wise that special attention is paid to them, for theirs is a problem which can be isolated and, in perhaps the majority of cases, dealt with successfully. The promiscuous type of family needs a whole battery of social expertise over a very lengthy period of time if progress is to be made.

Men of the psychopathic type typical of the 'promiscuous' family are in any case very difficult to treat, as it is almost impossible to make them see that their behaviour is wrong and must be changed. A team of psychologists working in this field told me they can usually recognize the type of man who will not respond and try to have them taken into hospital as they are too difficult to treat on a once-a-week outpatient basis. They describe them as 'cut-off' people, giving the impression of being 'flat, rigid, tight – you have a sense there's no emotion, there's something impenetrable about them.' There are of course some fathers in 'promiscuous' families who are not psychopathic but around whom violence or at least the family behaviour just described seems to occur. Obviously any of these descriptions and those following can overlap or be blurred: in real life human beings rarely fall neatly into any one category, but nevertheless classifications are useful as long as one remembers their limitations.

Cavallin (1965) consistently found in his endogamic patients the presence of paranoid traits and unconscious homosexual strivings. He describes a strong hostility towards their mothers whom they saw as neglectful and often absent: in later life they transfer this hostility to their wives and then to their daughters. He suggests the hypothesis that incest is primarily an expression of unconscious hostility that combines with unsolved Oedipal impulses, finally being discharged on the daughter. He also found in his patients a weak ego; certainly a lack of a clear sense of identity fits in with many other findings, as does the expression of hostility towards the wives which is frequently overt rather than unconscious. Hostility towards the daughter may well also be present, but is not usually admitted to.

What has become clear is that, just as with physical abuse, history endlessly repeats itself. An abused childhood leads to an abusive parenthood. One offender told the investigating policeman who took him in for questioning, 'I really hate myself.' When the policeman asked him why, he said, 'Because I hated my dad, and look at me now.' He told the investigator that when he was a boy his father used to sexually molest his two sisters. Everyone knew: his sisters told him about it, and he saw it happen – his father took no care to hide it. He asked his mother to make his father stop it, but she did nothing about it. It continued all of his childhood until his sisters left home. He said,

> You know, I hated my father for that, I couldn't stand it. But when I left home I put it out of my mind, got married and had children of my own. Then one day I was visiting home and my dad picked up my daughter, my own daughter, and put her on his lap. I was uneasy, but I didn't say anything. Then he started stroking her leg and began to put his hand up her skirt, just like that right there in front of me! I was outraged! I can't tell you how I felt! I pulled her off his lap, and had a real row. I told him what I'd thought of him all those years ago, and then I walked out. I've never been back since, never seen him again.
>   And now. I'm doing exactly the same with my own daughter. I can't stop myself. All I could do was to hope to God I'd be caught out.

His daughter was seven years old when he started molesting her.

Wenet found in his study of juvenile offenders (personal communication) that 54 per cent of those referred to him and his colleagues for actively sexually molesting young children had themselves been victims of either physical or sexual abuse. Those who had not actually been abused as children still seem to have experienced their childhood as though they were victims, Wenet said. Interestingly, only 12 per cent of sexually molesting adolescents of the less serious type (the exposers and the peeping Toms) had directly experienced abuse in their own childhood.

Early abuse in their own lives left these adolescents feeling very isolated, Wenet found. Abusive families of all kinds are usually socially isolated – from neighbours, workmates and, in the case of children, from their schoolfellows. And where, as often happens, one particular child is scapegoated, he is not only isolated socially but also within his own family. This leaves him with emotional needs that he has no idea how to deal with. Without treatment it is extremely difficult for victims sooner or later to avoid passing on their sad past.

The families within which the offenders themselves grew up are likely to have been large. Cavallin (1965) gives an average of over five children in the case of the twelve incestuous fathers he was treating. In the American National Study over 35 per cent of incestuous families had four or more children. It must be remembered however that these figures relate to fathers whose incest has been discovered. Socially disadvantaged families not only tend to have larger families but are also more likely to come to the attention of the authorities. It is possible that much incest occurring in small families is unnoticed, so these figures should be treated with some caution. Another of Cavallin's findings, that during the childhood of the incestuous fathers in his sample half of their mothers had either been absent or were dead and that another two mothers had been away from home working, was repeated quite frequently in serious case histories I came across. But I know of no other study which confirms or denies this pattern, so its general validity is open to question.

The following case history told me by a therapist illustrates some of the points discussed above. It is an interesting case and although I have altered a few facts to avoid recognition I have changed nothing of importance.

Paul was an unusual person in that in spite of having had such an appalling childhood he somehow managed to cope by himself, or to get other people to look after him. He was born in Yorkshire, but his parents didn't come from there. He knows practically nothing about his background as they were always moving – he never met his grandparents for instance. His mother died when he was about a year old, and he doesn't remember her at all. His father couldn't hold down a job for more than a few months at a time: he was a very restless man, never stayed in the same place for long. So the early childhood was chaotic, unsettled – he wasn't fed properly or anything like that. When he was about six his father remarried. The new wife soon took over the home, and for a while they stayed in the same place. Then problems arose between her and the father – he'd come home drunk or in a filthy temper – and gradually she began to seduce the boy. At first she'd call him into her bed and get him to fondle her breasts, that sort of thing. Sometimes it would be when they were alone, but at other times when his father was drunk she'd call the boy in and she'd lie in the middle between them both. By the time he was ten or eleven she was trying to have intercourse with him. Apparently it wasn't too successful at first, but she persevered. Whenever his father found out what was happening he'd beat the boy severely, which can't have helped him much! Obviously his stepmother was mainly doing it as a way of getting back at his father.

When the boy was about twelve he came home one day from school and found his parents gone. They had just packed their cases and left, with no forwarding address, gone just like that. It was a rented flat, they were overdue with the bills, so he couldn't stay on there. Extraordinarily enough, he determined to look after himself. He wandered the streets, did odd jobs, sold newspapers, that sort of thing. Various people took him in from time to time, but he doesn't seem to have come into contact at all with the social services, so he obviously managed to keep out of trouble. As soon as he was old enough he joined the army, took up an apprenticeship and learned a trade. It suited him, being within a community and not having much personal responsibility. He thrived until one day he was run over by a truck and severely injured. When finally he recovered he was invalided out.

It was a great shock to him, being alone once more. His relationships with women had never been easy, but he wanted a settled background again, so he married. His wife is a cold, distant sort of woman, very controlling, who soon took over the marriage, much as his stepmother had. They had four children but he was quite unable to maintain an adult relationship with his wife, either sexually or emotionally, although physically he coped well enough. He saw his wife as a mother figure rather than as a wife – she wrote the cheques, paid the bills, never encouraged him to develop. He had put himself into an infantile role and she was happy to keep him there.

He still felt very hostile towards his stepmother, though he had not seen her since she and her father walked out on him. He remained very angry with her, very resentful; to him she was just a bitch, a whore. He can't talk about her without using terms like that. He recalls no warm feelings towards her, and I think that was partly due to the loss of his own mother so young, and partly due to his stepmother's behaviour towards him.

It was unfortunate he had only daughters. He directed a lot of his anger towards the oldest girl, whom he was sexually abusing. She submitted to him, but she felt a tremendous anger. Eventually she told her mother, who reported it to the authorities. Whether or not the mother already knew I am uncertain: I suspect a certain amount of unconscious collusion. When the mother was a child she had had a sister of whom she was extremely jealous, and now with her own daughter the whole situation was set up again in her own home. Not long before the incest began the mother's father had died – she had been very close to him, seeing him as the only person in her family who had ever given anything to her. Her relationship with her mother was very cold and distant – there was no warmth in it at all. She was deeply upset by her father's death and she withdrew even further from her husband and children.

When the case finally came to court the daughter expressed great anger towards her father, while he blamed her for what had happened, said she had led him on. There was a strongly sadistic quality about their relationship together in many ways – they were both so angry with each other – and yet at the same time there was obviously a need, a dependency on the other.

Profiles of the father are often so contradictory that at first glance it seems impossible to reconcile them. We have on the one hand an image of the tyrant, and on the other of a weak, inoffensive man incapable of dominating anybody. On reflection we realize that a man who is obliging to the point of servility in the office may be a tyrant at home – such a figure is not unknown in literature. But what of the aggressive loud-mouth who bullies everyone, outside and inside the family? If Cavallin is right this type should fit more easily into the pattern of the 'promiscuous' family, although in fact in the few multi-problem families that have been described to me (both in Britain and America) it so happens that the fathers have been rather weak men pushed around in life.

Part of the confusion may lie in the assumption we make when we hear certain words. For example Muldoon (1979) writes of the sexually abusive father as

> typically overcontrolling and overly restrictive. Many . . . require their teenage daughters to come home immediately after school and forbid their participation in normal recreational activities that would permit interaction with boys of their own age. They maintain their control through excessive discipline, even to the point of physical abuse. Their wives are equally subject to their tyranny.

The picture seems clear – in our minds we see a big tough man, swiping his daughter round the face if she so much as stays ten minutes late at school to practise for the school tennis tournament. Although what Muldoon says is basically true – such restrictions are typical – the picture we imagine may be quite fallacious. For a start, we have already seen that physical abuse is thought to occur only in the minority of cases. And a man does not have to be big and tough to dominate a girl much younger and much smaller than himself and entirely under his control. By the time the girl is grown to near his height (and even then she will not have his muscle power) she will be too accustomed to his dominance to easily override it. Therefore, although his *behaviour* may be tyrannous, we should be careful how we visualize him. The story of the social worker in Chapter 2 may be recalled, who, after meeting an entire family which had been tyrannized – young males as well as females – by the father, went to the hospital to meet this terrifying ogre and was amazed to find a tiny, shambling creature with shaking hands. The man who to the outside world is weak, characterless, inoffensive, may in truth be perceived by his family quite differently. If, when reports are made, only the victim is seen and not the offender (especially likely in retrospective studies) a completely erroneous image of the offender may become a statistic, to be repeated again and again. This may not be thought to matter much, but if we are to help these men and their families (a three-year jail sentence is soon over) we need to understand the complexity of their characters.

Again, apparently clear definitions can still produce confusion. Julian and Mohr (1979) in their survey of the American National

Study, reporting on 'authoritarian methods of discipline' in incestuous and in physically abusive families, give the figures of 11.8 per cent and 16.8 per cent respectively. The first shows us that only just over one in ten incestuous fathers use strong discipline, which seems almost entirely to disprove the 'tyrant' image. But then we also notice that less than two in ten physically abusive parents use similar disciplinary methods. Since we know that authoritarian discipline (although usually intermittently applied) is sometimes thought to be symptomatic of child physical abuse, at least in two-parent families, it is obvious we must proceed very cautiously indeed. The same terms can mean different things to different people, and we cannot always know exactly what is implied.

If the reader is thoroughly confused by now it may help to consider the following comments made to me by Geri Hatcher, Child Sexual Abuse Project Supervisor, Los Angeles:

> We usually find there is some other kind of abuse going on in the family as well as the sexual abuse. It may be alcohol or drug abuse, or it may be physical abuse towards the wife, but in addition invariably there is emotional abuse, tremendous emotional abuse. You have to be there with the whole family to see it. It may not sound much, but if you watch the faces of the victims you can see how they are being hurt. Things like – when we're sitting around drinking coffee or in the groups themselves, the man may say something like, 'Gee, you'd be pretty if only . . .' or, 'You don't make my coffee right, you always . . .' It's a continuous put-down that goes on between the abusing father and the rest of the family.

I suggested this did not sound too severe and she agreed that the men, if challenged, would argue they were only teasing or making justified comments, but she added that it clearly affected the rest of the family badly:

> The wife responds with remarks like, 'Oh, apparently I'm no good as a mother,' or 'I'm not a good sex partner,' and you can see from their faces they're thinking, 'I'm just not a worthwhile person.' There is very low self-esteem in these families, and you have to stop this kind of interplay if you are going to get anywhere with them.

I said this still seemed fairly mild to me, although I could well understand its wearing-down effect over a period of time, but she explained, 'There's no talk-back to a man like that. He's head of the household, he runs it and what he says goes. He doesn't have to do a lot to get his way.'

Again we have a different kind of picture from the case history told two or three pages back, where the father left all the cheque-writing and management of the household to his wife. And yet at the same time his daughter, in spite of her extreme anger at him, did not find it possible to defy him until she was older. Nor did the mother, in spite of her apparent domination, find it in herself to break up a situation of which she was probably aware at one level or another.

It seems, then, that – yes, the man is perceived by the victim as dominating, perhaps tyrannous, certainly as someone who cannot be defied. Even an apparently dominating wife will be limited in the extent of her power. But to the outside world, even to those coming into comparatively close contact with the family, the father is likely to be viewed in an entirely different light.

Work done by Gene Abel on paedophilia will be examined later in this chapter. One finding that is worth mentioning now is that paedophiles who are not also incestuous show a noticeably higher degree of violence than do males whose sexual activity with children has been limited to members of their own family. This applies to the arousal patterns of both types of males when various scenes of seduction or rape were played on tape to them as well as to their actual behaviour. However, incestuous fathers were not entirely unmoved by tapes depicting violent scenes. Hostility and aggression does appear to play some part in their characters, but it is a part that is usually suppressed and may not even be guessed at by other people.

Alcohol, often linked with aggression, also plays its part in incestuous behaviour. There seems to be a general agreement that, in at least a third of incest cases, alcohol is consumed in excess. The American National Study gives a figure of over 32 per cent for alcohol dependence, Cavallin found one-third of the men in his study drank to an 'excessive degree' and Finkelhor (1978a) writes that almost all researchers have found a high degree of alcoholism among incest offenders, giving an average finding that between 30 per cent and 50 per cent of offenders are chronic alcoholics. Maisch (1973) quotes a variety of earlier research which supports these figures, and points out that although the offenders were not usually drunk or in a state of diminished responsibility when committing the offence, the alcohol intake may well 'indirectly favour incestuous activities' by reducing self-control and permitting the acting out of desires which may otherwise be suppressed.

Tyranny and aggression, expressed only when supported by alcohol – it is not an unfamiliar picture of the bully with a need for power. Time and time again incest victims use phrases such as: 'I felt so powerless'; 'There was nothing I could do to stop him, he just had power over everybody and he knew it.' It is difficult to sympathize with such a man until we begin to consider that in all probability he himself was abused, either physically, sexually or emotionally, as a child, and that he had no chance to develop feelings of well-being and self-confidence.

This need to express power, even if only over somebody weaker than himself has been one of the major findings of Gary Wenet, whose study of adolescent offenders has been mentioned previously. Wenet is director of a programme in Seattle, working with teenagers between the ages of twelve and eighteen who are referred for committing sexual offences. This programme is part of the work done by the general adolescent clinic which deals with every kind of adolescent problem. The victims of the teenagers with whom Wenet works are usually much younger than the offenders – six years or under – so the offence is not a question of two children or adolescents of similar age exploring each other's bodies or playing around. In two-thirds of the cases victims are not family members, but children whom the molester knew because they lived nearby or for whom he babysat. It is very rare for the adolescents to molest children unknown to them, perhaps because they simply do not have the confidence to do so, or because suitable situations rarely present themselves. We saw earlier that the gender of the molested child does not seem to be of much importance – one third of the victims are of the same sex as the offender. Most of the adolescents are boys, but there is a small proportion of girls among them. Molestation includes any sexual act short of intercourse: penetration of the vagina, anus or mouth is considered a rape charge, and is not dealt with in Wenet's programme.

As this programme for sexually abusive adolescents was thought to be the only one of its kind, Wenet and his colleagues decided to conduct a study which would look at five groups, each of twenty-five teenagers, randomly selected from clients coming to the general adolescent clinic, matched for age, social-economic status and size of family. One group had come to the notice of the clinic for rape or attempted rape; one for the sexual molestation of young children; one for exposure or peeping in at windows who had not touched the victims; one for delinquent behaviour such as car theft, house burglary, and the last who had been referred to the clinic for health problems such as stomach-aches or headaches but who had no behaviour problems.

We have already looked at some of the results from this study, in particular the finding that over half of the sexually molesting adolescents had themselves been abuse victims. Wenet and his colleagues talked to parents and examined social work files as well as talking to the adolescents themselves when researching this aspect. The kind of abuse revealed was mostly physical, from which the conclusion was drawn that it was not a necessary or even normal pattern for a sexual abuser to have himself been abused in a sexual manner. However, Wenet agreed that it is often some time before a background of sexual abuse is admitted by a client. In their treatment programme (as opposed to the study) they are normally involved with the offending teenagers and their parents for at least a year. It is rare for knowledge of sexual abuse (with the adolescent offender as victim) to emerge until the treatment has been continued for some while, often not until six months or more have passed, but the workers on the programme are becoming more and more aware of sexual abuse as part of the background of their patients. It is highly possible, therefore, that the number of sexually abused adolescents in the study was actually higher than was revealed at the time.

The molestation these adolescents commit is clearly not simple curiosity as to the physical make-up of another human being, nor do the offenders talk about it as though it were curiosity that had prompted them. The most common act is manual or oral manipulation of the child's genitals, or their having the child do the same to them.

Sexual reasons, however, do not seem to be the predominant cause of the offence: when asked why they commit the abuse they almost routinely reply they have been feeling angry, or were frustrated by something that is happening to them and about which they are powerless to do anything. The child is an object on which to vent their anger, something over which they have power and can manipulate as they will. Wenet speculates that they may hope sex will relieve their tension, but in fact they usually report that they were not satisfied or relaxed afterwards. Mostly they do not expect to have any real communication with the child – their development is too retarded for them to search out emotional involvement with another as yet. Basically they are very isolated individuals and quite unaware of the impact of their behaviour until they begin to understand their motivations through treatment.

Their own feelings of powerlessness as a child and their frustrated need to impose themselves on others, combined with a strong sense of anger, is repeatedly revealed as the driving force behind their actions. Wenet anticipates that without treatment these feelings will be carried forward into adulthood, when one kind of abuse or another will most probably be committed by them on to their future families, thus continuing the cycle.

Incidentally, when thinking about these adolescents it is worth bearing in mind that in Washington, DC, in 1979, out of 500 sexually abused children coming to a children's clinic for attention, 55 per cent had been offended against by teenagers, not adults – the offenders mostly being siblings or babysitters. The Seattle Assault Center in the same year found 30 per cent of the offenders to be teenagers. Incest and child abuse is normally thought of as an adult crime, but it is apparent this is not necessarily so.

Another frequently mentioned characteristic of these men is their immaturity. A picture is drawn of men with a sexual development of somewhere between three and fifteen years, basically scared of adult women to whom they cannot relate confidently either on an emotional or a sexual level, and who are unable or unwilling to take responsibility for their sexual offences. Much sexual abuse of children does not include intercourse: this may be because it is impossible to have intercourse with a prepubertal child without causing pain and probably physical damage as well, and most of these fathers do not wish to hurt their children in this manner. But Finkelhor (1978b) suggests that it is also partly 'because the offenders in most cases are motivated to seek a kind of childlike form of gratification that is not fulfilled by intercourse.' I do not know of any research which shows how many post-pubertal incest victims have full intercourse with their fathers as opposed to lesser sexual activity. It may be that in most cases the man naturally progresses to full intercourse as the years pass, as in John's case in Chapter 1. But Debbie, also in Chapter 1, was able to restrain her father from going beyond oral masturbation, though he too had wanted intercourse once he considered her old enough. It could be that the men gradually begin to gain confidence and wish for more adult methods of gratification, even if they still prefer to have it with their children rather than with their wives. Certainly the impression I have received from people working in the field and from talking to victims is that in general the offenders want intercourse when they consider the child is old enough, and that the victim's physical development is the main check to this rather than the father's infantile masturbatory desires, but this is only an impression and may be incorrect.

Incest is not only a question of sexual desires and gratification, but also of emotional needs. Some men romanticize their daughters and claim they are in love with them, but if so it is in an adolescent way, for they conspicuously put their own needs before those of the beloved, of whom they are scarcely conscious in any meaningful way. I was told of one father who had suddenly woken up to reality. He said,

> When I finally realized I was screwing my own daughter and that I was her father and that I shouldn't be doing this, I looked at her and all of a sudden I realized that she had acne on her face. I don't know how to explain it, but in all that time I'd never noticed it. Not once. I'd seen her just as a beautiful girl, not as a wife or a mother or anything, but as a very desirable, beautiful girl.

Another man who was married but had no children of his own did voluntary work with boys. His own father had been in the army and he had seen very little of him as a child. He related particularly well with young boys whose fathers were absent, giving them what he himself had not received. Unfortunately, he gradually became sexually exploitive with these boys – not, it seems, mainly out of a sexual drive, though that was present too, but mostly out of a desire to get as close, as intimate, as possible in order to give to the boys and to receive for himself what he had never had as a child. This combination of adult sexual drives and childish emotional needs are very confusing to the person to whom they are happening, and his underlying distress is, of course, compounded when he commits acts of which he is afterwards deeply ashamed.

In spite of this emotional immaturity, workers have often told me that offenders were regarded as solid members of their community until their offences were discovered. Often hard workers, even to the point of being called workaholics, they rarely make friends and do not attempt to socialize. When their work is done they go straight home and pull up the drawbridge – they do not gather in the pub or join clubs. It has been suggested that those who busy themselves with long hours of work do so to fight the depression they cannot help but feel; they do not want time to reflect.

Not all research draws this picture of the incestuous father as the hardworking reliable employee: some shows them to have poor unemployment records, that they change jobs frequently and are often dependent on their wives for financial support, but this is mostly earlier research reliant on families from low socio-economic groups. Surveys based on cases coming to public notice inevitably tend to be biased in this direction; surveys based on socially mixed groups point to different conclusions. For example, the American National Study already quoted in this chapter gives a median income of incestuous households in 1976 as slightly less than $9,000, the national median at that time being approximately $13,900. (Even so, over 25 per cent of the families had an income between $13,000 and $40,000 or above). Giarretto, on the other hand, dealing with a cross-section of the county's population, found that in the same year the household incomes of the incestuous families in his pro-gramme averaged $13,413.

The same comments apply to education: some researchers find the fathers to be mostly unskilled with not much education, but others – increasingly so – find otherwise. Cavillin (1965), for ex-ample, writes of his twelve fathers

> they were at least of average intelligence and education, with an average I.Q. of 102 and education of 9.2 grades. Compared with statistics on the rest of our delinquent population these figures indicated a level of intelligence and training decidedly superior to the average (I.Q. 88, education – 8th grade).

Ten had been semi-skilled or skilled labourers who had been steadily employed until just before the occurrence of the incest. The Amer-ican National Study found 41.2 per cent of the fathers to be either skilled or professional workers in spite of the fact that their incomes seemed to be surprisingly low on average.

The parallel may be drawn here with early ideas about baby battering. The cases that most obviously came to public notice were usually from deprived families, but it was soon discovered that physical abuse occurs at all levels of income and education. The same appears to be true of sexual abuse. People in the very profes-sions one might think ought to be free of taint repeatedly appear in the reports – teachers, policemen, boy scout leaders, ministers, lawyers, doctors. I have no idea what the proportions are, for I have seen no breakdown on occupations, but it does not seem inconceivable to me that people with personal problems might tend to choose professions which involve them in working directly with other people. One psychiatrist told me that after talking to a trainee group of social workers about incest last year she asked them if any had experienced any kind of sexual abuse (not necessarily incestuous) when they themselves were children and one-third of the class put up their hands.

Incestuous fathers of the endogamic type are seen as having 'middle-class strivings' as one informant put it: they want the conventional things, their children to do well at school, to have a car, a good house, to dress well. Whatever else happens, no one outside the family must know of the deviation from the norm occurring within. They work conscientiously, but are rarely pushing or overly-ambitious. They do not like to stand up for themselves in public confrontations and are unlikely to rise to the top of their profession because of this almost total lack of overt aggressiveness; a group worker described them to me as 'good company men'. One incest victim in telling me about her relationship with her father said, 'He was an intelligent man, a solicitor, but he was so quiet I could never understand why anyone used him. I don't know how they ever got him to tell them what they wanted to know, he was so quiet. But he seemed to do quite well, so I suppose he must have been efficient or they wouldn't have stayed with him.'

Incestuous fathers seem to be older on average than physically abusing fathers (Julian and Mohr 1979), with the majority falling between thirty-five and forty-nine years of age, although Lukianowicz (1972) puts the mean age at 32.6. However, this last figure was the age at which the onset of incestuous behaviour began, and I understand that Julian and Mohr's figures relate to the age at which the incest was discovered, which would account for the difference. Other research also places the ages of the fathers within the 35–49 age range.

Leaving aside the violent, socially disorganized minority the one characteristic that is repeatedly commented on by workers, then, is that most of the incestuous fathers with whom they deal are respectable, law-abiding folk. Various studies give an average of 80 per cent of families not ever having had any dealings with the police courts previous to the incest charge (Julian and Mohr 1979; Hatcher

– personal communication; Cavallin 1965 – where only two out of twelve fathers had previous convictions).

Their respect for organized religion – in America at least – is something that is referred to again and again by people working with them (Muldoon 1979) and during various personal conversations. Roger and Florence Wolfe, psychologists who work with incest offenders in their practice in Seattle, commented that they had found one of the characteristics of sexual offenders to be that they were more religious than other people. This went hand-in-hand with a surprising ignorance about sex – as they said, 'They know what goes where, and that's about it. They come from families where information about sexuality is strictly restricted. They believe in the most extraordinary myths, and have very few facts'. Someone else said, 'for some of these religious people all sex is sin, it's all bad, so what the hell difference does it make what you do? Screwing mummy when she's on birth control is just as much sin as screwing your 11-year old daughter.'

I do not know how far the same comments may be made about British fathers, but I did notice an article in *The Times* recently commenting on the fact that Roman Catholics 'are vastly over-represented among drug addicts, alcoholics, compulsive gamblers, prostitutes, night club strippers and convicted prisoners'. One in four convicted men in prison comes from a Roman Catholic background, according to this article (based on a book, *The Church Now*, published in 1980): an extraordinary statistic when you consider the Catholic population is between 4 and 5 million in England and Wales, out of a general population in those two countries of approximately 49 million. Since we know drug addiction and alcoholism is linked with sexual abuse, and later when we look at certain surveys we shall see half the prostitutes being interviewed came from sexually or physically abusive families, perhaps we may fairly expect incest also to be over-represented in this Catholic population. It would be interesting to know whether the American experience is repeated among members of other religious groups in Britain which exhibit something of the same fervour as that to be found in certain American sects.

Most of the studies referred to in this chapter have dealt only with natural fathers. It appears from the evidence so far available that children are more at risk from stepfathers than they are from their own fathers. Finkelhor (1980b) in his study of 795 undergraduates from mixed social backgrounds found that a stepfather was five times more likely to sexually victimize his daughter than was a natural father. In addition, nearly half the female students in his study who had stepfathers were victimized sexually during their childhood, though not necessarily by the stepfathers themselves. (It should be remembered that 19 per cent of the women students in the survey had experienced some kind of 'sexual victimization experience' as children.) The Wolfes, Seattle, told me that they frequently see stepfathers whom they consider chose their wives because they had teenage children. This was not necessarily done consciously, but on investigation it was often discovered that all the women the father had previously associated with had also had teenage children. Perhaps the Lolita syndrome is not as rare as Nabokov might have thought when he created his young heroine. The day I met him Roger Wolfe had received a report of a young man of twenty-two who had married a woman in her thirties. Within a month he had become sexually involved with both her daughters, one of ten years and the other of thirteen. The mother had remained unaware of this, and was still sleeping with him. Roger Wolfe commented that in most cases sexual interest in the wives soon evaporates as it is the children who really interest the men, not the adult women.

Because of reporting variations, both in Britain and in the USA, it is not known what proportion of incestuous fathers are natural parents – sometimes stepfathers and natural fathers are lumped together in reports while at other times only natural fathers are taken into account. Presumably one may expect to find a higher proportion of children who have been victimized by their stepfathers in the USA owing to the higher prevalence of divorce in that country, but Britain may soon be catching up in that respect.

There seems little doubt that the errant behaviour of most incestuous fathers is compulsive. They commit the act and afterwards regret bitterly what they have done. They swear never to do it again, but soon the compulsion returns and their will-power disappears. Comparisons have been drawn with alcoholics or other addicts. Reformed cigarette smokers will remember the broken vows, the brave attempts, the failures they endured before they succeeded in giving up the habit. Incestuous fathers have their temptations continuously in front of them, and the remorse they suffer when they have succumbed is insufficient to stop them offending again. Many express deep relief when they are finally discovered and treatment is promised them.

Part of their problem is the different values men and women are taught to place on sex. We cannot ignore the fact that many of the differences between men and women are of biological origin, much as some of us might like to: women who loved briefly then up and ran would not have made successful breeders. It is difficult enough to throw off a lifetime of social indoctrination; it is even more difficult to overcome the desire to settle and to consolidate, and to abandon the accompanying character habits which natural selection has bred into us. David Finkelhor summed up the differences between the sexes thus (personal communication];

> Women don't get off scot free with regard to undesirable sexual effects on their children, but I think it's very unusual for there to be explicit sex. The main problem is to do with male sexuality – the way men define their sexual needs, the sexual privileges they learn to think they have. One of the reasons why men are so much more likely to sexually abuse children is that men learn to abstract sexual and erotic experiences from the context of the relationship they occur in – this goes back to adolescence. When boys are adolescents they start to fantasize about and masturbate to fantasies of specific sexual acts – who it's with is not particularly important – they practise having these sexual fantasies on lots of women. But I think women see sex differently – they are likely to think about someone who's treating them well, someone who thinks of them as a special person, a whole romantic context. Later, as adults, some men visualize sex with very inappropriate partners like children, whereas women have a much harder time doing that. The fact it's a child interferes with their ability to incorporate that into any kind of sexual fantasy.

Another important difference is that women have more practice than men in touching other people without sex being part of the action. Girls hug each other, cuddle pets, sit on their mother's laps well into adolescence, and are encouraged to hold and cuddle babies or small children if there are any around. Boys are soon taught this is babyish or 'girlish' behaviour and, in Anglo-Saxon countries at least, overt displays of affection such as walking along arm-in-arm or kissing warmly on meeting are out of the question. This century's increasing openness about homosexuality has unfortunately brought with it a tightening up of behaviour among heterosexual males lest certain actions should be misinterpreted. For men this means that touching and sex are so linked that it is difficult to do the one without the other springing to mind. Most fathers of course can cope with this without trouble – the link may not be perceived consciously or, even if it is, its inappropriateness when it is their children they are touching is so clear to them they have little difficulty in acting properly. The tensions between adolescent girls and their fathers are notorious; the generation gap, out-of-date beliefs clashing with modern ideas – all sorts of reasons are given to explain why the air is thick with argument, but one of the basic motivations may well be a necessary distancing of the father from an exceedingly attractive nubile girl who herself has little idea of her own attractiveness to someone who, after all, is a normally sexed male with all his senses still intact. Probably few men are aware of what is happening – they block out such ideas from their minds – but ask any half-dozen men with teenage daugthers what their relationships are with their daughters, and their expressions will almost certainly be as rueful as they are fond.

There is one aspect of male molestation of children which is very little discussed, although strong views are held on it. Most professionals nowadays see incest as a problem of family dysfunction: inadequate people come together, react badly with each other, perhaps in addition are unfortunate in life experiences; eventually pressures on the father lead to his giving way to his desires, possibly with the other parent consciously or unconsciously colluding. There are some people, however, who are convinced that this is not the normal pattern. In their view the offending parent has a sexual deviancy, and it is that which causes the problems in the family, not the other way around. They will point out although you can spend a great deal of time treating the entire family the man may still molest his own or other children even though he has apparently sincerely regretted his past behaviour. This was expressed to me thus: 'Once a sex offender, always a sex offender. There are sex offenders who don't offend, as there are alcoholics who don't drink, smokers who don't smoke, but in our view there's always that potential there.'

Such beliefs frequently have a strongly feminist background – Karin Meiselman told me that she often finds it very difficult when lecturing to convince any feminists in the audience that women too play their roles in problem families. I can understand and share the anger feminists feel when told that women who have been rape or incest victims asked for it, wanted it and probably enjoyed it. But we have to face the fact that a large number, perhaps the majority, of mothers of incest victims have themselves been victims, and also that most victimized children eventually learn to be seductive and use this seductiveness. Undoubtedly there are some, perhaps many, cases where the man does have strong paedophilic urges, and where the wife is a thoroughly normal, happy, well-adjusted being, and where the deviancy may be laid entirely at the father's door. But I don't think that life is usually quite as simple as that. One might ask, why should such a well-balanced woman pick such a man for her mate? Is anyone really quite as blind as that, even in the throes of love?

But that some fathers do seem to be paedophiles in the sense that they prefer children to adult women as sexual partners has been shown by research carried out by Gene Abel of the New York Psychiatric Institute and his colleagues. A major reason for this study (Abel, Becker, Murphy and Flanagan 1979) was to discover how many victims child sex offenders had in comparison to other sex offenders. To obtain genuine figures it was necessary to assure the offenders of total confidentiality with no legal follow-up. The subjects were sexual deviates, the majority of whom volunteered for the programme, and who were under no pressure to participate. Indeed, Abel assured me that if there was any suspicion of coercion from the authorities who were putting these men forward he refused to accept them. None were severely mentally retarded or psychotic. Care was taken to establish a good relationship between the men and the interviewers to help ensure openness. Not surprisingly under these circumstances a far greater number of offences was admitted to than there would otherwise have been. Exhibitionists, for example, owned up to an average of 200 victims. Homosexual and heterosexual paedophiles had an average of thirty-one and sixty-two victims respectively, whereas previous evidence had suggested an average of under two victims per offender. Heterosexual incest offenders, however, had a much smaller number of victims – just over two per offender – though in itself even this number is important as so often no or little attempt is made when incest cases come to light to discover whether children other than the known victim have been molested.

An issue of particular importance to students of incest which was also studied was whether or not incest offenders were aetiologically different from paedophiles. It had already been shown that recidivism rates for heterosexual incest offenders was lower than those for heterosexual paedophiles: did this imply that while paedophiles were only turned on by young girls, and continued to be so after punishment or treatment, for incest offenders family dynamics were more important? If this was so then obviously treatment for the two types would need to vary – one treatment would need to deal mainly with family dysfunction, the other with a specific desire for young girls. To investigate this issue Abel's programme used methods they had previously found successful in identifying rapists, which were based on discovering the arousal patterns of the various offenders when presented with various sexual stimuli.

As the results are somewhat controversial I will explain in some detail how the study was carried out. Twenty-seven sexual deviates took part in the study, six of whom were cases of heterosexual incest, ten were heterosexual paedophiles and the remaining eleven were subjects with other sexual deviations, ranging from rapists to an obscene phone-caller. It will be objected by many that six is too small a sample to have any validity, but other work by Abel and other researchers elsewhere points in the same direction.

After an extensive clinical interview in which the nature of the research was explained and total confidentiality was assured, the subject was taken to a laboratory where he was seated comfortably then left alone. Over an intercom he was instructed how to wear a small device which encircles a part of the penis and records any changes in penile diameter. Any changes could then be compared with the man's own full erection, so that the exact percentage of whatever erection the subject was having could be accurately measured. The reliability of this method had already been tested successfully by Abel on other occasions and it is a technique used by many experimenters. Obviously the standard to measure by has to be the subject's own: it would be useless applying the standard set by a sexual athlete to a man ungenerously endowed by nature or one deeply inhibited by the laboratory setting.

One of a set of seven two-minute audio-tape descriptions of a variety of acts were then played over the intercom to the subjects. The first of these tapes has a child of eight to ten years initiating sexual interaction with a male. It is she who leads the man on, while the man is passive. The tape describes the child, attractive and blonde, approaching a man sitting in his car.

She is walking towards your car. She wants to talk to you and have a sexual experience with you. She is in the car, moving right up close to you. She is putting her arms around you, feeling your body; she really enjoys it, she really likes holding you. She is unzipping your pants, she wants to feel your penis. . . . She is eight years old, she is touching your penis and holding your penis. Now she wants to have sex with you . . .

The second scene describes a scene in which both the child and the man are equally participating, both equally enjoying the situation. The setting is the same. The third scene depicts non-physical coercion, though verbal force is used. 'You are watching an eight-year-old girl. . . You want to rape her. You are telling her to come over to your car. She doesn't want to . . . you tell her if she doesn't . . . you are going to hurt her, to beat her up.' She gets into the car reluctantly. 'She is really frightened and scared.' The same physical action of the child holding the man's penis takes place, but now the child is an extremely unwilling participant, though no actual physical force has been used. The fourth scene includes actual force. It starts in the same manner, but this time the man goes over to the girl and pulls her into his car. She is fighting to get away, 'but it's no use, you are too strong and powerful. You slap her across the face and tell her to be quiet. You are yanking her clothes off. She is screaming, trying to get away. She is eight years of age, blonde, very pretty. You are going to rape her and you slap her across the face. . . .' The scene continues but the force used is only sufficient to get the girl to do what the man wants. The fifth scene depicts a forced sexual act where more violence is used than is necessary to make the girl submit. It starts in the same way as the fourth scene but this time, although the girl is so frightened she says she will do anything the man says, the man has a sadistic urge to hurt her anyway, and he does. He twists her hands so violently the bones snap. He forces his penis into her mouth until she nearly chokes. The sixth scene describes an assault that has no overt sexual connotations at all. It describes the same scene yet again, but this time after forcing the child into the car the man beats her up. She pleads for the man to stop, but he continues to hit her, making her bleed. The final scene is similar to scene 2, except that the willing partner is an adult female, not a child. The emphasis is on her adult body, her large breasts, her rounded hips. The experience is mutually gratifying, and the scene starts with the woman already in the car so the subject may either visualize the scene as taking place between himself and someone he already knows or with a stranger.

There are several sets of tapes, with each set depicting the same victim but with varying actions. During the study, each individual session consisted of two sets being presented randomly to the subject. Following each two-minute audio scene the subject was asked to report verbally how sexually aroused he had been, using a scale of 0 to 100, and also to describe the extent of his actual erection, using the same scale. In all cases the subject's report of his sexual arousal closely paralleled *his reported* rate of erection and the two verbal reports were therefore dealt with as one result which was then compared with the electronically recorded erection.

The results for the heterosexual incest cases were as follows: actual erections varied from 11 per cent to nearly 24 per cent, with the more aggressive scenes (3 to 6) producing the lowest arousal. While the accurately measured erections and the subject's own self-report were close for the first three scenes, the self-report of arousal sank to virtually nothing by the scene of the physical assault (scene 6), although in fact the average erection was over 11 per cent, only slightly lower than that for scene 3 (non-physical coercion). The difference between accurate measurement and self-reports was also clearly marked in the response to the final scene involving a willing woman, when the reported arousal was quite high – nearly 25 per cent, but the actual erection was much lower, under 14 per cent, only slightly higher than for scene 4, physical coercion.

This last result together with the important fact that scenes 1 and 2 – which described sexual acts with girls who were not the men's own daughters – produced erections of nearly 24 per cent, leads Abel to ask, 'If incest cases involve themselves with close relatives because of family conflicts or their mere availability, why do they get erections to scenes depicting sex with young girls not related to them?' He points out that this last pattern, of a noticeably higher response to young unrelated girls than to adult females, is characteristic of the heterosexual paedophile, and that a classification which relied on sexual arousal pattern would redefine heterosexual incest fathers as heterosexual paedophiles. He also stresses how self-report is misleading, as socially approved acts such as sex with an adult female were reported as being quite arousing when in fact there was only a minimal response, while acts such as forced sex with a child, which were reported as not being arousing at all, in fact showed as much arousal as with a consenting woman.

After testing the remaining subjects, whose offence was other than incest, Abel found that the arousal pattern of heterosexual incest cases (in response to young girls) was at least as great as that of heterosexual paedophiles. He suggests that since it may be that the incestuous offences have occurred primarily because of a sexual preference for young girls, it is possible that the family problems have been caused by the incestuous offenders attempts to have sex with their own children, rather than by malfunctioning family dynamics.

His conclusion is that since the cases of heterosexual paedophilia and heterosexual incest were similar in their ability to be aroused by young children other than female relatives, treatment for both must include reduction of the sexual preference for young girls.

The study did show one vital difference between paedophiles and incestuous fathers, however. Heterosexual paedophiles are much more responsive to the scenes depicting violence than were the incestuous offenders, which fits in with the pattern as we have come to know it.

So what do we make of this evidence? It is not unsupported by other research. Summit and Kryso (1978) suggest that males are retreating from castration fears when they chose children for their sexual partners, and that many with this paedophilic urge are able to resist the temptation until they are overwhelmed by the continuous presence of their own children.

Like Abel, Lucy Berliner, a social worker at the Sexual Assault Center, Seattle, believes that frequently offenders do not tell the whole truth about the extent of their problems. She has told me that the experience of the workers at the assault center and of Roger Wolfe, who treats some of the fathers from the center, is that incest offenders are not necessarily different from paedophilic child molesters. She claims that most people who work with incestuous families see only certain types of offenders and families, usually incestuous fathers and their daughter victims, and from this limited experience they generalize about incest as a whole, usually regarding it as a fairly loving relationship. 'But what about the cases where there's violence present, and battering? What about when the offender not only molests his own kids, but other people's kids as well? When it's boys, or a three year old? We see 500 children a year, and deal with the whole range, and we have found there is no automatic difference between an incestuous offender and a paedophilic offender.'

The Wolfes point to the many cases they see of men who have molested their own children and after the first marriage has broken up they have remarried and gone on to molest their stepchildren. On the other hand they see very few men who have resisted touching their own children, but after remarriage have begun to molest their stepchildren. Where a childless stepfather molests his stepchildren and then has children of his own by that marriage they have found he is likely to molest them also when he considers them old enough. Other professionals have reported the same kind of experiences. The Wolfes also told me that the subject of incest and paedophilia has been researched in various parts of the country, and the same kind of physiological response to children in general was shown, not just with the incestuous fathers' own children. Audio-tape presentations, photographic slide materials and in one case video-tape presentations of children and adults have been used. Some subjects have been voluntary, some not, but this seemed to make no difference to the results.

People who disagree with the theory that most, if not all, incestuous fathers have at least some paedophilic leanings, are usually very adamant that in the majority of cases this is not true, and consider family dysfunction to be the primary cause. There is no doubt it makes one much more comfortable to be able to envisage incest as a problem of family dysfunction rather than to see the father primarily as a paedophile. It spreads the blame, for one thing, and perhaps makes a solution seem simpler – family problems can be sorted out, can't they? (Until of course one remembers that it is probable both mother and father have been victims of one kind or another in their own childhood, in which case we are back to square one in having to deal with very difficult character problems.) Julian and Mohr (1979) express this attitude clearly in their paper:

It is suggested that the social worker can alleviate the high level of apprehension and distaste associated with incest by focusing on the perpetrator's poor parenting skills and the family's dysfunction, rather than the sexual abuse per se. A dysfunctional family is unable to function effectively as a family unit in the pursuit of socially approved goals and in conformity with socially defined values.

I myself would have thought it possible that someone who would prefer to have satisfactory sexual relations with adult women but who finds his own self-doubts and unease make this difficult, and who for one reason or another eventually has sex with his own daughter, would after his experience with a young girl naturally respond to stimuli of the type presented during Abel's research because of the association of this material with his daughter. I also suggest it is possible that the poor response to the scenes with adult women in the studies may be more because of the men's fear of adult women and their only too certain knowledge that they simply aren't much good at adult sex, than because they necessarily prefer children as sexual partners anyway.

It certainly seems true that most incestuous males do not go outside the family for extra sex. It could be, of course, that this is because they are terrified of being caught – it seems a character trait of the endogamic type, at least, that they are unaggressive, and the father's responses to scenes 3 – 6 of Abel's study bear this out. Does this mean that the reason they stick within the family is because that is what they want, or is it because they are too frightened to do otherwise? If they are essentially paedophiles the last may be true; if not, then the first should be true.

Wenet, in talking to me about this issue, repeated that after five years of working with teenagers he and other members of the staff have come to the conclusion that most incestuous activity is not essentially sexually motivated, and that it is other issues which lead to the offence – issues to do with power, with anger, with not being able to deal with frustration, with not being able to effect any changes in their lives – and they believe this view is as valid for adult offenders as it is for juvenile ones.

Perhaps eventually we shall end with a composite view, allowing that because of early experiences an offender is drawn to young people in a way that most adults are not, but that it will take the concatenation of a series of circumstances to make his relationship with his children turn sexual.

I reported earlier that one of the excuses most frequently given by the fathers for their incestuous behaviour is that sex with their spouses is unsatisfactory. It is certainly true that I have never come across a case where it was reported that the offender was *enjoying* sex with his wife as well as with his child/children. I emphasize 'enjoying' because although some earlier studies indicated that incest does not usually occur until after sex has virtually ceased between husband and wife, other surveys suggest that many men do continue to have sex with their wives, but that it is neither mutually enjoyable nor satisfying.

The men, of course, blame their wives for this, but as we saw earlier many of the men have little idea how to approach a woman in such a way that she feels sexually turned on. Some women report that the only time their husbands ever touch them is when they want sex. Most women need other kinds of touch, a feeling of being desired and liked: if the only time they are given a hug or a kiss is when their partners want sex it becomes very difficult for them to respond warmly although many men cannot understand this and imagine the woman is being deliberately cold and unfriendly. Sometimes the men clearly show their aggressive feelings towards women by the kind of touch they use; the touch may not be overtly aggressive but there is a world of difference between a tender loving touch and the kind of rather impatient pat that means – come on, respond, let's get down to it.

Perhaps the basic problem here is that these fathers do not seem able to relate to their wives in the kind of emotionally giving way that makes a woman feel valued and wanted for herself. This in turn means that she will not respond to him in the way he unquestionably needs. The question of who does it first, or rather, who doesn't do it first, is irrelevant. Neither responds to the unspoken needs of the other, there is little mutual affection between the couple, and the result is a gradual withdrawal on both sides. The daughter, on the other hand, is likely to be responding differently to her father (if he has treated her well up until then). We saw how John in Chapter 1 had such a response from his stepdaughter – she fetched him cans of beer when he arrived home and petted him generally – which was markedly different from the response from his wife with whom, however, he claims he had a good sexual relationship until after the marriage had taken place (and the resulting increased availability of his stepdaughter?). When this pattern becomes established it is the father and the daughter who are the centre of the family and the mother who is on the periphery, a withdrawn, cold figure increasingly alienated from other members.

One might expect that in large families it would be the mother who remains at the centre while the father and daughter are separated out, but in fact in the large famiies I have been told about the father is quite likely to be sexually involved with all or most of the children, while commonly the mother retreats into illness or work outside the family which draws her away from them. I cannot recall hearing or reading of a single case where it is the father and daughter who are isolated from the rest of a united family – again research would be invaluable here. Certainly it is unquestionable that in most families if the mother learns of the incest then sex between herself and her husband becomes extremely difficult for her; there is the occasional surfacing of a family where orgies including both parents and sometimes other children outside the family as well take place, but this is rare. One mother commented that whenever her husband had intercourse with her she could not help imagining her daughter in her place.

A possible reason for the sexual incompatability between husband and wife is their ignorance about sex. Repeatedly we hear from researchers of the lack of sexual knowledge in these families: they do not know either because they have never been taught, or because they choose not to know for a variety of reasons ranging from religious strictness to imagined inhibition. Finkelhor (1980b) found that girls with mothers who scolded or punished them for asking questions about sex or for masturbating were 75 per cent more vulnerable to being sexually victimized (not necessarily incestuously) than was the typical girl in the study. It was the second most powerful predictor of who would be victimized, the first being to have a stepfather. No doubt these mothers were passing on the kind of sex education they themselves received when they were girls. Men share this ignorance and lack of understanding about sexual matters equally. We must also bear in mind that wives about whom the incestuous fathers complain have not only to cope with the prohibitions and perhaps a fear or disgust for sex inculcated in them by their own parents, but that in very many cases they were incest victims themselves. Under these circumstances, we cannot be surprised that sexual problems between husbands and wives are characteristic of incestuous fathers.

Some men see their wives as stronger than they really are. Psychologists suggest that fears of homosexuality and strong dependency needs that cannot be met make adult relationships with grown women difficult, perhaps impossible. Offenders see their wives as rejecting or threatening and have no knowledge of what their wives need in their turn. On their part the wives probably know of no response other than the one they give, having been taught that that is the way adult women behave. Since the men fear other women equally, and dread separation from what little security they do have, they mostly do not move out but remain within the family, searching for comfort from their own children.

In several case histories already given we have seen this pattern of the rejecting wife, the available daughter. Since it is virtually impossible to draw a complete picture of the father without looking closely at the rest of the family, especially the mother, in the following chapter we shall do just that.

Chapter 5

The family

Incestuous families bind themselves together with ropes of mutual dependence, fear of separation, and secrecy, and if any one member tries to break away the bonds are ruthlessly tightened. Locked together by their emotional relationships they insulate themselves away from the rest of the world. If their secret is revealed and the world tries to break in the usual defensive action is one of absolute denial. Often the entire family puts up a united front against officialdom: even the victim may join his or her family in denying incest ever took place, and unless clear evidence is available (and evidence in most incest cases is difficult to come by) no further action can be taken.

We have already talked a little about family dynamics and their importance in cases of incest. There are those who feel that too much attention is paid to them: what matters is rescuing the victim. But as I have said before, life is not as simple as that. For a start, there may be more than one victim in a family but others are unlikely to be discovered unless a considerable amount of time is spent working with the family. Undiscovered victims will not only receive no therapeutic treatment but will continue to remain in a thoroughly disturbed setting, probably continuing to be assaulted if the offender remains at home (as may happen if there is insufficient evidence to jail him).

Secondly, because these families are so tight-knit, a removed victim is likely to drift back to the family. If the offender has been removed the victim will be made to feel responsible for the absence of the father and breadwinner. If he is still present she will probably find herself being molested again. If the victim is prevented from returning to her family she is truly a bereft child who is going to have enormous difficulties fitting into an alien world.

Giarretto (1978), commenting on the refusal of the families to accept or admit the truth of the victim's story, writes: 'As I listen to the parents and tune in to the underlying confusion and fear, I realize that they desperately rely on the lie as a kingpin which, faulty as it is, keeps the family structure from falling apart.'

The victim, most commonly the daughter, is made to feel the entire stability of the family depends on her silence. This sense of her own vital importance begins well before discovery. The father will often insist that if she tells her mother what is happening the mother will either leave, throw out the father, or throw out the daughter – i.e. the family will be broken up. Often the daughter observes the unhappiness between her parents and notes that when she is 'nice' to her father he is pleasanter to everyone else, confirming how essential she is to the well-being of the family.

The daughter may suspect her mother knows, may suspect everyone knows, but probably will not talk about it to anyone. Other family members may be involved in the incest – sometimes simultaneously or sometimes the father will not touch children below a certain age – but usually a general pretence of innocence is maintained. And if the abuse of one of the victims comes to light the remaining victims will keep silent – whether out of shame, or fear of the family being broken up, or out of a desire to protect the father, or whether out of a mixture of all three, no one can be sure. But since these are families who stick together much more than most, having few friends or outside contacts, it is difficult to imagine how – when they are closeted with each other so continuously – individual members can genuinely be ignorant of what is going on.

Also, of course, in many families where incest is widespread demarcation lines become unclear, with barriers of age and relationships breaking down, particularly where families are poor and overcrowding severe. But even in better-off families the atmosphere can become such that all the family – brothers, sisters and mother as well – cross the usual boundaries of restraint. I was told of one family where general incest was only discovered because it was found out by chance that a twelve-year-old boy was molesting his four-year-old sister. Some months of treatment passed (in which the entire family – the parents and their six children – was involved because of the youth of the two known participants) when two other children independently told their teachers that their father had been having anal sex with them for several years. After further investigation it was discovered that he had had anal intercourse with every child in the family, including the twelve-year-old offender. At first there had been total denial that anyone other than the twelve year old and his sister were involved, but in fact every member including the mother knew about everyone else, but they had all banded together to protect the father.

This sticking together can last a lifetime. One victim told me how she had tried to talk to her surviving family – her mother, brother and sister – several years after her father had died and all the children were approaching middle age. Her sister had once told her when they were both adolescent that she recalled her father holding her as a child, and her feeling a certain amount of pain 'down there', but later she denied it. The victim was also sure her brother had known what was happening at the time, although he would never talk openly about it. Her own life had been nearly destroyed by what had happened to her, and although now after intensive treatment she was becoming able to take hold of herself she badly needed to have the backing of the remaining family to reassure her. But such was their own need to protect the memory of their father/husband and the image of the united family that all three insisted nothing had ever happened, refusing to talk about it or to discuss it at all. Unfortunately this kind of action is common, as many victims undergoing therapy know, and it can add considerably to the confusion and difficulty of the patient unles she has a very understanding and supportive therapist.

In fact, in this particular case, at a later date the victim was able to arrange another meeting with the same members of her family and a therapist in the psychiatric clinic of a hospital. It might have been the official setting, or the fact that the other members had a preliminary meeting with the therapist before coming face to face with the victim (a woman of forty or so), but this time although the rest of the family were still not prepared to talk at least they listened to what the victim had to say and made no attempt to deny her story. This woman now works with other victims, and she says that in a clinic or therapy setting (if the patients/family members agree to come at all) denial is unusual, even if previously they have always denied the incest. The mothers might say things like, 'Oh, I don't think you understand it quite right', but they don't turn to their husbands and attack them, or say 'How could you!' Out of the twenty victims who have been through this experience in the group where she works, not one has found their mothers overtly shocked or distraught, as presumably they would have been if they were faced for the very first time with a totally unexpected revelation.

Families refusing to admit the truth are terrified of disturbing the balance of the family. Psychiatrists both in Britain and the United States have found clear evidence of family role-playing, with each member allocated his or her role in an organic whole. Where self-regard is low parents cannot easily support each other or build up in their children a high self-regard. In these circumstances the continuing existence of the family is even more necessary than in self-assured families, and any threat to the family system puts everybody's role into jeopardy. However dubious the value of these roles may seem to outsiders, to the members themselves the demands of the roles to be played may be satisfying to the extent that they set boundaries within which the players can live and survive without rocking the stability of the family as a unit.

If the incest comes to light and the victim does not deny it, the role she must now play is the villain of the piece, the main cause of the trouble, so that the remainder of the family can close ranks and continue as they were. Only if the daughter absolutely denies the incest can the family return to 'normal'; pressure on the victim to do so is therefore immense. It is rare for the mother to defend the victim and insist on the removal of the offender, for with the incarceration of the main breadwinner the structure of the family, its wealth and perhaps its place of residence will probably have to change.

Family rules in incestuous families are strict and not easily altered. To be able to adapt easily to changing circumstances people need to have a high self-regard and not need to cling to what they already have. This is exactly the opposite of most incestuous families: change upsets them, throws their balance off kilter, and since they are poor communicators (there is too much to hide for free communication to be possible) they cannot help each other to change. Children brought up to follow family rules blindly are often confused when they find school friends have quite different family rules, which is yet another reason why friendship with outsiders is strongly discouraged. As children grow older and develop natural desires for outside relationships, so the more powerful is the pressure put on them to remain within the family for all their social and emotional needs. This is not out of simple fear of family secrets being revealed, though this of itself is sufficient to keep the family isolated, but more out of a dread of the family system collapsing. Eventually, of course, the children will grow up and leave home, but even then a powerful feeling of responsibility and involvement is likely to continue.

It seems that one reason for this dependency on the family as a unit is that many incestuous families have an actual history of abandonment. Fathers, grandfathers, mothers may have walked out in the past, leaving behind an ingrained fear of further abandonment (Finkelhor 1978a). Emotional abandonment or neglect, of course, also produces an intense need for security. Parents in incestuous families seem incapable of treating their children in a way that produces a secure and healthy unit, and all the members, young and old, are typically short of affection. Often the wrong kind of touching is used in an attempt to satisfy this need. When we read of very young children having sex with each other in these families it is more likely to be out of an unmet desire for warmth and affection, rather than for straightforward sex. Later other needs, such as a desire for power, will intrude and complicate the picture.

The parents, as much as the children, are searching for this comfort and nurturance, and the victims are very well aware of this. I have heard small children of five or six refer with worried frowns to the needs of their parents, in particular to those of the abusing fathers, without any consciousness whatsoever of how topsy-turvy this appears to someone from the outside world. Children of eight or nine will weep with pain at the thought of the desolation their offending parents must be suffering, and although some workers assure me this pain is not as straightforward an emotion as it seems, the children look sincere enough at the time.

Gottlieb (1980) reports that individuals in incestuous families have many physical ailments, such as stomach problems, hearing problems and headaches, as well as 'behaviours that are geared towards avoidance of each other'. It is important to bear this last in mind: it is easy to suppose that because they so deliberately isolate themselves from outsiders they must therefore be in communication with each other, but the opposite is true. The stress within these pathetic families may be imagined if one envisages the tremendous needs each member has for true contact, for warm touch, and yet sees how at the same time they avoid outsiders and also each other, being incapable of reaching out with genuine openness and asking for what they need most. The sex they take and give can only exacerbate the underlying sadnesses and needs.

An exception to the home-centred activity is sometimes made by the mother who occasionally withdraws from the family, either through outside work or other activities that take her away from the home, or through illness which confines her to her bed. This will be looked at more closely later in this chapter, but I mention it here to draw attention to the importance it has for the victim/daughter, who will probably under these circumstances emerge as the central figure in the family, taking over her mother's role. The absence of the mother and the role reversal of the daughter of course brings the father and daughter closer, encouraging the emergence of a dangerous relationship.

There are certain other facts that put families at a greater risk than might otherwise have been the case. Some have already been mentioned, such as having a stepfather, or being one of a large family, especially where there is considerable discord (apparent in 65 per cent of the families), or where alcohol dependence exists (32 per cent). Other less obvious risk factors are beginning to be discovered, such as the combination of a well-educated father and a poorly educated mother, which according to Finkelhor's research (1980b) makes the daughter significantly more vulnerable to sexual abuse by her father than if both parents had little education.

Finally, as has been pointed out elsewhere, it is in sexually severe, not sexually lax, families that children are most in danger of sexual abuse. Abel, Becker and Skinner (1980) refer to a study by McConahay and McConahay, in which seventeen primitive cultures were rated for the amount of sexual permissiveness, sex-role rigidity and violence contained within them. There was found to be no correlation between sexual permissiveness and violence, and no correlation between sex-role rigidity and sexual permissiveness. But there was a significant correlation between sex-role rigidity and violence (the latter being judged by the severity of punishment in child rearing, the number of rapes, murders, tribal attacks, etc.). Abel *et al* caution against generalizing from non-industrial to industrial cultures, but mention similarities with our present-day society. Certainly these findings seem borne out by the type of sexual atmosphere apparently common in most sexually abusive homes.

We concluded in Chapter 4 that there does seem to be some element of paedophilia in at least certain cases of incest, and that the father's possible attractedness towards young children should continuously be borne in mind. Nevertheless I feel it would be a mistake to attempt to put the question of family dysfunction into second place for the simple reason that time and time again we find that a family pattern is being repeated. Whatever has caused the perpetrator to have the desires that he has, not only will the family become adjusted to his needs, but in all probability it will have no chance to do otherwise because he will almost certainly have chosen and been accepted by a wife who herself was either sexually assaulted as a child or was physically or emotionally deprived, so that a whole new repeat of their own family pattern is set up before the question of child assault can even arise.

This multi-generational victim-to-victim pattern is mentioned by many researchers (Rosenfeld 1979b; Muldoon 1979; Finkelhor 1979b; Summit and Kryso 1978). Susan Mele-Sernovitz, Assistant Attorney General for the State of Colorado, writes: 'Like parent physical abuse of children, sexual abuse is the result of disturbed family psychodynamics and reoccurs with each new generation.' Roger Wolfe (Seattle) reported that 70 per cent of the homosexual paedophiles he had worked with had themselves been abused by an adult male either within their own family or from outside when they were children. Sexual patterns set up in childhood exert a strong force, and where incest – acknowledged or not – occurs among various members of a family it is not difficult to understand how such a pattern may be repeated in the new generation, whatever the conscious desires of the once-victim, now offender, may be.

One aspect of the results of incestuous behaviour which many people find distasteful and difficult to deal with is the seductive behaviour of victims. In the past it was common to blame victims, usually female, for the behaviour of their seducers, and although to out-siders this may seem outrageous and grossly unfair, when one has met some of the girls one begins to understand why observers with little or no understanding of the background took and often still take this attitude. It is occasionally argued that to use the word 'seductive' is misleading, since a small child cannot understand adult sexuality and therefore cannot be truly seductive. I think this is a pointless argument, although I well understand the motives behind it, since the fact of the matter is the children have learned, often from the age of a year or two, to make physical gestures and emotional appeals of a kind that a susceptible male will interpret sexually. The child, like any child in the world, wants love and affection, warmth and touching. She has been programmed that certain gestures being certain rewards: if a sexual response is the only response she ever gets then her needs will tell her that that is better than nothing. She probably won't even realize that what she is receiving is not what most little girls get: to her that is the way life is – adults do *this*, when all you want them to do is *that*, but adults are odd creatures and at least daddy is smiling at you and petting you and making you feel someone cares something about you.

There are those who see this whole subject in terms of child liberalization, who argue that children should be free to have sex and to behave exactly as they choose, but for the majority of child psychiatrists sexuality in an adult sense simply isn't an issue for children. The development of sexuality is a slow natural process of maturing that cannot be hurried without the eventual fruit being spoiled, as a peach plucked early from the tree and forcibly ripened can never reach its full potential. The kind of genital behaviour that excites and pleases adults is very different to the kind of genital behaviour small children enjoy. And the complicated desires and emotions behind adult genital behaviour are immensely different to the simpler feelings of the small exploratory child. A small child can be taught to imitate or accept adult sexual behaviour, but this does not mean he or she is being 'liberated' into an exciting world previously hidden from him by his ignorance. To many readers it will seem absurd that I even have to say this, but when people begin to concern themselves with other people's 'freedom' they sometimes get carried away beyond reality into the realms of fantasy.

There used to be a common refusal to believe children had any sexual feelings at all. The popularity of certain of Freud's, then Kinsey's, works put a stop to that. As we saw in an earlier chapter, Freud eventually taught that all children have fantasies of desire for their parents and that if incest actually occurs at all it is probably the victim's strong desires which are the root cause. When, later, Kinsey's reports proved to everyone just how common childhood sexuality was, it was not surprising that most professionals dealing with incest victims came to the conclusion that if the victims didn't actually ask for it, they certainly weren't the sort to give a firm 'no'.

Worker after worker reported on the seductiveness of incest victims, and this is still a common finding, though now it is interpreted differently. Earlier researchers were inclined to draw the conclusion that the victims either initiated the incest or were content to accept it (among them were Bender and Blau in 1937; Weiss *et al* in 1955; Lewis and Sarrel in 1969), describing the children as 'seductive' but not explaining exactly what they meant by that term. Rosenfeld (1979b) reports that in a fairly recent written communication Weiss stated that of the seventy children he investigated thirty years ago some behaved very seductively towards him during their psychiatric interview and then when they returned to their parents again they told them the doctor had tried to molest them. Gottlieb (1980) warns professionals dealing with victims: 'A seductive 15 year old may give many mixed and confusing messages to a 21 year old male counsellor who has not been trained in the area of incest' and that 'special training in self-awareness' is necesarry to be able to treat these girls. Foster-parents also need to understand the particular problems they may have to face when looking after incest victims – physical affection offered by either side may well be misinterpreted and acted upon wrongly. A group worker talking to me about children as young as three and four years stressed how amazingly seductive they can be even in court, 'being seductive just as young women are seductive', and that their play can be highly sexual, full of adult endearments and talk of boyfriends.

This seductiveness is not necessarily overtly sexual. I remember being captivated by a small six-year-old girl at a group I attended of half a dozen or so children of between six and twelve years of age. This particular child had only been to the group once before and was feeling shy. She crept close to me, smiling tentatively, not quite able to look me in the face at first. After a while she put her hand on my knee and, still standing, leaned against my leg. Later her hand slipped into mine, and when I squeezed it in encouragement (she had been trying to speak in group but was too bashful to force any sound out of her mouth) she gave me such a look of shy pleasure and sweetness I could hardly bear to contemplate the reason why she was at the group. She attached herself to me for the whole evening, and I found myself feeling intensely responsible for her, only just resisting the strong urge to cuddle her tight and 'make her better' (as a temporary visitor it would have been cruel to have encouraged her to imagine a relationship was beginning). I had not realized just how strong her appeal was until discussing her later with one of the workers, when I saw how totally she had won me over. I suppose I could say that in a sense I had been manipulated – that little six year old had a desperate need for affection and regard, and she knew exactly how to get it. She was a lovely, endearing child, and appallingly vulnerable, sending out dangerous messages to anyone who cared to stop and hear. Later we shall see how many rape victims had previously been molested as children, how many young prostitutes were incest victims.

I have stressed the fact that many of these children are strongly appealing. Occasionally the opposite effect is produced, when the child acts more like a little nun, but such children are in the minority. To deny this seductiveness is counter-productive: what is vitally important – and I emphasize this as sometimes the child loses the help and protection she needs because of her manner – is to understand that her seductiveness is the product of her training. Many adult women who had been incest victims report that the only kind of 'love' or touching they knew in their childhood was sexual. Apart from that they received no warmth, no touching, no affection. A child responds to the wrong kind of overtures made to her by a molesting adult because her needs for affection are as great as her need for food and drink. Researchers have reported that child victims are preoccupied with oral deprivation and the need for nurturance and support – obviously they do not see their parents as fulfilling these needs.

One of the side-effects of the children's open expression of their needs is that its very effectiveness increases their guilt. They know perfectly well they wanted some of the touching they received and, although they develop a deep anger as they grow older and begin to understand how they have been used, they also suffer guilt and remorse, believing themselves at least partly responsible. This will be particularly so if they also enjoyed some of the sexual activity, as some victims do. It is essential they are made to understand that however they behaved, whatever they did, the responsibility lay with the offending adult; that the affection they craved for is what any child wants and that, as children, they were incapable of making an adult evaluation of the situation.

A question is often asked: how do we judge between being too warm with our children and not warm enough? There can be no firm answer to this: communication between people is not something you can weigh up like cheese. I think the only possible reply is, do what you feel is right. What is appropriate behaviour for one person may be positively frigid for another or almost torrid for yet another. What has to be wrong is to hold back affection out of a fear of it being misinterpreted, and, at the other extreme, to touch in a way that you know is exciting you sexually. At times the difference between sexuality and sensuality becomes blurred – I mentioned earlier how erotic an experience breast-feeding can be. Summit and Kryso (1978) comment on the natural erotic impulses we all occasionally feel towards members of our families and on 'the vague borderline between loving sensuality and abusive sexuality. Just as both discipline and sensuality are vital to the growth of children, the backlash of these qualities by abusing parents can blight a child for life.'

I doubt if a normally loving father, well in control of himself, is going to cause any harm if once or twice he momentarily touches his daughter inappropriately. Humans are not obtuse – they pick up signals, good and bad, and even if that moment of unplanned touching is sexually enjoyed by the father, the daughter will know instinctively whether or not she is threatened. Sunday morning cuddling in bed is a happy normal part of family life; wrestling, playing around, snuggling up – it is a time of animal ease and warmth, something that is looked back on with great pleasure by millions of adults. The difference between that and harmful behaviour can be seen in the following, told to me by a young mother, Elizabeth. Nothing very dramatic happened, but the incident changed her feelings towards her father permanently.

Elizabeth was brought up in a busy provincial town in the south of England, and after moving to London she made a successful career for herself which she has combined with marriage and children. I have quoted her in some detail because of the interesting threads in the pattern of her life. She was not badly traumatized, was easily able to cope because of her reasonably successful upbringing, and later had few problems. The incident was brief, and, although it may be she is blocking some of it out, it was clearly neither violent nor especially frightening. All the same, it disturbed her deeply and she has never been able to forget it. Readers will see in the relation many typical patterns of behaviour – dominant father, 'doormat' mother, tyrannical behaviour when the girl became a teenager, strictly orthodox sexual instruction – but will also notice other atypical aspects – the father made a success of his career, she was given a stable early upbringing without apparent tension between her parents. This seems to be a borderline case, where had things been slightly different incest could quite easily have occurred, but a basic stability and strength of character saved all concerned. Even so, Elizabeth dropped out of school at seventeen and ran away from home.

It was quite normal to get into bed on a Sunday morning with my parents and have a cuddle, and it was just a continuation of that. I was ten or eleven when it happened. My mother had got up to make breakfast, and my father and I were just lying

there, chatting, I suppose. I can't remember things very clearly
– I'd have been wearing pyjamas or a nightdress, I don't
remember exactly, and he was in his pyjamas – I'm pretty sure
he kept them on. I picked up that something was different from
the way he was talking – I had a sense this wasn't the usual
Sunday morning cuddle even before he began to hug me and
ask me if I knew where babies came from. I remember
thinking, he knows quite well I know all about that – my
mother had told me a couple of years before – so why is he
asking me, and why is he getting hold of me like this? He
wouldn't drop the subject, he kept on about it even after I told
him I knew, and he was rubbing himself up against me. He had
his arms around me – it was an extension of a father cuddling a
child in bed – but it got beyond that and I was aware of his
genitals.

I remember wanting to get out of bed, sensing this wasn't
right, it shouldn't be happening, but I also wanted to please
him very much. I was very fond of him. I'd really had a very
good loving relationship with both my parents up to then, and I
believe I was an ordinary fun-loving child. But when you're
suddenly confronted with a large penis for the first time and it's
next to you, you instinctively feel worried, very upset. I'd seen
my father naked several times before, but when it gets big, you
know? It's not exactly shocking, but it does take you back a
bit. You think, my God, what's this? I think if I'd just *seen* him
naked with an erection I'd have been rather shattered, but to be
in bed and to feel this is a very bewildering experience: you've
no terms of reference to deal with it. As I said, my mother had
already told me about the mechanics of sex, so I wasn't
ignorant about it, but it was still shocking. Well, after a bit I
pulled myself away and got out of bed. I just knew it wasn't
right, what he was doing.

I don't think he actually touched me, but I can't be sure, I
may be blocking out exactly what happened. I think later I
denied it to myself – oh no, he can't actually have touched me!
– but I'm not too clear about it. If he didn't touch me, why was
I so worried I was pregnant? Because I *was* worried, I was
really frightened for three or four months afterwards that I
might be pregnant. I didn't really think I could be, but I
couldn't be sure I wasn't. I remember wishing I had somebody
to talk to about it, to clarify what had happened. I couldn't

explain it to myself, you see, I couldn't understand it. Of course I couldn't talk to my friends about it, though there were all sorts of stories told by the girls at school, that the man didn't actually have to put it in, you could get pregnant just by having the tip of the penis touch you. Since I was so worried, maybe he did touch me, just a bit? I simply don't remember.

A year or two later I told my mother about it, and how I'd thought I was pregnant, and she refused to believe me – she just laughed and said, 'Don't be ridiculous!' I haven't really thought about this before, but it was odd she laughed, because she didn't think sex at all amusing. For her, sex was dirty unless you were safely married. You'd have expected her to be angry with me, or shocked I could say such a thing, if she didn't believe me.

It certainly affected my relationship with my parents, especially with my father. I felt separate from them after that. I never mentioned it to him, but I wouldn't ever be in bed with him again alone: trust had gone for ever. I lost respect for him, too. I never felt guilty about myself, I felt it was entirely his doing. I suppose the truth is that they had given me a pretty good upbringing, and I was a fairly strong and stable person. Though later I think this aspect of me began to annoy him. The little girl he'd adored had suddenly become an independent difficult teenager.

He is a very powerful and opinionated person, while my mother's a doormat. He's a self-made man, immensely practical, and intolerant of people who aren't. I became very rebellious and when I was about fifteen he began to knock me around, grab hold of me and thump me on the back with his fist, while my mother tried to drag him off. I must have been very provocative – I know I was – but I'll never forgive him. It's deep inside me, that humiliation. He'd go completely out of control, as though whatever had set off the row no longer had any relevance.

He had very unreasonable rules in the house – I always had to be in by 10 o'clock at night, that sort of thing. He was very rigid, quite unthinking about my needs. When I was seventeen we had a big row. It wasn't really my fault. I'd quite genuinely misunderstood something he wanted me to do and we had a great scene, with him beating me. I'd already worked out a plan, and so I followed it. I rang up a hostel I'd previously checked on, booked a place, took a bus, and off I went to London, with £20 I'd saved up in my pocket. Next day I rang my parents, but my father was so mad with me he refused to have anything to do with me for several years after that. I'd been an only child for many years, and he had been extremely fond of me, so it shook him. I think he thought I'd get picked up or something ghastly. Now I've made a success of my life he likes to imagine it's his doing.

You know, it's always there, at the back of my mind. I don't know if it altered my relationship with boys at all – I think I have a basic lack of trust because of it. I wasn't revolted by what he did, but . . . it was unsavoury, that's the word, unsavoury.

And another thing – it's made me uneasy when my children get into bed with us, now they're getting bigger. My husband is terribly free, wanders about with nothing on without thinking anything about it, and I wonder what our eldest daughter is thinking – I warn him to be careful when he's close to her. Yes, I've told him about the incident, but he quite rightly refuses to get prudish with our own kids as a result. All the same, I can't help getting uneasy about it.

As to my character, I don't know if it affected it. How can I tell what I would have been like if it hadn't happened? But I know I'm not at all sympathetic to weakness, especially in men. With boyfriends, my husband, or colleagues at work, if they show they're vulnerable or want me to be supportive I cut off, I just don't have any sympathy with them. I'm not that way with women at all. Maybe it's a kind of punishment to men, or perhaps it's just the way I'm made. Who can tell?

The change in relationships mentioned by Elizabeth, even when practically nothing happened between her father and herself, is inevitable. Where molestation takes place normal parent/child relationships are inevitably destroyed. It is not possible for a parent's natural authority to be maintained under these circumstances, so violence or bribery will probably be used to ensure the victim's silence. As the child grows she is likely to be faced with the combination of affection when sex is wanted, at the same time as increasing strictness, even tyrannical behaviour, as she attempts to turn outside the family for her adolescent needs. If the incest is solely between father and daughter, the father will dread losing her, and will try more and more to ensure her dependence on him. Many fathers fear this loss, but incestuous fathers, having so little in their lives, feel it more than most.

'Incest is a relationship among at least three persons, the two participants and the nonparticipating parent' (Rosenfeld 1979c). The bitterness that many incest victims feel towards the nonparticipating parent, usually the mother, has only recently begun to be appreciated. Tsai and Wagner (1978), working with fifty women who had been sexually molested as children, found that the thirty-one who had been molested by their fathers and stepfathers felt as much, if not more, resentment and bitterness towards their mothers as they did towards the molesting parent. Some of these mothers had known what was happening, some had not, but either way the daughter felt they had been sacrificed in order to keep the family intact. Henry Kempe in an address to a meeting of the Ciba Foundation (unpublished, April 1981) spoke of the immense anger incest victims feel towards their mothers, and how they are far more ready to forgive their fathers than they are their mothers. Barbara Myers, an incest victim who runs a programme called 'Christopher Street' helping other incest victims in Minneapolis, gives us a clue as to how this anger builds up in her account of why she persistently ran away from the foster homes in which she was placed after discovery of the incest (Myers 1979).

> I was afraid I would destroy those other families with my pain. I preferred taking responsibility for not wanting them, rather than risking the possibility of their rejecting me. (In the same way, it was always easier for me to be angry and tell my mother to go to hell than have to face her inability to protect me from my father.) I was afraid that if I stayed too long in a foster home, others would see how ugly and evil I was inside and wouldn't want me any more. I was often afraid to start running again, but I was more afraid of staying.

The relationship between the mother and her molested child is of great importance, particularly when the victim is female. Therapists following the Giarretto model of treatment usually make the building up of a successful mother/daughter relationship their prime target, which they then use as a core for rebuilding the rest of the family.

The way in which mothers in incestuous families reverse roles with their daughters is a commonplace, and modern research has not disproved this phenomenon, although it is not of course invariable. In the past it has often been seen, at its crudest, as a desire of the mother to free herself from an unwanted sexual relationship. While this is undoubtedly true in some cases, there is disagreement as to how universal this is. What has been commented on less is the desire of the mother to be mothered herself: she turns her daughter into a 'little mother' for her own needs as much as for her husband's. Most of these women have in one way or another suffered emotional deprivation as children, and since they so frequently choose husbands similar to themselves they do not receive in marriage the nurturance and warm sympathy they yearn for. They become disillusioned with a relationship that does not give them what they so badly need, and since they cannot change this pattern (for they are as incapable of nurturing the husband as he is of nurturing them) they turn elsewhere. Frequently they gradually abdicate their duties to their daughter – usually the eldest, but not always – handing over the housekeeping and even the upbringing of the younger children. They may actively encourage the daughters to fuss over the fathers, even to take over their sexual role, or they may opt out of this side of the affair altogether, consciously or unconsciously. The daughter thus takes on the well-being of the entire family including that of her mother, and it is only later, when she comes to understand how unfairly she has been used, that anger surfaces. In many cases she is never able to acknowledge her anger at all, and it remains the buried cause of future miseries.

The daughter, who in this type of situation now becomes the central figure in the house, finds it extremely difficult to shed her responsibilities, even when the incest is discovered. I have been present at several group therapy sessions where daughters recently removed from their homes have cried out in distress at the thought of their abandoned families whom they were certain could not cope without them. Discussing this with a therapist who dealt only with aggressors, he commented that he himself rarely saw any evidence of the 'little mother syndrome' and that he failed to see how an eight year-old could run a family household. I suggested that the aggressors would probably not see their daughters in this light at all, at least not when they were very young, but that to the children themselves the fact of their responsibility is clearly apparent to the therapists I have spoken with who work with victims, either women who were molested as children or youngsters whose molestation has only recently been discovered.

Summit and Kryso (1978) suggest that as the young girl takes on the wifely duties, greeting the father warmly when he returns from work, bringing him his dinner and tucking up the younger children in bed, she reminds him of his wife when she was still his bride-to-be, especially if she takes after his wife physically, and that the excitement the mother once aroused in him is now aroused by the daughter. Whether the path to most incestuous sexual relationships follows this pattern, or whether in general it is far more complicated – as discussed for example in the previous chapter when we explored the possibility of incestuous fathers having paedophilic leanings – the result can only be a basic confusion in the child as she takes on an adult, caring role for which she is not emotionally ready. She becomes, as one adult victim put it to me, 'the caretaker of all of them, especially the caretaker of the family secrets. Even now I feel responsible for the entire family, though they don't want that, they broke away years ago, they want to forget the past as though it never happened.' She spoke as one bereaved, who could not yet come to terms with the emptiness of her life.

One may ask why, since so many of the mothers were themselves victims once, they cannot put themselves into their daughters' place and help them? It is suggested by some psychologists that denial has been such a lifelong part of these women's lives that they cannot see what is happening under their noses, neither the sexual inter-action between their husbands and daughters, nor how totally they have abrogated their maternal responsibilities.

How far these mothers are consciously aware of the sexual activity is a subject for disagreement. Some professionals consider virtually all mothers know at one level or another, others say that at least half have no idea at all. Gottlieb (1980) writes: 'Mothers are usually aware there is some problem in the family, although they strongly deny what is often clear and blatant evidence of the incest.' Rosen-feld (1979c):

> the mother often denies any knowledge of the incest and may even act the martyred victim, but this denial often seems to represent her attempt to preserve self-respect, since clinical experience frequently suggests that she was fully aware of the relationship.

Giarretto (1978), discussing the subject of group therapy with mothers, writes: 'As a general rule, the mother will admit eventually that she was party to the incestuous situation and contributed to the underlying causes. Certainly, something was awry in her relationship with her husband and daughter.' In a conversation with Helen Alexander at the National Center for the Prevention and Treatment of Child Abuse and Neglect, Denver, she told me that out of seventeen adult women who had been molested as children, fourteen had told their mothers about the molestation but they had done nothing about it. The mothers had accused the daughters of lying, or said they were having hallucinations, or simply ignored the charge. One woman said it was as though her mother were stuffed, and she seemed so totally uninvolved in what was happening around her. The women who had never told their mothers reported that their relationship with them was so remote it was not possible for such an intimate communication to take place. One of the victims reported how, when her mother (previously divorced from the incestuous father) took a new lover, she went home on a visit and was amazed to find the new boyfriend making a pass at her. Now an adult, she was strong enough to refuse him, but when she reported the incident to her mother she again refused to believe her, saying, 'You're *always* making up stories, what are you talking about!'

On the other hand, Karin Meiselman, psychologist and author of *Incest* told me that she believes that 'a small majority' really do not know about the sexual relationship between father and daughter. She considers that for many mothers the idea is inconceivable and it literally never crosses their minds, although in retrospect they can recognize symptoms that, had they been alerted they would have picked up. Geri Hatcher, project director of Los Angeles Child Sexual Abuse Programme, agrees with this finding.

It is possible that the mother who herself was once a victim is the mother who at one level or another knows what is happening, and who is most likely, because of her own insufficiencies, to deny the existence of the current incest; while the mother who was never a victim is the mother who genuinely does not recognize the signs, but who at the same time is most likely to accept her daughter's story and go for help to the authorities. This is purely a hypothesis, but perhaps one worth investigating.

We must not underestimate the importance economics has in the decision a mother makes as to whether or not to take action. Quite apart from her own emotional reactions to what her daughter has told her, in the great majority of cases she knows that bringing in outside help probably means losing the main breadwinner's salary. Even where she and her husband earn roughly similar amounts if he is removed from the home the loss of his money will still mean a considerable reduction in the family's style of living. There also arises the almost inevitable loss of status, the scandal, and even a change of home because of financial difficulties or the need to move to an area where they are unknown. In addition to these practical considerations it seems that most of the mothers are extremely reluctant to live without a man. As one psychiatrist put it to me, the mother is often incredibly dependent on a man. She believes to the bottom of her toenails she's got to have a partner, and she's going to hang on to the man she's got, no matter what. If she continues with her household duties she is likely to behave submissively, a 'doormat', even if outside the house she holds down a good job. I was told the following by a social worker:

> I'm thinking of a particular lady, she works for a bank, has a very good position supervising people, and as a working person she feels pretty good about herself, but when she gets home she's like a slave! Her husband has usually got home before she does, and he's taking a shower and kind of lounging around waiting for her to run in with a TV tray meal for him. If it's not exactly the way he wants it he sends it back, maybe two or three times so she can get it right. If he had a different wife perhaps he could look at what he's doing and grow up out of the infantile modes of behaviour we so often see with our offenders, and if the wife had married someone who could make her feel good about herself, then a lot of the abuse just wouldn't have taken place.

But they didn't marry different people, they chose each other with the unerring accuracy with which so many of us choose our spouses, and certain events followed with the unsparing inevitability of Greek drama.

The result of all these pressures, factual and emotional, is that if they are forced to make a choice most of the women elect to stay with their husbands. Either they deny their children's stories, or, if the truth comes out into the open but the husband is allowed to stay at home they remain with their spouses and it is the child who is sent away. Thus the daughter is usually faced with the fact that if she wishes to continue to live with her mother and the rest of the family she will have to accept living with her father too. And this is the decision she usually makes in the end, even if it means continuing with a sexual relationship she detests. If the father is removed, the daughter may not be much happier as she will almost certainly be left in no doubt as to the destruction she has caused.

Although the type of mother we have been describing, one who is relatively dependent on her husband but who abdicates her responsibilities to her daughter, appears to be the most common, there is a second type of mother who is stronger in personality, and who often removes herself physically from the family either by working away from home or by taking on outside activities that absorb a great deal of her time. Others escape by becoming ill whenever tensions are at their greatest, taking to their beds or going into the psychiatric ward of the local hospital. As we saw earlier, many of the incestuous fathers had mothers who had absented themselves in this way, and they tend to marry women of the same type. When the mother is physically absent it is of course more difficult still for the daughter to keep away from her father. Even when mothers of this type are around the house they usually cut themselves off from the family so successfully that neither daughter nor father has any sense of communication with her. In several of the case histories I have given this pattern shows up clearly.

It is interesting that when Giarretto and his colleagues brought together the first group of three mothers of molested children (the beginnings of Parents United) it was suggested the three should meet with a woman who was the mother of a physically abused child and work to set up a new chapter of Parents Anonymous. This was done, but the incest mothers came to feel that their problems were too different for them to feel completely at ease with the other mother, and that there needed to be a separate group for incest families. Among themselves the incest mothers found they recognized many similarities and they were able to experience the relief of discussing problems they had never before been able to share with anyone. This joining together was to be the source of the regeneration of thousands of other women's lives.

Chapter 6

Incest other than father/daughter

Because family dynamics are of such importance in the study of incest regardless of the relationship of the offender and victim, the fact that we have so far concentrated almost entirely on father/daughter incest makes most of what has been said no less valid for other types of incest. But, having said this, I have to admit it is easier to be certain of the similarities than of the differences, for there has been too little research into other kinds of incest to be sure of what those last are.

Part of the reason for the paucity of research is that incest is a new field and researchers have to work with what they can get. The law is mainly concerned with intercourse between a male and his closest female blood relatives – daughter, sister, mother. People do not seem to take brother/sister incest anything like as seriously as father/daughter incest, and son/mother *intercourse* appears to be rare, while other forms of incest such as father/son, mother/daughter, are not even considered, therefore the great majority of cases coming to the public eye are father/daughter. Even where the law has a wider mesh, such as in certain states in America which use the word 'caretakers' rather than 'fathers', for example, other relatives such as grandfathers, uncles, aunts, brothers or elder sisters are usually excluded.

Where we do have reports on other types of incest they are mostly based on very small samples which tend to be biased towards socially disadvantaged groups: better-off people seek private advice and do not figure in such research. Another problem is that the great majority of victims come to the attention of researchers because they are known to be in need of help and they are rarely compared with control groups of unmolested children sharing similar backgrounds and problems. It may be that many of the symptoms exhibited by the molested children are due to growing up in dysfunctional families rather than to the incestuous acts themselves. Neither do we know much about victims who are not sufficiently disturbed to come to public notice – work of this nature is only just beginning to be undertaken.

Yet another difficulty is that because of the smallness of the samples many of the findings are contradictory. In addition study methods differ considerably, and different data is given (such as the sex and age of the child, the acts involved, the relationship of the molester, the duration of the molestation), making it very difficult to compare results. These problems still exist in the study of the whole of incest, including father/daughter, but they are particularly noticeable when we come to look at other forms. There is virtually no research at all into entirely female incest since it is so rarely reported and case studies are not available: because of this many people assume either that it doesn't exist, or that if it does it causes no problems. These assumptions may be true or they may be untrue – how are we to know?

In the following pages I will report on some of the available studies on incest other than that between father and daughter, but it must be borne continuously in mind that in most cases these are based on small samples from biased groups which were not compared with normal population controls.

Multiple sex, occurring simultaneously or consecutively, is far less uncommon than was once thought. In a study of fifty-eight patients seen in a psychotherapy clinic which dealt in the main with only mildly disturbed people, Karin Meiselman found that nearly thirty per cent of the patients had either themselves been sexually involved with more than one member of their family or they knew of other incestuous affairs occuring within their immediate families. Of the father/daughter incest cases 15 per cent were multiple in the sense of the father moving on from one daughter to the next in sequence. Meiselman points out that since in 31 per cent of the father/daughter cases there was only one daughter in the family the figure of 15 per cent seems even higher, and that in the remaining 54 per cent probably quite a few daughters remained ignorant of the father's possible approaches to their sisters and brothers, secrecy being so important a factor in incestuous families.

Once in a while both parents are involved in group sex with their children, occasionally with excuses that they are being 'modern', free, expressing themselves, educating their children, etc. Pornography may be used, films made, unrelated children brought in from outside. Summit and Kryso (1978) quote a case where a mother and father led their children through ever-increasing 'orgiastic adventures' then used them as 'bait to draw in neighbourhood boys to provide the father with a continuous harem'.

In other families the mothers do not join in the sexual activities, but neither do they stop them. Summit and Kryso quote a case of this kind: a highly religious man, a fundamentalist minister, was having a sexual relationship with his nine year-old daughter, and in spite of entreaties to the mother from the girl and her eldest sister the mother refused to intervene. Thirteen years later when the older girl found her own seven year-old daughter and the sister's three-year-old child had also been molested by their grandfather (her father) she at last sought help. She blamed her father for the family's many problems: she herself was promiscuous, her sister was beaten by her husband, one brother was schizophrenic and the other homosexual. A third brother at the age of fifteen had tried to seduce the woman's seven-year-old child. As Summit points out, only one member out of two generations of the family was able to seek help, and that was through an anonymous helpline. Similar cases have been quoted elsewhere in this book.

We have seen that quite frequently a father who is assaulting his daughter is also assaulting his son, and that this is far more prevalent than had been thought earlier. Maisch (1973) wrote that simultaneous father/daughter and father/son incest was very rare, and does not even appear to consider the possiblity of father/son incest occurring alone at all. In fact the extension of father/son incest through the interchange of young boys among a group of men is causing concern among some professionals. Summit and Kryso refer to a case which was opened up when a vice-officer and his son joined a group advertised in the underground press, where men brought their young sons to arranged meetings and then traded them among themselves for 'extended orgies'. 'Sex rings', as they are called, are not all that uncommon, involving perhaps a scoutmaster, a neighbour, a teacher or a local businessman who do the boys favours – provide recreational sport, give parties, or in some way indulge them, and in return boys are expected to do what the man or men ask. I understand that more often than not nothing more serious than masturbation takes place, but for boys brought up with the usual social expectations the fact of having been forced to be passive partners in sex can result in traumatic after-effects, although at the time the activity may not have seemed so very disturbing to them.

What little research into the after-effects of father/son incest there has been, has mainly consisted of descriptions of individual patients seen in a psychiatric clinic or hospital. These patients are usually highly disturbed, perhaps suicidal, psychotic, often with an intense fear of becoming homosexual. Father/son incest victims who marry sometimes have sexual relationships with their own sons who may themselves become disturbed to the point of hospitalization, when the whole cycle is revealed. Meiselman (1979) quotes a case investigated by J. B. Raybin which is typical in many respects of various reported cases. When a young man of twenty had a psychotic breakdown after taking LSD his father became so depressed he needed hospital treatment, during which he admitted he had had homosexual relations with his son when he was younger. The father himself had been molested by his own father, a successful 'respectable' businessman, who used to enter his bedroom at night and manipulate his genitals. Stimulated by this, he initiated sexual relations with his younger brother and later with a male cousin, both of which affairs continued for several years. As an adult he had a number of homosexual affairs outside the family. He also had some heterosexual desires, however, and married twice, but after a while lost sexual interest in the second wife. Although he was physically affectionate with his son it was not until the boy admitted that he himself was having homosexual relationships that the father approached him sexually. It was after they had developed an incestuous relationship that the son had his breakdown, which was then followed by the father's depression.

Meiselman, summarizing the sparse literature available, suggests that in general the initial sexual approach is almost invariably from the father, who will have had homosexual desires since childhood but who has put up a convincing show of being heterosexual to the extent of marrying and conceiving children. Often he himself was an incest victim. The research suggests he is usually intelligent, good at his job and until forming an incestuous relationship with his son has shown no signs of severe psychological difficulties. He is strongly attached to the son he has chosen, and becomes guilty and depressed when he perceives he has harmed his boy and spoiled their relationship. The son usually goes along with his father for a while, whom he wants to please, but sooner or later he persuades his father to stop it. In late adolescence or early adulthood he often suffers severe disturbance and is very frightened of becoming homosexual, although mostly he is not, or at least not exclusively so.

While some of this pattern holds good for a number of the father/son relationships I have been told about it hardly covers the many cases I learned of where the father indiscriminately abuses whichever child is available. Such families as these are usually labelled 'chaotic' or 'promiscuous' by researchers, as compared with 'endogamic' families, and I have the sense that homosexuality as such is not a predisposing force in this type of molestation. The father in endogamic families who has sex only with his daughter/s certainly appears to have problems with forming mature relationships with adult women, and often also has fears of possible homosexuality, but since only female victims are chosen one might assume that the pull towards homosexuality in such cases is less strong than in those fathers who molest their sons.

The Harborview Sexual Assault Center (Seattle, Washington) presented three very interesting papers on sexually abused males at the Third International Congress on Child Abuse and Neglect held in April 1981 in Amsterdam, Holland. Harborview were kind enough to give me copies of these as yet unpublished papers so that I could include their results in this book; their present titles being: 'Psychosocial sequelae in intrafamilial victims of sexual assault and abuse', 'Intrafamilial sexual abuse of male children and adolescents: an under-reported problem', and 'Sexual abuse of adolescent males: an overview'. The four authors are Shirley Cooke Anderson, Carol Mosier Bach, Sandra Griffith, and David Paperny, all members of the Department of Pediatrics, University of Washington.

Between 1974 and 1980, seventy-two males with ages ranging from thirteen to twenty came to the Sexual Assault Center. Male victims were rarely seen in the first few years of the centre's opening, and forty-two of these seventy-two came for care during 1979 and 1980. It was decided to do a retrospective study of these seventy-two youths, during which comparisons were made with 151 adolescent female victims who had been the subjects of a previous study. 21 per cent of the boys and 41 per cent of the girls were intrafamilial victims (reporting of incest cases was a late development – thirteen out of the fifteen were seen during 1979–80). The number of male victims seen between 1974 and 1980 was 373: 250 were twelve or under, and 51 were twenty-one or over.

Of all the adolescent victims seen between 1974 and 1980 4 per cent were male, and this clearly is a minimum figure as none were seen at all during 1973–4. In the following years the numbers increased rapidly and, in 1979–80, 5.5 per cent of the adolescent victims were male. If previously quoted research is valid we may expect this percentage to rise further as young males find the confidence to report assaults which at present are kept secret. Harborview report that most molestation takes place at an early age: only seventeen out of the seventy-two adolescents were in the seventeen to twenty age bracket. Children aged six to twelve were at the greatest risk.

Although there was a slightly higher than average number of adolescent victims receiving public assistance, it was reported that sexual assault occurred at all social levels. Of the adolescent male victims 7 per cent (5 per cent female) were developmentally disabled, either intellectually, emotionally or physically.

It was found that the adolescent males were more likely to be abused by acquaintances than females who were likely to be abused either by strangers or by family members. Of the adolescent male victims seen during 1979 to 1980 31 per cent were molested by family members, as were 36 per cent of the male children aged twelve or under. Equal numbers of natural parents and step-parents were responsible for the sexual molestation of the male adolescents, but offenders against the younger children included other family members – grandfathers, uncles, siblings and cousins. Of the abusers 6 per cent were female, including baby-sitters, mothers, cousins and one sibling.

As with all incest, early molestation mostly began with fondling and increased in seriousness with age. The type of assault differed considerably between intrafamilial and extrafamilial contacts: whereas 59 per cent of sexual contacts with extrafamilial males were purely oral-genital, 12 per cent anal, 10 per cent forced masturbation, and 3 per cent multiple type, only 8 per cent of intrafamilial abuse was purely oral-genital, and a further 8 per cent anal, while 23 per cent consisted of forced masturbation and 31 per cent was multiple type. An interesting difference was discovered between offenders' approaches to male and female victims – more attempts were made to involve the males by masturbation or oral contact to the point of ejaculation. Also more males were persuaded to perform sexual acts with other victims, or to watch the offender have sex with another person.

Far less force was used on young males within the family than was used by offenders outside the family. Only 8 per cent of the adolescent intrafamilial victims suffered force, while 92 per cent were persuaded to cooperate by the sheer use of adult authority. Of the total of thirty-four youths who were given a medical evaluation (those who were seen for counselling only were not medically evaluated) eleven had injuries of one kind or another. No injuries were found in male victims of intrafamilial sexual abuse.

Being abused by family members, however, caused more psychosocial complications than when the assault was made by someone outside the family – 77 per cent as against 52 per cent. The figures for adolescent girl victims were very similar, being 78 per cent and 51 per cent respectively. The older the child the worse he was affected. Major psychosocial symptoms included sleep disturbances, fears and phobias, needs for reassurance, regression, depression, guilt and anger. Externalized problems were difficulties at school, problems with peer relationships, truancy, running away, family conflict, chemical dependancy, delinquency and prostitution. Sexual acting out sometimes involved victimizing other children – previously mentioned findings that many, if not most, sexually abusive adolescents have themselves been victimized, is confirmed here. Although all these symptoms were shown by both female and male victims, among the males there was less guilt and depression but more acting out behaviour, including sexual aggression. Anxiety about their sexual identity, including fears about homosexuality, was higher among the boys, particularly when they had been forced into active participation or if they had been successfully stimulated into a physical response. Girls were more concerned about being 'damaged goods' or that 'people could tell', and had greater difficulty with intimate relationships.

Harborview consider that the new professional understanding of problems of this kind, particularly those relating to sexual identity, is a major reason for the steadily increasing reporting of intrafamilial molestation, and feel it is essential that help be given at as early an age as possible in order to break what they regard as a cycle of abuse continuing from generation to generation. They are equally convinced that, as with other types of incest, male victimization is at present under-reported.

Finally, it seems that many of the boys used in pornographic modelling for magazines and films, and many, perhaps most, of the boys offering themselves for paid sex have already had relations with their own fathers. B. and R. Justice (1979) report that in Houston, USA, it is estimated there are 200 boys involved in prostitution, and that in big cities such as New York or Los Angeles telephone orders can be placed for local boys to be 'delivered' in various parts of the country, and that such sex 'can be bought with a credit card.' They state that many of the boy prostitutes and the men who buy sex from them have backgrounds of sexual abuse.

Incestuous relationships with grandfathers as the perpetrators are even less well charted than father/son incest. I found they were mentioned quite frequently by caseworkers and other professionals when I asked them about incest other than father/daughter, but their incidence is impossible to estimate since theirs are so rarely reported officially. A mother finding her father molesting her daughter is likely to whip the child away, making sure by their absence that further repetition is impossible, without feeling any need to call in the authorities; there is not the same urgency that there would be if the offender were the husband.

The few studies available are all on grandfather/grand-daughter relations; I know of none on grandfather/grandson. Tsai and Wagner (1979) found that in a study of 118 sexually molested women just under 10 per cent had been molested by their grandfathers. In another study of theirs, involving fifty women reached through the media, 11 per cent had been molested by their grandfathers (Tsai and Wagner 1978). Lukianowicz (1972) discovered five cases of grandfather/grand-daughter incest in the twenty-nine subjects who had had incestuous relationships of a kind other than father/daughter in his previously mentioned survey of patients in Northern Ireland (it should be recalled that their incestuous activities were only indirectly discovered). This figure is somewhat misleading from the statistical point of view as in fact all five cases were from one family, and all were molested by the same grandfather. The man was mentally normal, certainly not senile, and physically in excellent health. He had also had incestuous relationships with two of his three daughters and it seems that at least one of his grand-daughters was also his own daughter. The Justices (1979) refer to a grandfather who sired a son on his daughter. Later one of the daughter's other children, a girl of thirteen, was molested by her own brother (the grandfather's child by his daughter). At sixteen the girl's grandfather moved in on her too, using her as he had her sisters, calling the girls into his room one after the other.

Meiselman found five women in her sample of fifty-eight psychotherapy patients who reported incest with their grandfathers, two of whom had also had relations with other family members, one with her father, the other with an uncle. One of the other women's grandfathers used to fondle her genitals when she paid weekly visits with her parents when she was supposed to be having an afternoon nap; this continued for about a year until she was about five or so. She loved her grandfather and enjoyed the presents he gave her, as did her older sister whom later she learned had received the same attention. It was not until she was older that she developed various psychological problems as a direct result of the molestation. The remaining women – one from a rich, the other from a poor, background – also were manipulated genitally by their grandfathers when they were around five or so, the molestation in the second case continuing until the victim was ten. All three women suffered intensely from guilt as adults and made unsatisfactory marriages. None of the grandfathers were senile, mentally defective, psychotic or alcoholic. They were all gentle, never attempted to have intercourse, and the girls were not uncooperative at the time, which later added to their guilt. Meiselman adds that this group of five women were the most middle-class, most intelligent and best-educated group in the entire sample of sexually molested women.

The literature on uncle/niece incest is thinner still. Tsai and Wagner (1978) found in their group of fifty women that the same number had been molested by their uncles as by their grandfathers, i.e. 11 per cent. In their University of Washington Study (1979) of 118 molested women eight uncles (nearly 7 per cent) had molested their nieces. In Lukianowicz's study of twenty-nine subjects who had been molested by relatives other than their father, four women had been molested by their uncles. One of the uncles was 'mildly immature', one was an alcoholic and a psychopath, and the other two were normal, as were the four nieces. Meiselman points out that while Kinsey, in his 1953 *Sexual Behaviour in the Human Female*, reported uncle/niece incest to be the most common form of incest among women not selected on the basis of being psychologically disturbed, she only found five women in her own psychotherapy sample of fifty-eight patients who had had sexual relationships with their uncles. From this she suggests there may be large numbers of women who have had such experiences but are not sufficiently disturbed by them to seek help. She postulates that this may be so when the uncle has no direct part in the child's upbringing (thus avoiding many of the child/parental conflicts that arise with fathers) and when the uncle has approached her with gentleness. Where the uncle is caretaker of the child, or where he uses force, then severe problems are likely to arise.

Mother/son incest has been a subject of artistic and popular in-

terest from the telling and retelling of the tragedy of Jocasta and
Oedipus onwards. Playwrights, novelists and nowadays film makers
have used it as their main theme, some more overtly than others.
It has also been written about more frequently in professional papers
than the other types of incest we have just been looking at, but
again there has been very little actual research. Most people regard
it as the rarest and most taboo form. If intercourse is the criterion
for the definition of incest, then it does seem true that it happens
between mother and son rarely, though even here I suspect its actual
incidence is minimized in the statistics because of the already discussed reluctance of males to admit to having played a passive sexual
role. The more usual kind of relationship seems to be an intense
kind of flirting, which can occur with girls as well as with boys.
This was well described to me by a therapist who had worked with
a boy and his mother who had brought her son in for treatment
because she claimed he had been forced to submit to fellatio and
anal intercourse by a homosexual male friend, and exhibited to and
possibly molested by her boyfriend:

> He was a very deeply disturbed boy, five years old. We weren't
> at all sure that although she accused others she herself hadn't
> been sexually involved with him. She was very suffocating of
> him, used him almost like a father figure. She'd ask his
> opinion, what to wear, whether to move from one apartment to
> another, wanted him to care for her when she was sick. Often
> during the night she'd have fears and then she'd have him come
> into her bed. They slept together a good deal of the time. She
> treated him as a husband – she was a very busty woman and
> she'd wear little or nothing around the house with him. She'd
> be very seductive, extract comfort from him, getting him to pet
> her, make a fuss of her. There was a very definite role reversal:
> she'd ask him to do errands for her way beyond his
> development level, and she made her dependence on him quite
> clear. Their relationship was defined in terms of what she
> needed rather than what he did, and she'd play the heavy
> mother if he deviated from what she wanted. She was very
> erratic in discipline. The point is, you could pick out a different
> quality about their relationship that made it quite different from
> that in normal families – there was no question just how
> seductive she was being with him.

Theorists consider mother/son incest to be probably the most harmful of all, some believing that almost invariably the victim will become psychotic as a result of the relationship. A mother actively involved in incest is also considered highly disturbed: 'The basic psychological profile of the mother who aggressively seeks out her son for incestuous activity is that of psychopath', claimed one professional. We discussed earlier how women seemed to sexualize relationships with their children less than men, and I shall not go into this again except to remind the reader of the central role the oedipal situation continues to play in psychoanalytic theory, and that for many the very first years involving mainly the mother and child are considered the most important as far as development is concerned.

Meiselman writes that in nearly all the reported cases where the son initiated the incest he was either schizophrenic or severely disturbed prior to the incest. The mothers in such cases were usually not grossly disturbed though they were sometimes promiscuous, with the result that their sons were both tempted and antagonized by them. The father was away from home at the time of the incest in all the reports she examined. In occasional cases of this type the mother and son have been separated for years and it is only on the son's return that he sees his mother as an eligible sexual partner.

The more common pattern is for the mother to initiate the incest. The reader will remember the case history of the man whose real mother died when he was a baby, and whose stepmother began to be seductive towards him when he was about eight, the behaviour finally leading to intercourse when he was physically capable of it. In this instance the boy was a very reluctant partner, as the stepmother's main interest seemed to be to annoy his father who would beat him severely if he caught him in his wife's bed. When grown up and married the man eventually had intercourse with his own daughter.

Deborah Anderson, programme director of Hennepin County's Sexual Assault Services, told me she had had around ten cases of males, boys and men, within the last year who had had intercourse with their mothers. She described the effect on one of them:

He is absolutely beautiful, a beautiful young man, but a whore! He has sex with women all the time, but he's not really there, he's the equivalent of a prostitute. Not for pay. He takes care of them, of their warmth needs – that's what he's been brought up to do – though his own needs aren't taken care of. He actually described himself to me as 'the community whore'.

Everybody knows he and his mother have had sex, and he talks about her as a terrible person.

Many workers in the field told me their experiences are that mother/son and mother/daughter incest are by no means rare, and I suspect that we shall be hearing far more about it in the future. Certainly at the moment very little is surfacing: Harborview Medical Center found only 4 per cent of the offenders in their 1977/1979 survey on child sexual assault to be female, although even this figure may surprise many. Obviously a major difficulty is to decide whether a certain activity is incestuous or not. It is normal for a mother to wash or bathe a young child and take him into her bed for a while. It is not normal for such a boy to sleep regularly with his mother, though he might well come into her bed after a bad dream or for a family romp. Many of the women who keep their sons in bed with them long after they ought to be sleeping alone are single women whose touch and comfort needs are not being met, and who drift into this pattern out of loneliness.

Sometimes excessive concern with hygiene is reported, when a mother might insist on regular inspection of the boy's penis to see if it is 'growing properly' or manipulate his genitals unnecessarily when washing him, and sometimes when he is older actually masturbating him to the point of ejaculation. She might have him sleep regularly with her, and while some women never overtly stimulate their sons, others gradually introduce mutual masturbation. It is difficult to know which is finally the more disturbing. Boys who have spent their early and even late adolescence (a time when sexual fantasies are intense) lying next to a woman whom they may not touch, are likely to develop severe problems later and will find it very difficult to make successful approaches to other women. The available evidence makes it appear that most boys who have experienced direct sex with their mothers end up deeply disturbed, but we must always bear in mind that there may be many who cope with any problems that do arise and are never seen by therapists, and who therefore never enter the statistics.

Of Lukianowicz's sample of twenty-nine patients, three were males who had had intercourse with their mothers. One boy was schizophrenic (but whether he became so before or after the relationship is not explained), one was educationally subnormal and one was normal, marrying later when he left home. The first mother in these three cases was normal, though later she developed depression and severe guilt feelings, the second was herself schizophrenic and the third was clinically neurotic. Lukianowicz adds that while in the other twenty-six cases incestuous sexual relations occurred several times a week at least, in the three mother/son cases they occurred only sporadically.

Homosexuality sometimes is connected with mother/son incest, as is a fear of women and an inability to achieve orgasm. Often there is a deep anger at having been misused by so important a caring figure as the mother. Meiselman, while acknowledging research showing that sexually *seductive* behaviour in a mother may produce a homosexual orientation in the son, argues that in the few reported cases where actual intercourse has taken place most of the sons when adult have had a heterosexual orientation, and she suggests research into the question of why there should be such an apparent difference in the effects of covert and overt maternal seduction. I suspect that it may be related in part to the boy's basic sexual orientation, and that whether or not sexual activity leading to intercourse takes place depends considerably on the boy himself as well as on the desires of the mother. After all, unlike girls, a boy has at this point to be sufficiently aroused by the female to be able to take an active part if the affair is going to be fully consummated.

Either way the mother is likely to hold him to her, and to discourage him from making outside contacts, not wanting him to grow up or away from her. The boy will probably feel insecure outside his home and have difficulty in making friends, especially female friends who will arouse in him ambivalent feelings of desire and prohibition.

This same problem applies to girls who are exposed to sexual behaviour from their mothers. There are very few reports of mother/daughter incest and no research, as far as I know, but in talking to various people, professionals as well as victims, I have the impression that seductive behaviour at least, is not that uncommon. The few cases that are written up suggest that adult problems arising from such incest are similar in nature to those caused by other forms of incest. I spoke at length with a woman whose perception was that she had experienced both father and mother incest, although as far as she was conscious her mother had never molested her sexually. The importance of this case is that she nevertheless perceived her mother's seductive behaviour as being more damaging to her than her father's actual molestation. As she explains, she became an alcoholic at a young age, and when I saw her she was extremely fat.

She was happy to accept her lesbianism (she worked in what had originally been a self-help group for lesbians only but which has now become a therapy group for sexually abused women, straight as well as gay) but rejected the alcoholism and has overcome it. Her fatness she saw as a direct revolt against her mother, and was preparing to tackle that also. She was an intelligent, middle-class woman in early middle age, active in spite of her weight.

With women there are ways of being sexual without touching: men are far more overt. What's so agonizing about mother/ daughter incest is that it's one oppressed woman doing it to another who is even more powerless than she is, a little kid. What lots and lots of us here have discovered as we go through the programme is that we weren't the only one whose mother set us up to be her caretaker. Little bitty girls having to take care of our mothers when we're not ready to – they set us up by flirting with us and teasing us, making us give them emotional support.

I was my father's wife and my mother's husband at the same time, and that's common, we find it a lot here. I was the oldest child in our family, and I had to look after the house a lot as well, because my mother used to get out of the house and do civic activities – voluntary stuff. It's really confusing, playing two sexual roles, being both a little boy and a little girl. It's very different when it's from the mother; all my friends who are incest victims love their mothers still in some tangled way, and feel empathy for them, though it takes a lot of work here for us to reach that stage. After all the anger there's still love left, and it just doesn't feel that way with the father, it doesn't go as deep.

To this day my mother will say to me things like, 'Darling, I don't see how you can do a thing like . . .' you know, silly basic things like calling taxis. She still uses little girl talk to me, and she's sixty-five. She does a whole lot of seductive flirting as though I were some escort. She does that with everybody of both sexes, but I was her little girl, she should have looked after me, not the other way round. Yet in her civic work she's on a school board, she's confident, has responsibility – she's a real hard worker, but she just hates herself and thinks everything she does is no good, phoney. You know, I love her a lot. I was brought up to it, to take care of her, and we were very close.

No, she didn't touch me genitally. But there was lots of flirting. Like having me watch her when she took baths, watching her while she got dressed. There was lots of stuff about clothes – she'd ask me what to wear – that seems to be a common thing. She was a watch-but-don't-touch person, but sometimes she'd sweep in on me and want to do something like dance, and that would embarrass me. I felt like I was always on guard, waiting to be pounced on. She'd grab me up – I mean there was no respect, I didn't like it because I had no control over it. I was entirely at her disposal, ignored if I asked for things for myself, but had to do what she wanted when she wanted it. It probably doesn't sound that bad, but it was . . . there was something wrong there.

She's like a dragonfly, my mother, the feelings come out in little fragments and she can't stay with them. She and her sister were orphans, brought up by relations and she didn't like them, and I think the only two people who've ever mattered to her were my sister and me. It's a very incestuous family, mine. There's lots of intermarriage with cousins, and I suspect that the oldest son of the family she was brought up in had sex with her and that her aunt was covertly sexual with her. Cold but seductive, as she is with me.

My father's family? It was very abusive, physically and emotionally. All eight children, professional people all of them, grew up to be alcoholics, him included. They couldn't stand each other but they were very entwined with each other. I don't remember everything yet – the counsellors here say you only remember what you can and memories will come back as long as you live because you can only let some of it out at a time. I know my father used to read to me every night, and I remember him being aroused and that he'd kind of pat me around my breasts and I think between my legs, but I'm pretty sure he didn't actually have intercourse with me. I think that he kissed me a lot and that I had to have oral sex with him, because I have lots and lots of choking here [she touched her throat]. When I get nervous I kind of strangle, I still do. [In fact several times while she was speaking to me she would break into repeated coughing as though trying to remove something from her throat but she seemed quite unaware of

what she was doing.] It must have started when I was real
young, about two or three, and stopped young, too, when I was
seven or eight.

My mother was always a much more essential person to me –
she had a lot of contempt for my father, saw him as a weak
person and an alcoholic, although she herself was also very
dependent.

When I was sixteen I knew I was lesbian but I didn't think
anybody else was, only weird people in books. I married for a
while but he was killed. I realize now he must have been gay;
he was a really neat person, but sexually no. It was so boring.
It was more like brother and sister between us – it feels
incestuous when I look back on it. I find that a lot of the
lesbian women here are oldest daughters, like myself, and I
think if there's any ambiguity between the parents it comes out
on the oldest child.

I'd say the relationship between being an incest victim and an
alcoholic is high, and promiscuity too: most of us have been
promiscuous at one stage or another. Lots have been prostitutes
– I mean, why not? You've already lost your sense of
boundaries. I was always being invaded. I never knew when it
was coming, from my mother or my father, and there was no
way to be my own discrete person.

In treatment I've learned to see that my different self-
destructive behaviours throughout my life were survival
strengths for me, not really weaknesses. Drinking, for instance,
kept me alive. Without it I'd have killed myself in despair. I
started at fifteen, and it anaesthetized a lot of the pain that I
had no one to talk to about. My mother is small, and my fat is
a big issue between us. It was one of the ways I consistently
defied her, and of course she used it back to torture me.
Sometimes I get to be the right weight, but right now I'm
trying to like myself just as I am so that I feel good about
however I am. After that I'll see what I do. We learn here that
all these bad things we did weren't really bad, they were ways
of coping. It's helpful to understand that.

When I began treatment here I cried a lot, I was good at
that, but I wasn't much good at being angry. It was really
difficult for me to get angry but when I did I screamed a lot at
my father, that I was glad he was dead, that it was finished,
that he was to leave me alone, get away, that kind of thing. I

said before I only thought he'd done those things to me, I couldn't be sure, but I know inside myself that he really did do them – I knew it clearly enough in those sessions, but afterwards you can't quite accept it, you've hidden it for so many years, from yourself as much as from other people.

Of the eighty women who've been through here I only know of one mother who had repeated genital sex with her daughter, made her four-year-old daughter make love to her. With the rest, though some of them have rather hazy memories of things like fingers being stuck up them when they were babies, for those who felt their mothers had behaved incestuously it was mostly covert seductive behaviour they got. But it came through to us like incest, it felt like incest, though we don't always use that word for it.

We will look in more detail at the group mentioned above and how it set about helping the women who came there in Chapter 9, where various types of treatment will be described. Meanwhile it might be noted how many familiar points were raised in this last story, points of character and of family interaction that have come up time and time again during this investigation into incest, regardless of who the two main protagonists were.

Finally we come to the sibling incest. There are two frequently asked questions – how common is it, and does it matter? I cannot answer the first for the usual reasons, and therefore cannot answer the second. That is to say, there are not many cases reported, and that may be because although there is a great deal of sibling incest it causes so few problems we never hear about it. Or it could be that it is more rare than one might suppose, considering the opportunities siblings have, and of those few who do commit incest most become disturbed, and these are the cases we learn about. Finkelhor (1980a) found in his survey of 796 college undergraduates (already detailed earlier in the book) that 13 per cent reported a sibling sexual experience, 15 per cent being girls and 10 per cent boys. Tsai and Wagner (1979) report that 8.5 per cent of their study of 118 victims had been molested by their brothers. Tsai, Feldman-Summers and Edgar (1979) studied two groups each consisting of thirty women who had been molested as children. One of these groups had sought clinical aid, and one had not. In each of the groups there were two women who had reported sibling incest, i.e. 6.7 per cent. Meiselman found that eight out of fifty-eight in her survey had experienced sibling incest, or just under 14 per cent. Lukianowicz had fifteen cases in his group of thirty-nine incest patients, but these did not include cases of father/daughter incest. We can see therefore that a substantial number of incest victims reporting disturbance to official sources have experienced sibling incest. Only Finkelhor's figure of 13 per cent represents sibling incest in a normal population, but as he himself points out a college population has to be sufficiently psychologically healthy to have passed their entrance grades, and that it is bound to be unrepresentative of those who have been badly disturbed by childhood sexual experiences. We may therefore make the assumption that if Finkelhor's figure is representative of college students at large (and it does not necessarily follow that this is so) then 13 per cent is the absolute minimum number of cases of sibling incest in the general population, and that in all probability the real figure is larger.

Interestingly, sibling incest is the only type about which people commonly ask – does it matter? I think this is because it is very easy to visualize it in terms of amiable exploration between two free, inquisitive young animals, sniffing out each other's bodies on a summer's day in a kind of Garden of Eden. If that were the way it happened, it is certainly difficult to see the harm, but in fact I doubt if there are many such cases of innocent comings-together.

Fox (1962) puts forward the hypothesis, 'The intensity of heterosexual attraction between co-socialized children after puberty is inversely proportionate to the intensity of heterosexual activity between them before puberty.' That is to say, children who have been able to romp freely together, who grow up in a close intimate atmosphere, do not desire each other physically after puberty, while children who have been brought up apart, either at some distance or in the same household but without being allowed to touch, do after puberty desire each other and suffer strong anxieties about their desires.

There is not the space to report him fully, but starting from the work of Westermarck and Freud and taking evidence from various anthropological studies, most particularly Spiro's work on the behaviour of children in a kibbutz, Fox puts forward a convincing argument. His own hypothesis is based on the idea that sexual desires are aroused in prepubertal siblings who are allowed to play intimately together, but because of their youth these desires cannot be consummated and as a result they develop mutual antagonisms and quarrel. Eventually sexual feelings towards the siblings become associated with angry frustration, so that by the time they reach adolescence they turn away from each other to outsiders who do not carry the same associations. None of the children from the kibbutz, for example (who had done everything together from babyhood and had, as it were, an intense sibling relationship) married each other, nor, as far as anyone knew, did any of them ever have sexual intercourse together. This behaviour was an entirely natural development – there was absolutely no outside pressure on them to abstain from sex. On the other hand Freud's work, based on his own very different experience of growing up within a strict Jewish family system, postulates intense incest anxieties as an inevitable part of human development. If we accept Fox's theory we now see that our picture of innocent animals exploring each other in the Garden of Eden is unlikely to occur at or after the age of puberty since in such free circumstances they will most probably have been doing just that since they were tiny, and by puberty will have arrived at a natural parting of the ways as far as sexual exploration is concerned.

If we also bear in mind the typical background to endogamic incestuous families in which it is common for sexuality to be repressed, where mothers see sex as dirty, something not to be discussed, then we can see how likely it is that in such families the children will indeed be kept apart from each other, as a result of which frustrated sexual desire towards the siblings may eventually develop. Given other factors also generally present in incestuous families, such as a lack of healthy touching and of reassurance, we can see how some children may turn to each other for warmth, while others in a dominant position, such as older brothers or sisters, may forcibly take from younger siblings what is not being given to them voluntarily. A weaker sibling may not be much of a conquest, but at least the need to express power over something in their lives is temporarily satisfied.

Meiselman reports in her survey of studies on sibling incest that the most common finding is that the children lack proper supervision, especially where sex play is concerned. Often the father is weak or absent, and in such cases, particularly where there is a younger sister and older brothers, the girl is bound to be more vulnerable. Mothers were frequently reported to be rigidly puritanical in their views on sex, and it is likely that in addition to the repressed desires we would expect to build up, according to Fox's theory, sheer curiosity about the wicked, forbidden unmentionable leads some children to explore sex in secret. So convinced were the eight sisters in Meiselman's therapy group of the implacability of their mothers' attitudes that seven submitted to their brothers' threats rather than risk their mothers' wrath by informing on them, though all eight wanted the behaviour to stop. Three of the eight said the incest had originally developed out of a curiosity about sex, implying they were not at first unwilling partners. Two referred to the act as rape, but it was thought from her attitude that one of them was not telling the truth.

If force is used, the effect on the victim in later life is more traumatic than incest entered into as part of a mutual experimentation. Finkelhor (1980a) found in his survey of undergraduates that a quarter of those reporting sibling incest said force was used, the great majority of these victims being girls. Sisters are more likely to enjoy the incestuous sex than daughters, presumably because they are far more likely to initiate the activity or to want to satisfy a curiosity about sex than daughters. Also they have less sense of betrayal, and can more easily refuse their brothers than their fathers, though this is not always so.

In Meiselman's group the majority of the sisters found it a 'slightly negative' experience. In Finkelhor's study 30 per cent found it positive, 30 per cent found it negative, and the rest had no strong feelings about it being either. Not unexpectedly, those who had been threatened or forced, or whose sibling partners were much older, were four times as likely to find the experience negative as those who were not forced. Girls are more likely to find the experience unpleasant than boys, as they usually had less choice in the matter.

From Finkelhor's study it appears that the age at which the incest occurs makes no difference to the outcome, provided the relationship between the siblings is close enough for neither of them to be exploitive or exploited. Nor did it matter whether it was a homosexual or a heterosexual sibling experience. Surprisingly, having full sexual intercourse did not increase the negative outcome either, although cases where the sexual activity was confined to exhibiting the genitals were more likely to be remembered positively. Such mild sexual behaviour mostly took place in early childhood: exhibiting genitals – 40 per cent up to eight years old, 24 per cent between nine and twelve years, and only 5 per cent between thirteen and seventeen. Other activities were: fondling and touching genitals – 53 per cent up to eight, 60 per cent between nine and twelve, and 64 per cent between thirteen and seventeen. But for intercourse and attempted intercourse the figures were: 5 per cent up to eight, 15 per cent between nine and twelve and 18 per cent between thirteen and seventeen. Finkelhor points out that sibling sex should not be thought of as simple sex play among very young children, as most of the activity takes place among children of an older age – the median age of his sample was over ten years – while more activity occurred during what Freudians consider to be the middle of the latency period – eight to eleven years – than in any other period. A third of these experiences happened once only, while over a quarter continued for more than a year. Two affairs continued for ten years. These figures fit in with other research work, including Meiselman's group of eight, of whom two reported only one incident, five remembered the activity as continuing over several months, and one affair lasted for several years. Sex between fathers and daughters, on the other hand, usually continues for long periods once it has started.

It appears that sibling incest has some effect on the later sexual behaviour of girls. Boys appear in later life to have been less affected by the incest itself, but this may be due to the fact that they were usually the initiators and there may well have been some disturbance already present before the incest took place. Meiselman told me that in later life there seemed to be a fair amount of what she called 'wild sex', and there are many reports of promiscuity. Although there is usually some difficulty with adult sex relationships this is not usually as severe as with victims of father/daughter incest. Of Meiselman's group of sisters all of those over eighteen had married at least once, whereas 40 per cent of the daughters had never married. Once married the sisters stayed married longer. However, she reports that this was not because they had happier marriages but because they were more prepared to put up with lengthy unhappy relationships. Of the daughters 42 per cent were classified as masochistic, as against 71 per cent of the sisters.

Finkelhor's study showed that the students who had had sibling sex were more sexually active than those who had not, but the indication was that this difference evened out after some years. This higher rate of activity occurred with all types of sibling sex, negative or positive, except for those who had had negative experiences of early sex with much older siblings. In order to find out whether or not this higher activity implies good or poor sex the investigators attempted to measure what they called 'sexual self-esteem.' The results showed that positive experiences, with a sibling of one's own age group were associated with a significantly higher level of sexual self-esteem, but where the experiences were negative or with non-peers self-esteem was the same as or lower than those who had not experienced sibling sex.

Without knowing more about the students involved it is imposs-ible to draw valid conclusions: as Finkelhor himself points out, it may be that only people who have high self-esteem anyway have the courage to report or even to remember early sibling experiences, and that it was this self-esteem which led them to experiment with a sibling experience in the first place. It would not be valid to conclude from these results that sibling sex is good for a very large number of people. Equally it would not be fair to condemn it out of hand. It could be that much of the positive sex was a result of early non-consummated experimentation before puberty, followed by a normal pattern of breaking away afterwards, and if Fox is correct there would appear to be no reason why if the siblings are not made to feel guilty any disturbance should follow. It would be very interesting to do an in-depth random study of a large segment of the general population to find out if this is so, and how common in fact it is. Certainly it is clear that there are also many victims of sibling incest, particularly where non-peers are involved. Leaving aside the severely disturbed, many participants in sibling incest suffer sexual problems such as difficulty in achieving orgasm; as mothers they often find extreme difficulty in relating to their sons, and there are also problems of self-esteem – all of which seem to be directly related to early sibling sexual experiences.

I think that in today's freer climate where any manifestation of sex is no longer automatically frowned upon a certain amount of exploration among children in well-balanced families will in most cases be perfectly safe. In disturbed families, in promiscuous chaotic families, the dangers are obvious. What people do when they are adult is up to them: if two siblings who have a genetically sound background and who have been brought up apart want as adults to marry each other I don't see that the law has any reason to interfere. Even if two siblings who have grown up together want to marry, although there is almost certainly some disturbance present and they may be in for an unsatisfactory marriage, again it seems to me that as adults the choice is theirs. But children need to be protected, sometimes even from themselves. That some people appear to have come successfully through the experience of sibling incest does not make the misery of those who did not any less intense.

Chapter 7

The pro-incest lobby and the after-effects of incest

Recently there has been much discussion, particularly in the United States, as to whether or not the laws against incest ought to be changed or even abolished. This had led some people to ask, does incest inevitably cause harm and should we change our attitude to it? The truth is, it is impossible with our present level of knowledge to judge the effect on the majority of people who have been involved in incestuous activities (assuming the incidence to be as high as I speculate in Chapter 3) since most never present themselves for treatment. This ignorance, however, does not deter many writers from plunging into the fray. To the fury of most therapists who have to deal with the severely damaged, it is currently being suggested by a variety of authors that the general attitude towards incest is simply a Victorian legacy, without justification in today's moral climate. Magazines mainly concerned with sex publish glowing letters from readers who recount their own happy experiences, most with sibling sex. Why should we deny children what we so much enjoy ourselves, it is asked.

As we saw in the last chapter a small number of people claim to have found their incestuous experiences positive, nearly all of these having been involved in sibling sex. Articles appearing in magazines such as *Penthouse*, *Time*, and *Psychology Today* examine what little evidence exists and draw conclusions which could have been anticipated, bearing in mind the vehicle in which they are printed. *Penthouse*'s article by Philip Nobile, for instance, is highly influenced by work favourable to the idea of 'positive' incest (though the same researchers are criticized by other authors for being imprecise, unrepresentative, etc.) but it attacks Giarretto whom Nobile depicts as a man revelling in misery, stubbornly determined never to find a good word to say about incest. Some of the figures quoted seem highly dubious to me bearing in mind other research – mother/son incest, for example (almost invariably thought to be the most destructive of all) is, according to Nobile, considered by researcher Warren Farrell to be positive for the sons in 70 per cent of the cases and only negative in 10 per cent. Farrell apparently claims that the 'boys don't seem to suffer, not even from the negative experience.' This is the exact opposite of every other piece of research I have ever come across. But even Farrell is pessimistic about father/daughter incest, to the distress of a Dr C. Tripp, a sex researcher who according to Nobile demands, 'Do you talk about rape and courtship in the same breath? Both are defined by intercourse, but the consent and spirit are vastly different . . . coercive and noncoercive incest . . . shouldn't be lumped together as two aspects of the same phenomenon.' *Time* quotes anthropologist Seymour Parker, University of Utah, as saying

It is questionable if the costs [of the incest taboo] in guilt and uneasy distancing between intimates are necessary or desirable. What are the benefits of linking a mist of discomfort to the spontaneous warmth of the affectionate kiss and touch between family members?

The importance of warmth and touch in family life has already been discussed at some length in this book, and I think my own attitude to this question has already been made clear, so it is unnecessary for me to deal with Parker's question except to repeat yet again that there is no earthly reason for anyone to feel guilty about 'affectionate kissing and touching', but that there is a world of difference between that and erotic touching done by adults seeking to gratify their own sexual desires. It is adults, not children, who are asking for 'child sex liberation', in particular men, who relate how happily their daughters have received their 'progressive sex education'. But I have not yet seen a single quotation *direct* from any daughter saying how much she had enjoyed the whole experience and how she would recommend incest for her own daughters.

People who put forward such ideological views tend to be very defensive: there exists a society called the Réne Guyon Society, for example, to which I have written but from which (in common with other researchers) I have received no reply. The society apparently still exists since one researcher told me that after persistent attempts he eventually received an uninformative note on headed notepaper. I will quote Summit and Kryso's (1978) comments on the society, which were written before the society closed its gates.

Based on the writings of Guyon [*Sex Life and Sex Ethics*, Lane, London, 1933] and a grotesque distortion of the early work of Freud, the society claims that children need sex with compassionate adults to reduce violent antagonism supposedly aroused by social repression and guilt. Sexual repression is advanced as the cause of depression, suicide, delinquency, gang warfare, assault and a host of other social problems. Under the slogan 'Sex by year eight or else it's too late', the group advocates sexual rights for children, including abolition of laws restricting incest and sexual abuse. The Guyon Society claims a membership of '2,000 parents and psychiatrists'.

These comments on the society sum up the main arguments put forward by other proponents of incest for all. Some of these arguments appear, debased, in pornographic books which, depicting father/daughter incest, typically have the girls joyfully thanking their fathers for their sexual education, while begging in the crudest possible manner for more of the same. It is as well here to point out that Finkelhor (1978b) shows that 66 per cent of his sample of 795 students rated their childhood sexual experiences as 'negative, unpleasant and noxious', the predominant reaction being fright, while a quarter 'registered shock'. Gratitude was not mentioned.

One of the problems in researching incest is that we all start from such different bases. For example, I was amazed to read in another paper by Finkelhor (1979b)

There are many new frontiers to be pushed back . . . many in favour of sexual reform of the family have begun to promote the idea of family nudity. They have mounted an assault in recent years against the psychoanalytic convention that adult nudity is harmful to a child because it is overstimulating or 'arouses oedipal anxieties'. On the contrary, say the reformers, nudity fosters sexual comfort, and positive gender identification.

The paper then refers to intercourse in a child's presence as being an 'even more radical proposal' which the same reformers are putting forward.

Now, although I have come across the occasional Freudian analyst who still thinks about family nudity in the above terms, it had hardly ever crossed my mind that most modern intelligent parents who were not themselves disturbed would have thought twice about their children seeing them naked, and I assumed nudity among children in such families was the norm. When reading Finkelhor's figures on sibling incest I thought about this and concluded that those students who referred to exhibitionism must be referring to deliberate showings off of the sexual parts rather than to casual sharings of the same bath or running around naked on beaches on holiday. To talk in the same breath of what to me are such totally different situations as fathers shaving naked in the bathroom while the children wander in and out, and of the parents having intercourse in front of the children, separating the second from the first only as being 'even more radical', seems to me extraordinary. If innocent family nudity really remains a 'new frontier to be pushed back' for many, even most, people, then indeed more reforms are still to be achieved than I realized. All the same, for these reformers to claim, as they do, that this necessary growth of openness is seriously threatened by those whose primary aim is to protect children from sexual abuse, is nonsense. It is the self-styled 'children's liberators' who are trying to go too far who in fact are likely to bring about the reactionary repressive climate they fear, activated as a defence reaction by the vociferous minority who will jump at any opportunity to stamp out the growth of a genuine sexual freedom.

To me the final argument against the pro-incest lobby is one advanced by many people who work in the field. Basically, it is that sex is only legitimate when it is between two freely consenting people, and children are incapable of giving their true consent to an incestuous relationship because: (a) they have no means of knowing what sex is really about; (b) they have no conception of what their feelings will be about any incestuous childhood experiences when they are grown up; (c) they cannot as yet begin to comprehend the importance of social pressures, and (d) it is almost impossible for them to deny their fathers, even if the request is made gently and without obvious coercion. Children submit time and time again to incest without overtly objecting because it never occurs to them they can do so, though the behaviour distresses them. Even if they partially enjoy the sex this does not stop them simultaneously feeling emotional distress, as many adult victims, still riddled with guilt, have told me. Finkelhor (1979a) referring to the need to protect children from experiences they cannot control, writes:

> the concern . . . is not part of a Victorian resurgence. It is compatible with the most progressive attitude towards sexuality currently being voiced, a position that urges that consent be the

sole standard by which the legitimacy of sexual acts be evaluated.

And there is no way in which a young child can be said to have truly consented to a sexual act initiated by an adult.

I doubt if those who work towards the ending of all restraints on sexual activities between adults and children have spent much time working with child victims, whose distress is immediately and painfully obvious. It is possible, however, that some therapists working only with adults whose lives have been maimed by childhood incestuous experiences may come to the conclusion that guilt has been the main cause of these people's sufferings, and that since guilt (it is commonly claimed) is caused by society's attitude, they may postulate that if we change that attitude the guilt will not occur and there will then be no bar to incest for anyone who wants it.

Unfortunately I do not think it is as simple as that. If by society we mean the neighbours, the old lady down the road, the ministers of our church, perhaps indeed we may eventually change its attitude – today's generally accepted morality is very different from that of a hundred years ago, and no doubt will be very different again in fifty years time. But the kind of guilt these adult victims suffer from goes much deeper than simple fear of what the neighbours will think. Of course that is important, but more important is the immensely complicated set of guilts arising from the relationships within the family. These have already been touched upon in various passages in this book – a certain amount of overlap is inevitable – but I would like in the rest of the chapter to concentrate on the after-effects of incest, not only in order to combat the claims of the pro-incest lobby, but so that a fuller understanding may be achieved of victims who still bear the scars of their early experiences.

The most obvious cause of guilt in a child is her belief – the incest having been discovered – that she is the cause of her father being sent to jail. The entire family may round on the victim and accuse her of betraying them, of having led the father on in the first place, of causing the whole family to move house, of them losing their best friends, their chances in examinations, their comfortable life – every misery will be laid at the 'offending' child's door. The father himself will most probably have already laid the foundations of this guilt from the beginnings of their sexual relationship by threatening the child that if she tells just such a break-up will occur, so that when at last the incest comes out into the open, even though it may be through no fault of her own, she cannot avoid feeling guilt. It is essential to make it clear to the victim that it was not she who put her father in jail, but the father who put himself there by his own actions. It is not always so easy to do this, however, especially if the workers who deal with the child find her 'seductive' and ambivalent in her attitude to her father – they may betray to her their lack of conviction that she is entirely innocent, which will confirm her guilt in her own eyes. Often this laying on of guilt, from the family and others, is so intense the child withdraws any charges she has been persuaded to make and refuses to give evidence against her father. She may then end up with a reputation as a lier, a trouble-maker, and thus suffer even worse guilt. This was related to me as a typical happening, both in Britain and in America, by doctors, police, lawyers and therapists who repeatedly found children (whose truthfulness they believed in) going back on their earlier stories.

As a child, the victim is more likely to feel guilt about putting her father in jail and breaking up the family than about the incest itself, though the full horror of that will come later as she learns more about society's attitudes to what she has done. Another cause of guilt is her feeling that she has deprived her mother of what rightfully should belong to her – of the sexual attentions of her husband and the loving tenderness that the child herself has probably received, at least occasionally. She may at the same time hate her mother for allowing the incest to continue, but this will not lessen the guilt she feels at the usurpation of her mother's place. If the incest is still secret and she suspects that her younger siblings are beginning to receive her father's sexual attentions she may feel guilty at doing nothing to protect them, combined with an understandable jealousy that she is no longer the only desired one. If, as frequently happens, she receives especially favoured treatment from her father while her siblings are ignored or badly treated, she may feel some guilt about her advantages, even while being grateful for her 'luck'. Victims removed from their homes after discovery will often cry to be returned, convinced their families cannot manage without them. 'Little mothers', they long since accepted their role, and what anger they feel at the injustice of life is buried deep, intensifying their inner confusion and future distress. Alone for the first time, away from the family with its incredibly complicated relationships, they feel existence is meaningless.

It has been suggested that the guilt a child feels for having 'permitted' incest is worse than when there has been no overt coercion, and she will be less traumatized if force was used. In fact, available evidence shows that when any kind of force is employed the effect on the child is much more traumatic than when the approach is gentle (Rosenfeld 1979b; Rosenfeld, Nadelson and Krieger 1979; Finkelhor, 1978b, 1980a, and Meiselman, personal communication). This is not to say that when – as often happens – sex begins with gentle touching at a very early age and progresses to intercourse after puberty the victim will not be psychologically harmed. But the damage done seems to be noticeably less severe than that suffered by a child who has been forced or even raped.

There are some who believe strongly that because of the power difference any incest between father and daughter has to be an act of force. Doris Stevens of the Sexual Assault Center, Harborview, Seattle, told me,

> I don't think a dichotomy between force and no force exists. It all has to be force. There is more there than people realize – it's just that the families don't talk about it, they don't see it that way. It's much more than just emotional. I think the men do whatever they have to do to get what they want.

This is probably so, but the fact is that victims do perceive their molestation in various ways and those who claim that force was used are reported as suffering deeper trauma than those who do not. Rosenfeld et al. (1979) report specifically that in cases where the incest experiences were loving and gentle and there was no legal involvement, they were not remembered 'as starkly' as other types of incest especially if the incest occurred before puberty and there was no penetration. They go on to write that what seems to make the event traumatic is where the child suffers pain and fear, leaving them with a deep sense of having been betrayed by one whom they ought to have been able to trust. Incidentally, it is as well to remember that force is quite frequently part of the incest experience in relationships other than father/daughter – for example, Finkelhor (1980a) writes that 25 per cent of the victims of sibling incest reported force was used.

There is one after-effect of incest not often considered that has a very powerful effect on the victim, and that is if she becomes pregnant. It appears that in general fathers take care to avoid impregnating their daughters, and the availability of contraception must mean there are fewer pregnancies than previously. Neverthe-

less pregnancies do occur – Adams and Neel (1967) while researching into incest pregnancies at the University of Michigan estimated
twenty such pregnancies annually in the state of Michigan alone.
These girls are usually very young and in addition to the general
trauma of the whole affair they also stand a higher than normal
chance of giving birth to a defective child. Any mother of an abnormal child will testify to the strains involved – obviously, even if
the infant is institutionalized (in Michigan a child cannot be adopted
unless it is normal) for the young incest victim mother the emotional
stress will be even worse.

I have not been able to learn of any studies specifically relating
to what happens to such girls after childbirth. Medical interest
seems to be confined to the physical and intellectual capabilities of
their incestuously-conceived babies, and even here research is very
limited. Adams and Neel (1967) investigated eighteen such births
which were compared with a carefully selected comparison group of
babies born to eighteen unmarried non-incestuous girls, matched
for age, intelligence and social class. In twelve of the incest cases
the father of the baby was the mother's brother and in six cases the
father was the mother's own father. Six months after the births only
seven of the eighteen babies were considered normal and suitable
for adoption. Two had died within a day of birth; a third died at
two months; another had a cleft lip, and two were severely retarded
mentally with spastic cerebral palsy (there was no family history
contributing to these cases). Three were not so severely retarded,
having IQs of around seventy. None of the comparison children
died or had to be institutionalized, and none had an IQ of less than
eighty. Altogether six out of the eighteen incest children either died
or had a major defect: of the control group none died and only one
had a defect considered major. A British study, by C. Carter (1967)
of the Institute of Child Health, of thirteen children (seven with
sibling parents and six the children of father/daughter couplings)
showed one child to be severely subnormal and four educationally
subnormal, while three died in infancy. The remaining five were
normal. An article in the *British Medical Journal* (1981) refers to a
third study of 161 incestuously-born children carried out in Czech-
oslovakia in 1971, which showed less than half the children to be
normal.

The article in the *British Medical Journal* also compared the increase in recessive disorders (totalling between three and six cases
in thirty-one children) in the Carter and the Adams and Neel studies

with the expected incidence of two or three per thousand in the general population. Two of the thirty-one children had congenital malformation, as against an expected 2 per cent in the general population. The article also states that the lowering of the IQ observed in those studies below that of the parents has also been found in studies of first cousins from Japan and Israel. The inbreeding between relatives as close as father/daughter and siblings is four times as intense as that between first cousins, which in itself is significantly higher than between unrelated persons.

I have occasionally seen dismissive reference to the dangers of inbreeding in articles discussing incest, but with evidence such as this it does seem that quite powerful contrary evidence needs to be produced before the risks can be ignored. The families in Adams and Neel's study were not from the tiny inbred communities of folklore but were mixed socially, and, in the sibling matings, there was no family history of disease. Yet only seven of the eighteen babies were normal enough to be adopted.

There is another occasional after-effect of incest that has rarely been discussed, that is, the increased likelihood of the incest victim also to be a victim of rape. Although there are a few figures available on the incidence of prostitutes having had incestuous experiences as children, I know of no papers specifically relating to rape victims and incest. But in fact I have been surprised how frequently I hear about adult women who have suffered both experiences, and how often in various written case histories a rape (committed by someone outside the family) is included as part of the background of a victim who is being studied primarily as an incest victim. When I discussed this with various professionals many agreed they had noticed occasional links between incest and rape, and connected this with the seductiveness a child incest victim is taught or learns. Perhaps one of the reasons the subject has not been studied is that any positive findings could be appallingly misused. A typical defence of rapists is that the woman 'asked for it'. Feminists have fought against this but have not always won, partly because of ancient prejudice, partly because the rape victim sometimes by her manner, her dress, her appealing air, gives an apparent lie to her outraged denial that she wanted sex. There still exists a frequent male belief that a woman who is not adverse to a little flirting, perhaps even allows a kiss or two and a little fondling, necessarily is wanting intercourse but feels it is not 'nice' to admit it. If, when pressurized, she fights and shouts 'No!' it is assumed she actually means 'Yes'. If she gets hurt fighting against her aggressor it is considered she only got what she deserved for behaving provocatively in the first case. There are still many police, lawyers, judges who take this attitude, as rape crisis centres will testify. Leaving aside the different sexual and emotional aspects of men and women and looking at the problem at its crudest, if a shopkeeper displays his goods on an open counter and a shop-lifter pleads that the shopkeeper 'asked for it' and 'only got what he deserved' I doubt if the same police, lawyers and judges would understandingly let the man off, but this is exactly what happens in too many rape cases.

Obviously many – probably the majority of – rapes are unpre-meditated and the choice of victim entirely fortuitous, but the fact is that a number of rapes occur after the victim has been watched for several days, her routes followed and her habits noted. Policemen tell me that it is the nervous girl who shows her fear, who wanders uncertainly exuding lack of confidence, who is the more likely victim. The woman who strides out, busy and self-contained, does not appeal to a rapist who is searching for a victim he can easily humiliate. Rapists are not brave men and are not looking for a fight.

The incest victim is not only likely to have less confidence than an unabused woman, but if a potential rapist were to approach her she is probably going to apply the same technique she has learned to use in the past – to appeal, to placate, to use her sexuality in a disastrous attempt to save herself. Summit and Kryso (1978) dis-cussing how incest leads to feelings of being fundamentally bad and unworthy, write that

> sexuality, tainted with guilt and fear, becomes exaggerated as the only acknowledged aspect of attraction or power. The child grows up expecting and deserving abuse, often searching endlessly and hopelessly for a redeeming experience with an older partner.

Mary Johnston, talking of work carried out at the National Center, Denver, told me that it had become clear that a lack of family affection predisposed children to sexual mistreatment outside as well as inside the family, as they would desperately try to procure the sense of being loved from any adult around. Thus they unwittingly become vulnerable targets for any potential rapists, both as children and later as adults. The conclusion was that if a child is raped by an outsider its family should be carefully investigated for signs of emotional deprivation, because if the last is a problem and it is not dealt with the child stands an above average chance of being further abused.

The whole set-up can be very complicated. The reader might remember the case quoted in an earlier chapter of a man who first battered his daughter when she was tiny then over-protected her until she was raped at eight years old. He was only able to assuage his rage at losing 'his little virgin' by making the child watch him and his wife having intercourse; later he himself had sex with the child. Other girls, already incest victims, are raped by neighbourhood boys or men, or by other less close family members such as uncles or cousins. It is as though they do not feel they have permission to fight, to deny their bodies to any man who demands it. I attended a combined group session for rape and incest victims, and I was surprised at the similarity in the attitudes of the two types of victim. The therapist and the older-established members of the group were trying to prod the newest member (a rape victim) into standing up to them, but she passively continued taking whatever was given her. There was no way they could make her react aggressively to their baiting. When finally they explained to her what they were doing and why, she said, amazed, 'You mean I could just have told him to . . . shove off?' They nodded in delight, and she looked pleased at the discovery of this possibility. She then admitted that yes, she had previously noticed the man hanging around her flat; yes, she had asked who was it when he rang her bell but she'd opened the door anyway because she hadn't been able to catch his name and hadn't liked to insist on his repeating it, and finally, she'd quite forgotten to put the chain on. Yet this was a girl who admitted she had always been terrified of rape, had often thought about it, and who took all kinds of protective measures against it, except the vital one of actually applying them when needed. I don't know whether it eventually turned out that this girl had also been an incest victim, but from the way she tried to win the sympathy of the group by appealing to us with her 'little-girl' big-eyed look of wonderment (at odds with her heavily overweight, sloppily-dressed body), and from her incessant desire to agree with whatever anyone told her, she may well have been. In her vulnerability and her determination to satisfy, she reminded me absolutely of the little victims I have met in incest children's groups.

As I wrote before, there are no statistics to prove the connection between incest and rape, but one of the happiest results of bringing incest into the open would be to ensure that more victims receive early treatment. Few projects could be more rewarding than building up the self-understanding and confidence of these girls with their low self-esteem, their vulnerability and their sad ingrained habit of trying to protect themselves by using their sexuality, until they are no longer easy victims for any man – no matter how aggressive or unsupportive – who comes along.

One difficulty that complicates research is that many of the problems sexual assault victims suffer from are also experienced by people who have never been sexually assaulted. Marital discord and sexual difficulties, for example, are a common phenomenon, and it may be impossible in any particular case to tell whether the cause is mainly the incestuous experience or whether other facts such as environment, genetic inheritance or pure chance are more important. As we have seen, many mothers of incestuously assaulted children have themselves suffered similarly as a child. The mother in the case just quoted (where the father had sex with his eight-year-old daughter whom he had battered as a child) had herself been a victim of incest, and had suffered rejection by her family. Which, if either, of these two factors was primary in causing her to marry such a disturbed man?

Eunice Peterson, of the Santa Clara County Juvenile Probation Department, whose growing concern about incest first brought Hank Giarretto into the field in 1971, told me she thought incest was always harmful: 'I am convinced that the potential for severe psychological damage exists in the great majority of cases and that actual long-lasting trauma does result which interferes with that victim's ability to form satisfactory personal relationships.' How universally this is true is unknown. The few researchers such as Mavis Tsai and her colleagues who managed to get into contact with incest victims who have not had any treatment found a number of people who were coping perfectly well without any signs of trauma. Of major importance to the successful outcome of such cases is the support of an understanding mate. Even so a good marriage is not always sufficient – the reader will remember the case of Debbie, whose story was told at length in Chapter 1. In spite of a supportive, kind husband she still needed professional therapy before she was able to free herself of her past.

One study yet to be made that could be of great interest would be a comparison between the lives of sisters who have both been incest victims. In the previous chapter, for example, I quoted the woman who became a lesbian and an alcoholic, having experienced incest with both her father and her mother. Her life has been so full of unhappiness that more than once she has contemplated suicide. Yet her sister, whom she was certain had also been molested by her father, was able to live a normal, settled married life. An important factor here is that the woman who became alcoholic had always felt herself responsible for the entire family, and is still not able to free herself of this feeling. Her sister, on the other hand, has moved away and is very reluctant to be involved at all with her family. How is it their eventual fates have been so different?

I met another woman who is still deeply disturbed by her early experience, but whose sister also found the strength to overcome these same experiences. Not only did the sister become a highly successful lawyer at an unusually early age but, after she had established her career, she found a kind supportive man to whom she is now happily married. The life story of the disturbed sister is typical: her father began to fondle her sexually at around four years of age, but when she complained to her mother she was told she was lying. When at puberty the father progressed into intercourse, she told her mother at once. This time it seemed she was believed but no action was taken. A Mormon, the girl informed her priest, but he said to her 'That's your cross, and you must learn to bear it. It won't last long.' (For readers who find this unbelievable, I was told an almost identical history by another victim whose family was equally religious. The father also, as in this present case, was the local policeman). The family lived in a small town, and having told the priest and her mother – the offender himself being the local representative of the law – there was no authority left to help the girl. She knew her sister was being assaulted as well, although the sister refused to discuss it until later, when at law school, she finally admitted it. However the sister has never told anyone else, not even the man she married.

The disturbed sister is a pretty, blonde girl with an appealing air of vulnerability, who stammers appallingly – the speech defect began when she was four. At times it is impossible for her to force any sound out of her mouth and she has to struggle for as long as a minute before words come. The word 'dad' always glues her up, which made our discussion particularly difficult. Her father had ensured her silence as a child by threatening that if she informed on him he would go to jail and that as he was a policeman he would be killed by his fellow prisoners. She has already been married twice, but the current marriage is breaking up as her husband frequently batters both her and her daughter from the first marriage. However, since the husband threatens to kill himself if she deserts him (using the same threat of death as her father) she has not yet quite found the courage to leave him. She is not without resources: recently she became a counsellor and she is helping others with similar problems, but she still has a very long way to go before she herself reaches anything like stability. Her sister, on the other hand, found her own driving force early on and has succeeded in everything she has tried. What made them react so differently? Was it a question of differing intelligence? Of different genetic endowments? Of different perceptions about their family responsibilities?

All the adult female victims seeking help report difficulty in relating to members of the opposite sex. Women victims tend to sexualize their relationships with any male they deal with and some researchers have commented that it is common for them to hold other women in contempt, considering them mere sex objects – which is how they see themselves. There is also an immense anger left over from their early feelings towards their father and mother – sometimes the anger at the mother remains more intense than that at their father. Even after treatment the effects of the early trauma may reoccur at each new life crisis – marriage, childbirth, the death of either parent, divorce – any powerful change can stir up old pains and fears. For women the overpowering sense of guilt returns, and their mistrust of men combined with the likelihood that they have chosen a mate incapable of supporting them as they need to be supported means that sooner or later the marriage will be in trouble.

Women victims coming for treatment almost invariably report sexual dysfunction with their husbands. Debbie, from Chapter 1, was typical in that although she loved her husband and had a good relationship with him she was unable to respond sexually to him, and frequently had flashbacks of her father when her husband touched her. Victims often comment that they don't really want the sex part at all – they want physical affection, but when it goes further they panic or freeze. They find it very difficult to say 'no', but resent any sex their husbands 'take' (sex as something to be shared is a concept their early training prevents them from believing in, even when that is exactly what they are longing for). Some women find they can only enjoy sex when they are 'on top' and in control as a contrast to their early experience; others report that although they reach orgasm they do not find it really enjoyable and they would as soon not have any sex at all. A sex therapist said he had never known this to be true of any woman other than an incest victim.

In spite of this general lack of enjoyment many, perhaps most, incest victims have been through promiscuous periods. Tsai, Feldman-Summers and Edgar (1979) found some interesting differences between three groups of women, two of which contained women who had been sexually molested as children. One of these groups contained only women who had sought clinical help, while the women in the second group had not. The third was a control group of unmolested women. In the clinical group 43 per cent had had fifteen or more sexual partners as against 17 per cent in the non-clinical group and only 9 per cent in the control group. But in spite of this sexual activity the clinical group reported a significantly lower proportion of orgasms than the other two groups. They were also less responsive sexually to their current partners than were the others. Similar results were found both with investigations into the women's satisfaction with sexual relations as a whole, and with the three groups' perception of the quality of their close relationship with males – in both investigations the clinical group was significantly less satisfied than were the other two groups. In an interview Tsai told me that some incest victims who answered a questionnaire for her reported they had had between 50 and 300 partners, while others had one or at the most two partners only – this tendency to go to one extreme to the other seems to be a common finding.

As we have seen, the major division between those who manage to cope without help and those who do not seems to relate to their ability to choose supportive partners. Incest victims are likely to have an impaired capacity to relate to others, and they will need to be very fortunate in their choice of mate if they are to build up a warm, soundly-based marriage. Too often they pick men who themselves have been abused; once children arrive and the wife is unable to give out a motherliness she herself never received as a child the marriage is likely to deteriorate rapidly. Even if the husband is potentially a good father he is likely to find himself uncomfortable with his children as they grow, knowing that his wife will be worrying about how he behaves with them. If the couple can talk about this together the marriage will be straightforward; if not, the strain may be greater than the marriage will bear.

Summit and Kryso (1978) writing of their conviction that substantial harm can be caused by incest, comment on the 'striking prevalence of incestuous experience in the childhood of parents who now have problems with physical and emotional abuse of their children' noted by various Parents Anonymous groups, and refer to a therapeutic shelter for physically abusive families where 90 per cent of the mothers had been sexually abused as children. The worst tragedy, then, is that the pain does not end with the current victim, but in one form or another will probably be passed on to yet another generation.

We have been looking at the domestic problems faced by incest victims, mainly females, but for many victims of both sexes their disturbance is so deep that from a young age they run foul of the law. Running away from home, stealing, prostitution, addiction to drugs or alcohol are common among the more disturbed. This delinquency needs to be seen in its true context.

> Children seldom demonstrate adult forms of depression before the age of 16. Rather, their depression appears in the form of depressive equivalents, such as acting-out behaviour. For purposes of identification, we have separated running away, truancy, drug abuse, and promiscuity from depression and withdrawal. For purposes of understanding these children, however, all these symptoms are best seen as manifestations of the same depressive process. Incest victims are almost always depressed (Muldoon 1979).

Prostitution is perhaps the most dramatic form of acting out. As yet there are only a few reliable surveys available, but these suggest that between a third and a half of all prostitutes will have suffered sexual abuse in their childhood. An early study found that 51 out of 103 'promiscuous' women arrested by the Chicago vice squad had had their first sexual experiences with their own fathers (Rosenfeld 1979a). A 1912 Swiss study of girl prostitutes reported that 30 per cent had been sexually abused (Weinberg 1955). In 1975 Dr James of Washington State University, interviewing 200 prostitutes in Seattle, found 22 per cent had been incestuously assaulted as children (Giarretto 1978). A recent study in Minneapolis discovered that as many as 75 per cent of adolescent prostitutes had been victims of incest (Weber 1977). In 1978 the results of a study by the Minnesota task force on juvenile prostitution were published (Enablers 1978): seventy-five out of the eighty women interviewed had turned professional before they were nineteen, and sixty were under nineteen at the time of the interview. Nearly one-third had

been sexually abused by a family member, a quarter of these relationships involving intercourse. The molesters had been fathers (one
third), stepfathers (one third) and brothers (one quarter). Three-
quarters of the girls had been to juvenile court for various reasons
before they began prostituting themselves, by which time one half
were already in out-of-home placements. It is not easy to find suitable places for these disturbed girls: some had had as many as eight
placements, and the median was three. Most of the girls aged between thirteen and fifteen had been put to work by pimps to whom
they gave all or most of their money, who sometimes beat them but
on whom they felt psychological dependence.

I was told by more than one professional (police and social
workers are only too familiar with the routine) that pimps are expert
at recognizing girls whom they can seduce into working for them.
Most have run away from home and are looking for somewhere to
stay, someone to care for them. The men wait at railway stations or
search through the bars, easily pick out the 'lost' ones, approach
them in a friendly way, feed them, take them out and sooner or
later sleep with them. They are too clever to force themselves on
the girls until they have won their trust. Once they have made their
victims dependent on them (very quickly done, for these youngsters
have such gross needs that it does not take much to convince them
they have at last found what they are looking for) they ask them, as
a favour, to sleep with a friend. This request is then repeated with
other friends until the girl is finally turned out to earn money. If
she refuses she is beaten, but mostly she is treated reasonably well.
The girls rarely run away, and if they do the pimps don't bother to
follow them as they know they will soon return because they have
no other relationships to turn to, even such pitiful security seeming
worth the exploitation they are subjected to.

Barbara Myers, who runs a successful programme for victims of
childhood sexual abuse known as Christopher Street Inc. writes
openly about the experiences which led to her becoming a prostitute
(Myers 1979). Her father began to molest her sexually when she was
seven, and by the time she was eleven he was having intercourse
with her. He had always been a physical bully and she did not dare
defy him, but she used deliberately to hurt herself in order to cause
herself such pain she could ignore what was happening to her
sexually. She would spray perfume into her eyes and thought if she
went blind her family might take more care of her. She pounded at
her foot to try to break the bones; she jumped off a garage; she

soaked herself then sat around hoping to get pneumonia. But all that happened was that when she succeeded in making herself ill enough to stay at home it merely gave her father more opportunity to abuse her. She cried continuously, sick with anxiety and fear that she would become so unpleasant everyone would hate her. But by the age of twelve the anxiety had been replaced by anger towards herself and towards everyone else. The self-abuse became worse. She wanted to show she was tough, that nothing could hurt her any more; she had herself tattooed, and burnt herself from her wrists to her elbows with a cigarette so severely she still carries the scars. She began to make suicide attempts, but no one took any notice – they just told her she was crazy.

Several times she ran away. Once she hid in a shack local boys had built and they let her stay there provided she had sex with them. Whenever she returned home her father always beat her and kept her indoors for long periods. She began to steal, hoping the police would catch her and help her. On her run-away trips she used to take money from strangers, and some of the men who picked her up raped her. She writes,

> My vulnerability must have been quite obvious in those days. I didn't much care what happened to me, and, as a consequence, a lot of other people didn't either. . . . I felt marked. I knew that, wherever I went, men would find me and abuse me. So, my attitude towards prostitution was, 'Why not?' If I had to have sex, why not get something for it?

She felt that, as long as she didn't care about them, making men pay for what they wanted was the only way she could have control over them. She had learned to separate her mind from what was happening to her body at such an early age that selling herself to strangers presented no problems: it was a situation in which she felt she at last had power over the men who had need of her.

She had been eleven when she first started taking drugs, finding that by sniffing glue she could get high and imagine she was happy. Drug taking also gave her a group to belong to, a gang of other unhappy kids like herself. When she was warned that taking drugs could 'burn out your brain' she pictured herself as a head of lettuce and thought how marvellous it would be not to be able to think. Later she deliberately used dirty needles in order to get hepatitis. She had begun to drink as well, and being too young to buy alcohol legally she would get older men to buy it for her, and pay them with the only currency she possessed. Her physical self-abuse increased – she deliberately picked fights with boyfriends so they would beat her up, and she continued to make suicide attempts. Sometimes her intention was to be found and helped; at other times she simply wanted to die.

She was lucky. In the end she did find the help she had been searching for all her life, but not until she had been through a great deal of pain and distress. At least she has been able to use this to alleviate the pain of others. The programme she originated, Christopher Street Inc., was begun in an attempt to help women with their drug abuse problems, and it was soon discovered that a surprising number had been sexually molested by the family members in their childhood.

This link has been confirmed in various studies. The Odyssey Institute in New York found that 44 per cent of 118 female drug users had experienced incest as children. In many cases there had been more than one molester – sixty out of the total of ninety-three incest offenders (there were fifty-two victims) were of the parental generation, and of this group 21 per cent were fathers or stepfathers (Giarretto 1978). A family therapist, John Siverson, who has treated over 500 cases of adolescent drug addiction, reported that around 70 per cent of his clients had been involved in family sexual abuse (Weber 1977). The Minnesota Correctional Institution for Women found 50 per cent of the participants in their drug abuse programme had been either incest or rape victims (Muldoon 1979).

At Christopher Street it was found that most of the clients who drank too much also took other drugs – aspirin from over the counter to go to sleep, stimulants to wake them up, marihuana, cocaine, anything they could buy. There seemed little point in separating out alcohol addicts from drug addicts in this programme, as the root cause was the same.

It seems absolutely clear, then, that many cases of incest are followed by various forms of delinquency on the part of the victims. Boys as well as girls follow this pattern but apart from Wenet's work I have not come across any statistics concerning male adolescents, only the mention, in various case histories relating to male incest victims, of drug addiction, prostitution, pimping, stealing, etc. In Wenet's study, as already reported, the delinquency took the form of the sexual molestation of younger children – 54 per cent of the adolescent molesters were themselves found to have been victims of sexual or physical abuse (personal communication). The Wolfes found that 70 per cent of the homosexual paedophiles they treated had been abused by an adult male in their childhood.

The delinquency usually starts with running away (according to one survey incest is one of the three primary reasons why children leave home) while stealing is often the first criminal offence. Policemen undergoing training courses at a centre in Colorado are taught that around 80 per cent of delinquent girls who run away from home or have been in trouble have suffered some kind of incestuous experience. Giarretto told me,

> The story is almost repetitious as far as those of our female adult clients who were molested as children are concerned. Usually there is promiscuity during teen-age, drugs, sometimes recourse to prostitution, followed by marriage then problems with sexual dysfunction. We see it again and again.

Jay, a quietly spoken volunteer working with Parents Anonymous (England), talked to me about the period of delinquency she went through in her adolescence as a result of incest with her father when she was eight years old. Her parents' marriage had broken up when she was small and she and her mother, with whom she had a close and good relationship, went to live with the maternal grandmother in the Midlands. Jay was happy enough in spite of the change, and she got on well with her peers at her junior school until her father reappeared in her life. After his repeated molestation of her her behaviour changed radically, but once it had ceased she so successfully blocked out the incestuous experiences that by the time she was being repeatedly arrested for shoplifting she had no memory whatsoever of them, and might never have recovered the memory if it had not been for drug treatment by a doctor in a mental hospital.

She recalls the day she saw her father again after a lengthy period of separation:

> One day coming home from school a man drew up beside me in his car. I recognized instantly who it was and said hello to him. He told me he'd been to see my mother and she had been very upset. He said he had to go away again, and that he wanted me to do something for him, so I got into the car simply because I knew it was my father and I had no reason to be afraid. He took me to the cricket pavilion, which was on the way home, and he put his arm round me and began to pet me. I was very

afraid, I didn't understand what was happening. All the while
he was telling me my mother loved me very much and that
whatever I did it would be because I loved her, and because she
hadn't got anybody else in the world but me. Then he had
intercourse with me. I was shocked and afraid, but all the time
it was in my mind that I was doing it to help my mother: he
kept on telling me that it was because my mother loved me and
I loved her.

Before they had parted she and my father had had frequent
rows, which came to a head when he threatened her life. I
didn't know about any of this at the time, neither when it
happened nor when he was taking me to the pavilion; as far as I
knew he was seeing my mother and she was in agreement with
what he was doing, although he always told me it was
something between him and myself, something I must never tell
anyone about.

He met me on a number of occasions, so I was often late
home from school. Gradually it got later and later. I always
made the excuse I had been playing with a friend who lived
near the school. My mother knew her, so at first it was OK,
but then my mother began to get worried. One evening when I
got home about 8 o'clock I was confronted by my grandfather
and my mother. They were both very worried people. They had
been in touch with the police who had started looking for me,
because earlier that day while I was at school there had been a
very bad argument with my father and he had threatened to
take me away with him. I didn't know that, of course, all I
knew was that he'd met me and as usual intercourse took place
– not only intercourse, but . . . other things as well.

The next time I saw my father – about a week later – I told
him what had happened. Straightaway he said he was going
back to Australia, and that when I was older I would be able to
go and see him, but that at that stage I couldn't. I never saw
him again after that.

Gradually I put everything that had happened to the back of
my mind. Soon I had literally forgotten what my father had
done to me. I continued through my life always being a little
rebellious, not getting on with my stepfather whom my mother
married three years later, and generally making life unbearable
for everyone around me. Nobody could understand why at one

time I had been a happy little girl and then suddenly I had changed so entirely.

When I was about fifteen years old I started to shoplift. I did it continually, I got caught continually, I was continually put on probation. I was fined, I was sent to a probation hostel for twelve months. It didn't make any difference, I couldn't stop myself. The things I stole weren't things I needed or wanted, or even things I cared about. I just had to keep on punishing myself, and I didn't know why. At the end of a long, long road of probation and suspended sentences, I went to prison for twelve months, finishing in the hospital wing because I was so very depressed.

When I came out I went back to the Midlands. By this time I had a boyfriend who didn't know about my previous life. But it didn't work out well – on one occasion he beat me so badly I had to go to hospital. As soon as I came out I started to shoplift again. As usual I was caught, and went back to court. But this time there was a difference – I had a very, very good probation officer. I really owe my life outside of a prison wall to her, because she arranged for me to see a doctor at Aston Hall in Derby, who was quite different from anyone else I'd met. He was very kind, and asked me again and again why I kept stealing. I said I didn't know. After a very lengthy and harrowing hour he agreed to help me. He sent a report to the court saying I was willing to go in as a voluntary patient for six months. The court agreed, and made an order that I should do so.

When I went in I felt very bitter – I don't know why, because the doctor was very good. After I had been there about a week and had settled in they decided to give me what they call the treatment. I was taken upstairs to a large room that was shuttered except for a small square which gave light to the room. I was put into a canvas nightie which just had a hole for your arms and a hole for your legs and lay down on a large mattress on the floor. Then the doctor came in with the sister who was in charge of the ward. He had a very quiet, calming voice and he told me he was going to give me an injection which would make me feel very drowsy and also make me want to talk. During this time the sister knelt down beside me and was very nice and kind to me.

When the injection was working the doctor began to ask me

about when I was young and took me back to the time when I was five years old. I went through the period of being five to seven with him, then they gave me another injection and left me. I slept until the next morning, when after breakfast I got up, had a bath, put on my own nightie and was left to stay in my own bed with my meals brought to me. The next treatment was about a fortnight later, when they took me through the ages of seven to nine and so on, until eventually my life was fitted together like pieces of a jigsaw.

What my father had done to me came out in one of the sessions and the next day I was called into the office. When the doctor told me what I'd said under the drugs I couldn't believe it, because although I had heard what I was saying in one way, yet in another way it wasn't me that was saying it. He played the tape back to me and explained that I had pushed the truth to the back of my mind until all that remained was that I had to keep persecuting myself, hurting myself all the time without knowing why.

I stayed at Aston Hall for six months and continued to have treatment for a while afterwards. The doctor told my mother about me and she was very upset. At first she and my stepfather refused to believe it. For myself, I felt much calmer, had much more confidence in myself. Since then I've never been in trouble again, nor ever wanted to be.

I would like people to understand that incest is a very painful experience, and that I suffered badly all those years. Not only me, but all my family suffered, my mother especially. It wasn't just an incestuous experience, it was an experience of mental hospitals, of prisons, probation, suspended sentences, fines, living in lodgings because I couldn't live at home as I couldn't cope with the family environment. It's left its mark on me in a lot of ways, but I've come through it. I've learned to live with it.

I am very lucky. I have two very happy children, and although my husband has his own problems – he was born from an incestuous relationship between his mother and her own father – we have each other. Fortunately there have been no complications on the genetic side. I am still very cold in some respects about love-making, though. I'm not at all a cold person towards my children or people I know, but towards men I am always a little nervous. I am very uneasy if I am left alone in a room with a man I don't know – even to this day I find it very difficult to be with my stepfather, although he had nothing to do with it.

But I suppose it is not to be wondered at, considering what happened.

Chapter 8

State involvement

Possibly the most vital question to be asked about incest is: is legal intervention necessary? This is a highly controversial subject, and one which is far more complicated than might be supposed. We have already considered the arguments of the pro-incest lobby, most members of which certainly wish incest to be decriminalized, but there are many others who while considering incest to be harmful feel that the intervention of the law can only be damaging to everyone concerned. Currently in Britain the laws are being examined with a view to changing them, but it seems unlikely there will be any dramatic changes in English or Scottish law within the forseeable future. In England in October 1980 the Criminal Law Revision Committee produced a paper on sexual offences, but there was very little relating to the sexual abuse of children.

At the beginning of Chapter 2 we saw that in English law incest is very narrowly defined as being either intercourse between a man and his daughter, sister or half-sister, grand-daughter or mother; or intercourse between a woman over sixteen with her father, brother or half-brother, son or grandfather. Illegitimate children are covered by the law of incest, but stepchildren and adopted children are not, nor are relationships between father and son. Sexual molesters not coming within the legal definition of incest may be charged with rape, buggery, unlawful sexual intercourse, indecent assault or indecency with or towards a child under thirteen, the maximum sentences for which range from two years to life.

In America the situation is even more complicated as the laws on incest vary from state to state, as does the definition. It is mandatory to report physical abuse in all states, but if a child is not physically damaged she may not come under the physical abuse reporting laws. Forty-two states do include sexual molestation in their child abuse reporting statutes, but thirty-four of these do not define it. Punishment varies considerably from state to state.

The English DHSS have suggested that by including emotional abuse in their definition of child abuse, sexual abuse which does not involve physical trauma will automatically be covered, but many working in the field find this highly unsatisfactory. They argue that emotional abuse is far too vague a concept to be of any use in very many cases, and that unless incest victims show obvious signs of mental breakdown many will go without help. Precise but broader terms and comprehensive reporting laws are clearly necessary both in Britain and in the United States on a national level: most professionals have no doubt that every victim of incest needs support and help, however minimal. But whether reporting should result in offenders facing criminal charges is a subject around which much argument rages.

In most areas the basic concern of those connected with law enforcement is to secure a conviction of incest offenders. Apart from certain enlightened areas they are not concerned with the well-being of the rest of the family. This single-minded attitude prevails both in the United States and in Britain.

> Throughout the country the typical repertory of law enforcement officials in the handling of father-daughter sexual abuse is ineffective and inconsistent. In the majority of instances, the police officer and/or the district attorney drop the cases because of insufficient evidence (the father usually denies the charges), even though there is strong suspicion that the victim's accusations are based on fact. The emphasis on a provable law violation has the effect of the community turning its back on the child and family and leaving them in a worse condition than before (Giarretto 1978, USA).

> Certain groups of professionals do not seem to refer on to other professional groups. For example, because the police surgeon's role is to collect medical evidence, he may not see the child's needs as paramount and may not consider referral to either a paediatrician or a child psychiatrist (Beezley Mrazek, Lynch and Bentovim, 1981, UK).

We have already seen how under these circumstances the child suffers from the reactions of her family. It is sometimes argued that if the police decide they have a viable case the position of the child is even worse than when the case is dropped. The main objection is that generally the child has to tell and retell her story, often to

people totally untrained in extracting evidence from children, sometimes over a period of months. As Lucy Berliner points out (Berliner
and Stevens 1979), while there are special courts for juvenile *offenders* because it is realized that juveniles need special treatment,
if a juvenile has been *offended against* however young she is she has
to go through the court process just as though she were an adult.
Victims are likely to face interrogation first by the patrol police,
then again at the police station or department, then by social
workers, doctors or police surgeons. Later there may be preliminary
hearings, discussions with lawyers, and finally the court process in
which the child yet again will have to repeat publicly all the sexual
details of what happened to her and to be cross-examined by a
hostile defence counsel.

At home she may well be submitted to a continuous barrage of
criticism by her family who tell her she ought to deny the charges
for the sake of the family. Grandparents, uncles, and aunts, the
immediate family, all may pressurize the child in an attempt to
avoid the inevitable scandal that will follow once the case becomes
public. It is understandable that some professionals believe the legal
process does more damage to the victim than the actual molestation.
There are, however, those who argue that it is therapeutic for a
child to tell her story several times instead of burying it deep, and
that it helps her to know that society is supporting her by trying
her molester. Children, they say, have a deep sense of justice, and
feel it right that if a wrong has been done the law should step in to
punish the offender. In some cases this is undoubtedly true – in
others the desire for justice will be mixed with a desire for revenge
compounded with misery and guilt for causing a once-loved (and
possibly still-loved) father to go to jail.

Obviously there is no easy answer. If incest remains a crime, then
committing it is a criminal offence and the legal process must be
carried out. Video-tapes are not sufficient evidence at a trial; a
defendant has a right to defend himself face-to-face against his
accuser. Since children need protection from those adults who wish
to molest them it is difficult to see how in practice this can be
achieved without the criminal law being involved. And if it is, then
we cannot take away an accused man's right to a fair trial.

Various ways of coping with this problem have been put forward.
The most urgent is to prevent the victims having to tell their story
repeatedly, and to ensure not only that it should not have to be told
more than two or three times at most but that these tellings should

be treated as part of the therapeutic process and only be conducted by professionals trained to deal with children. Because of the requirements of the legal process one of the professionals should also be trained in legal investigation to avoid further interviews necessitated by inefficient questioning. Several American states have already adopted processes of this kind – one method is to have several investigators in the interview room at the same time, with only one talking to the child but the others being able to ask questions if necessary. Another is to use a single investigator only to help the child feel more relaxed, but in fact to have members of other disciplines listening behind a one-way mirror so that if there are any unclear points they can afterwards come in and clarify them, thus keeping the questioning of the child down to a minimum. It may be considered that this last method is unethical if the child is not told what is being done – similarly children's statements are sometimes taped without them being informed, at least until afterwards – but we have to consider that different ethics may apply to the treatment of children who are too young to fully understand what is happening to them. When a child has been properly questioned and the statement taped, it appears that in the great majority of cases the father when confronted with his child's statement admits his guilt and the child is not then forced to appear in court.

However, if the questioning is not done properly and a confused and contradictory statement is all that is obtained, the defendant is likely to be advised by his lawyer to deny the charges, and either the case will be dropped because of insufficient evidence or the child will be forced to testify in public. Children are often accused of lying, simply because they may not have understood the interviewer's questions or may have been unintentionally using words wrongly. We saw earlier that children can confuse rape with a struggle, or may not at all understand what intercourse actually consists of. The concept of time means little to young children so they can easily contradict themselves without realizing they are doing so. Investigators have to know how to help the children pinpoint details necessary for legal purposes, such as when a molestation took place, perhaps by reference to a particular television programme or to an outing or someone's birthday (Muldoon 1979). Another complication is that children may be too embarrassed to tell the investigator the truth: they fear they will be blamed for having permitted something to happen they know to be forbidden, and may not understand that the questionings are intended to help them, not to persecute them.

Obviously very strong reasons are needed to validate forcing a child to face a variety of strangers with her story, even when the number of repetitions is limited. Therapeutic telling could be more simply and probably better achieved by sessions with a single trained child therapist. And since, as far as justice is concerned, a victim may easily feel she is suffering more than the offender even if the latter is sent away from home, she may well consider that the opposite of justice has been done. This is especially so when (as often happens) it is the child, not the offender, who is removed from the home. This may only be a temporary removal, or it may be for a considerable period of time if there is insufficient evidence to secure a conviction but the social services consider the home unsafe. Several times at children's groups I heard children saying that they felt it was they who were being punished, not their fathers, and that it was they who were being made to feel like criminals. This sense of injustice rankled bitterly even among girls whose stay in children's shelters did not last more than a week or so. The initial shock of being removed from all they know and plunged into a totally strange environment where they were closely guarded and not allowed out on their own made a very powerful impression that far outweighed the brief time the experience lasted.

I admit that when I first started researching this book I felt strongly inclined to the view that the police had no part to play as far as non-violent incest was concerned. It seemed to me a family problem which could best be dealt with by therapists, counsellors, psychiatrists, groups. How could the police help?

I found this viewpoint was shared by those who either have had little direct experience of dealing with incestuous *families* or by those who have never worked with cooperative policemen and members of the legal profession. But, where this last benefit is available, experienced workers who themselves were originally anti-police now agree that there is one overriding benefit to be had by legal involvement, and that is that it keeps a father coming for treatment and the entire family in therapy. Without legal sanctions nearly all perpetrators gradually drop out of treatment, whether they undertook it voluntarily or whether it was suggested they should take treatment but could not be pressurized to do so because of insufficient evidence to secure a conviction (Giarretto 1978; Meiselman, personal communication; Wenett, personal communication; and many similar personal communications of other therapists and psychiatrists as well as the directors of several social work departments.)

As Geri Hatcher (Sexual Abuse Project, Los Angeles Department of Social Services) pointed out to me, some therapists – not yet familiar with the process of waning enthusiasm for treatment on the part of offenders and their families who are attending voluntarily – are unwilling to undertake what they see as 'coercive therapy'.

> But when you think about it, there's already been some coercion in getting the men to therapy even when the law has had no part in it. There's usually been someone pushing whenever anyone goes into therapy: it may be a wife who says, 'look, I'll leave you if you don't get some therapy', or a school who say they'll expel the kid if he doesn't get some help. And there's another point. People are traditional in their thinking: when you commit a crime you're supposed to pay. I've only come to see this in the last two or three years – before I wouldn't have gone along with this point of view. But people themselves seem almost to want it. And in parents' groups they can give something back to the community, to help other parents. It's their way of saying, 'I'm sorry, I was wrong.' But without some coercion they'll come to a few meetings or treatments full of remorse, then after a bit it fades, and you don't see any more of them. And at home it starts up all over again. That doesn't help the victim any.

How do we set about getting this desirable police help, and does it really work when we have it? As with physical abuse, Americans have pioneered the way, but only in certain fortunate areas. It is always difficult for the English to realize to what extent laws differ from state to state in the USA – apart from certain federal laws, of course. This discrepancy is so marked that to an English person (and I'm told to Americans too) it sometimes seems that one is dealing with different countries rather than different states. In the field of incest there has been far more progress with regard to police cooperation in the west than in the east, which is not surprising considering the generally more open-minded and experimental attitude of westerners.

Much of the new-style cooperation springs from Hank Giarretto's work in San José. It was clear to Giarretto that men finishing long jail sentences had not been cured by their incarceration, but that equally without some kind of court order treatment outside of jail was usually abandoned. Gradually policemen and other professionals connected with the law were introduced to the various groups that Giarretto and his colleagues were setting up and they were able to see for themselves that the kind of treatment which was becoming available to the entire family was producing far better results than anything previously achieved. Many became convinced, and as a result shorter sentences were given or in certain cases were suspended entirely, provided the offenders agreed to undertake treatment. The pattern is for the offender to be involved in the whole family treatment as soon as possible after his arrest, and this will be continued during and after his incarceration if he is jailed. The reader may recall John, the father whose story is told in Chapter 1, who himself went through this process and who eventually ended up working professionally in the crisis intervention field. In most cases the police, probation departments and courts cooperate whole-heartedly, while the first two are major sources of referral to what became the Child Sexual Abuse Treatment Program (CSATP), of which Giarretto is director. Even more importantly, because of the changed attitude of the law enforcement agencies, workers in other disciplines and private individuals who previously would not have reported cases now do so.

Giarretto agrees that it is by no means easy to convince others that a compassionate supportive approach is the most socially useful way to deal with offenders.

> You will get much opposition at first. You will be challenged by many red, angry faces accusing you of permissiveness, of protecting child molesters, etc. You will hear, 'How can you even consider returning a child to a mother who set her up for abuse by her father?' and 'The only thing to do with that son-of-a-bitch is to let him rot in prison.' This will be said to you . . . with everybody nodding their heads in self-righteous agreement. How can anyone miss making points with an audience if he says he hates child molesters? (Giarretto 1977).

His answer is to be patient, to persevere, and to get to know objectors personally. He likes to take people out to lunch while he explains his point of view, then to have them come to groups and see the reality for themselves. He has found few hard-liners who could not eventually be converted by this gentle persuasion.

The El Paso County Department of Social Services, Colorado Springs, has over recent years achieved an increasingly successful rapport with their local law enforcement agencies. Anne Topper, social services administrator, has commented on the amazement of workers from other areas who have observed the standard of cooperation between the social services and law enforcement agencies, including the district attorney's office. In addition to the obvious advantages to the families concerned, this cooperation has saved public money through the sharing of resources and the avoidance of repetition of questioning, etc., and has also increased the mutual understanding of the difficulties under which the different disciplines work.

So successful has this coming together been that recently the social services department and the various law enforcement agencies have set up an 'Incest Diversion Program' which allows the non-violent, first offender the chance of avoiding jail providing he is willing to follow and complete the course of treatment considered necessary for him. The document setting out this programme appears in full in the appendix, since it is one which I imagine many police and social service departments would like to study. In brief, it points out (a) that families and others will not report incest if they fear the perpetrator will be jailed, and (b) that the judicial system is devastating to a child who must testify against her parent; it concludes therefore that if possible the judicial process is best avoided. The circumstances in which this may be achieved are as follows: the perpetrator may not have a previous history of incestuous offences, must not have used any violence including intimidation implying bodily harm, must admit he needs help and voluntarily agree to follow the treatment including family counselling programmes for up to two years. The agreement has been very carefully worked out, clarifying important points such as the fact that the perpetrator has admitted to responsibility will not be used against him in any criminal prosecution if it is decided not to admit him into the programme, but that if, once having been admitted, he fails to cooperate or comply with the conditions explained to him then criminal prosecution may be instituted against him. It also clarifies that the agreement will not last for more than twenty-four months and that once the programme is completed the district attorney will not prosecute him for the incident that brought him into the programme in the first place.

This programme has been widely publicized and it is hoped that it will greatly increase the number of families coming for treatment. It would be interesting in a few years time to compare the results from Colorado Springs with those areas which, although believing in cooperation among the different disciplines, prefer to weigh up each case individually in court without any previous guarantee of freedom from imprisonment if guilt is admitted to. Quite a few people mentioned to me their sense that many victims seem to need to pay publicly for their crime, a view expressed a few pages ago by Geri Hatcher. Few of these were the type of person who could have been expected to express such a viewpoint – they had arrived at it with some sense of surprise after working for some time with offenders.

There are some people who are unhappy about the coercive aspect of diversion schemes. Deborah Anderson, for example (director of Sexual Assault Services, Minneapolis) is worried about the implications of making someone agree to accept treatment when they have not been legally tried and found guilty. She considers it a real possibility that an innocent man could be blackmailed into accepting treatment because circumstances look bad against him.

> A social worker may have a very different value system from the family she's seeing, and there may in fact be nothing wrong. You can't just shift a whole bunch of people off to treatment because you happen to think they need it. And you are asking people to incriminate themselves. You tell them you are there to help them, but in fact it's possible they'll end up in jail. What I question is that anyone has a right to walk into people's houses and tell them they have to have therapy. You don't do that to a burglar – why should you do it to an incest parent? Would you like somebody knocking on your door, saying I want you to go to this treatment centre because I think you ought to? Personally I couldn't stand to go to some of those treatment places – I'd rather go to the workhouse! If someone said to me, you will visit this place every week, you will go there and you will bare your soul, you will not deny, and you will not stonewall, and you will let those people know you and share your innermost feelings and thoughts – to me it's very important to safeguard people from that. I think it is very scary and we've seen it on gigantic scales in the world when people's basic rights haven't been protected. In order to achieve what seems a good system you cannot go ahead and violate people's rights just because you feel they need help. What may help me may be absolutely terrible to you, and who is finally to decide?

If people have a trial and are given a fair choice, then it's OK. If they decide they want to change their behaviour – fine. If they choose jail, I agree it won't do him any good, but the important thing is he has to be able to make his own choice.

Against my argument that the victims whom he might molest after finishing his sentence have an equal right not to be molested, she said you cannot in any case successfully force a man to change his behaviour if he doesn't want to do so. Not everybody is treatable, and for some there is no alternative to prison; they are a danger to the community and at present, at least, there seems nothing else to be done with them.

For others these doubts about individual rights of personal privacy have little relevance, and they state openly that they would have no qualms about insisting that an offender accept treatment, if necessary threatening to take the children away from the family or to call in the police. For them the benefits outweigh any ethical doubts, as they believe that most people after undergoing family therapy will improve, even if initially they were unwilling participants in the programme.

It certainly seems to be true that without court involvement treatment is unlikely to be persisted with. Wenet (personal communication) said that 45 per cent of the molesting teenagers he dealt with and their families do not follow through with recommended treatments unless legal pressure is put on them. He feels very pessimistic about the future of those who do drop out, but for those who continue to receive treatment for a year or two he feels hopeful.

Roger Wolfe commented,

You're asking a guy to give up a behaviour that is essentially very pleasurable, very arousing to him, and to make some major changes in the way he functions, the way he looks at things. It's a difficult thing to do. They're very compulsive folks. They go through cycles of offending, then of remorse, then – they can't help it, they're like alcoholics – they do it again. People come to us sometimes in the remorse period, but their resolve rapidly fades and on average we'll maybe see them twice – half of them don't even show up to keep the first appointment they made. They need to have something making them continue to come for treatment. But we do like to see people *before* they've been sentenced so that you can work with them as an ally. Whereas if the judge raps his gavel and says 'I sentence you to treatment' – well they regard you as part of the punishment process, and you usually don't get anywhere much with them after that.

There is one snag to this ideal of cooperation leading to family treatment, however, and that is that although it is cheaper than each discipline going it alone, it still costs money. At the moment there is a great deal of 'blindness' as far as incest is concerned, and while in many cases this is undoubtedly caused by the profound embarrassment, sometimes almost terror, that incest arouses in many an otherwise stalwart chest, very often it is due to a probably unacknowledged fear as to the size of the vast area of need that might be revealed. The explosion in the number of reported cases of physical child abuse that occurred after Henry Kempe first publicized the 'battered child syndrome', rising in the United States from fewer than 7,000 cases in 1967 to 200,000 by 1974 (Rosenfeld and Newberger 1977) put a great strain on everybody's resources everywhere, and since it is apparent that acknowledgment of the real prevalence of sexual abuse is likely to lead to a similar explosion it is no wonder that on the whole the already overpressed social services are not rushing around enthusiastically looking for new clients. Indeed, if some of the figures suggested in the chapter on incidence are correct, showing for example that perhaps as many as one in eleven women have had some incestuous experience in their lives, it is impossible to imagine how any state system could cope with the huge numbers that might be involved, even if only a fraction of all incest victims were to be in need of some kind of state intervention.

Many organizations, of course, have always been reluctant to involve themselves with sexual abuse because of the criminal law. The British National Society for the Prevention of Cruelty to Children, for example, which has been one of the leaders in the treatment of physically abused children and their families, was at first unwilling to include cases of sexual abuse because of the severe legal punishments which would make casework with the families very difficult if not impossible. This complication, together with an increasing shortage of funds leading to an even greater strain on already overworked and overstressed social service departments, has contributed to the slow recognition of a problem that is at least as severe as physical child abuse was found to be in the late sixties. Beezley Mrazek, Lynch and Bentovim (1981) in their survey of

English Area Review Committees (multi-disciplinary teams set up to review policy on child abuse and oversee the management of cases of non-accidental injury to children) found that many did not include sexual abuse within their definition of child abuse, some because of this problem of overload. They quote one committee which wrote in its reply that it was

> 'worried about over-loading the special child abuse procedure . . . and thus possibly missing a serious case involving a small baby.' These committees are holding firm to a strict definition of non-accidental injury, excluding sexual abuse unless it involves physical injuries. . . . In some areas sexual abuse was considered to be primarily a criminal matter and, therefore, dealt with almost exclusively by the police and police surgeons.

As a result only 12 per cent of the Area Review Committees who responded to the request for information were able to give statistics about the incidence of sexual abuse in their area. The figures involved are so small that they are a clear indication of how few cases are being picked up. They range from no children at all to twelve. One committee wrote that there was a 'fairly high incidence of incest' in their area, but they had no statistics available to show just how high.

From the figures on police files in the UK it is clear that very few cases are being made known to them. Most policemen seem to be aware there are more cases than they hear about, but few of them have any idea of just how far they are still underestimating the problem. One, for instance, told me that while he was aware many social workers – although officially supposed to inform the police of any new case of incest – in fact try at first to deal with it on their own, he was sure that sooner or later in order to ensure the protection of the child or children they almost always bring in the police. It was clear he had not taken sufficiently into consideration the other ways in which a child can be protected by the social services, though these often mean the removal of the child, not the offender, from the home.

Police attitudes are by no means as necessarily traditional as many people like to think. When presented with new ideas they react like any other mixed population: some dig in their heels and refuse to budge, while others are interested and want to know more. But even in areas where great strides have been made in cooperation between police and others as far as physical abuse is concerned, the police attitude that they have no choice but to investigate and prosecute if they have sufficient evidence makes collaboration with them extremely difficult. Dr Hugh de la Haye Davies, Principal Police Surgeon to the Northamptonshire Police who was one of the progenitors of the first liaison scheme in Great Britain to bring doctors, police and social workers to case conferences during the late 1960s states that, 'largely due to the rigid police attitude which does not leave much room for manoeuvre, in the question of sexual abuse we are back where we were in 1965 as far as cooperation between the agencies is concerned.'

Nevertheless Northamptonshire police, while insisting they have no discretion in the matter of incest, are now attending case conferences under the chairmanship of the NSPCC Special Unit. As Hugh Davies says,

> although in the case conference doctors and social workers are still inhibited about cooperating fully with the police because of the strong possibility of family break-up, at least the police have the opportunity to make their attitudes clear, in particular their fear that other children in the family might be molested.

The result of this growing cooperation is that although cases do not escape prosecution, the courts are now taking note of the recommendations of the case conference which will be contained within the probation and medical reports presented to it, and acting on them. At the time of writing neither Dr Davies nor I know of any other area in the UK where such advanced treatment is available, but while even in Northamptonshire there is no certainty of outcome as far as sentence is concerned, the following case history given me by Dr Davies shows that Britain too has its enlightened men and women who are prepared to override prejudice and act as seems best for each particular case.

A father who had been having incestuous relationships with his two daughters, aged eight and nine, was charged with gross indecency (it will be remembered that in Britain intercourse is necessary for an incest charge to be filed). The mother, who claimed she had not known what was happening, because of pressure from neighbours, family and social services reluctantly filed a suit for divorce, but later felt very guilty about not standing by her husband. She blamed herself for not realizing what was going on, as in both families there was a history of incest. Her own mother and aunt having been sexually molested by her grandfather, and her husband's mother by his grandfather, she decided the whole affair was simply a hereditary characteristic.

The father was out on bail but separated from the children, who were in the care of their mother. All of them, including a third child of three years, bitterly missed their father, and the younger of the two victims particularly blamed the older who had given away the situation by talking to a neighbour's daughter. They developed psychological disturbances of a serious nature, which resulted in psychosomatic illness. At the first case conference the police felt that although the man would probably receive a prison sentence it was likely the mother would take him back when he was released, even if the divorce went through, and thus the children would be in danger for many years to come. Discussions between the police surgeon and the family doctor resulted in the latter putting forward the view that the whole family should be assessed and treated, using the services of a consultant family psychiatrist attached to the NSPCC Special Unit. At a second case conference the psychiatrist agreed, and undertook to coordinate the management of the family in liaison with the father's probation officer, the psychiatrist in the Child Guidance Centre, family doctors and the social services. Everybody took rapid action and soon the whole family was in treatment.

It was fortunate that for reasons outside the police control the case was delayed in reaching the crown court, and by the time the accused came to trial, at which he pleaded guilty, it was clear the treatment was being very successful. The judge, on reading the reports, passed a suspended sentence so that the family could stay together and continue to receive treatment as a family. The prognosis is good, and the children's psychological state has greatly improved, attracting favourable comments from their teachers. To guard against the father slipping, a care order was placed on the children which will remain in force until they are eighteen, ensuring that some control will continue. Family counselling is helping both parents redefine their family roles and the mother is receiving social training to help her with child care. Marital counselling is aiding the marriage, and sexual counselling for the whole family will help them cope with what has obviously been a long-standing problem.

All the professionals concerned have been very heartened by the progress of the case, and Dr Davies suggests that the accidental delay in the court proceedings could be deliberately adopted in future as a means of allowing the court a better opportunity of 'balancing its punitive function with reform of the offender and rehabilitation of the family.'

The police role can be a positive one. In many instances they are the first representatives of the state to deal not only with the perpetrator, but also with the victim and the rest of the family. The way they treat the situation can make a tremendous difference to the outcome for everyone concerned. In certain areas in the United States specially trained policemen are sent out to deal with incest cases whenever possible – these policemen are few in number and the areas covered large, so that inevitably on occasion only untrained policemen are available to go out and pick up a case, but someone from the special unit takes over afterwards. The special training may not consist of more than a weekend attendance at some course, but if a man or woman is receptive they can learn quickly enough what they basically need to know.

One such policeman works with a colleague in a sprawling area in Colorado. He was not at all happy when first chosen:

We didn't volunteer, they just picked two of us out. My first reaction was – hey, no, I want to be a cop, I want to work homicides, something like that. But after we'd been to a two-day course where they had workshops and so on we talked to each other, and we said, you know, we can either make this a boring terrible type of thing or we can get involved and try to do something. I think it's come a long way in this past year from what it was. We've got our own little office – it's not much but we're the only detectives that have our own personal office and personal files. When they chose us, we didn't have any choice, it was sink or swim, so . . .

He shrugged his shoulders. 'Since then we've brought in a lot of new ideas. Before, it was low priority – now it's different. And it's getting known about. My colleague puts out articles to newspapers, and we've both done talks to schools.'

When he was taken off his usual routine he was an ordinary patrolman; he has now been promoted one rank up to detective, which is below the rank of sergeant. Nevertheless he and his colleague, of the same rank, have responsibility for all the family investigations (including physical and sexual abuse) coming into the juvenile bureau at his police headquarters. Sexual assault committed by non-family members will be dealt with by other detectives. His enthusiasm was obvious from his manner and it was also clear how

knowledgeable he has become about the whole subject of incest in
the short time he has been involved in it.

He told me that his first concern on receiving a report is to see
that the abuse stops instantly. The usual procedure is for him to be
called by a school or the social services. Whenever possible they go
out in civilian clothes (though being American police they still carry
a loaded gun under the informal jacket) in order to play down their
official status. They interview everyone they can get hold of who is
likely to be helpful before making the decision as to whether it is
best to remove the child or the offender from the home. At this
stage they have the entire responsibility for this decision. If an
urgent call comes in and neither member of the special unit is
available a patrolman in the area will call at the home or school and
take the initial report. He will not go to the father's office and take
him away – such treatment can defeat any hope of later cooperation
– but the safety of the child being considered paramount the child
in all probability will be taken straight to a shelter or children's
home where she will be kept until it has been decided what action
needs to be taken.

But the more usual practice, when the special unit are able to go
out personally, is to take the victim to the police headquarters first.

> Usually we bring the child in here before she goes to the shelter
> and we get the mum and dad along if possible. We like to have
> the mother contact the daughter before she goes off to the
> shelter, or, in some cases, the dad, if that's what the daughter
> wants. We're aware what a shock it is for the girls – on the one
> hand we're saying you didn't do anything wrong, but on the
> other hand we're removing them from their house, their school,
> their friends. But we can't risk letting a girl stay in the home
> and maybe coming back next day and finding something
> terrible happened to her.

As far as behaviour towards the offender is concerned, the special
unit puts the needs – present and future – of the child first.

> I look at it, what's going to be best for the child six years from
> now? It's not going to be best for her if I bend my frustrations
> on this guy because he's been screwing her for the last six years
> or he's burnt the kid or whatever, because we shut parents off
> if we try to come on big and strong – you know, we're the
> police department, by God, and we're going to do this and that.

In the long run it ends up hurting the child. We've had deaths, we've had children of three or four months who've had terrible things done to them, and it takes a lot of conditioning to become professional enough to the point where you don't let your emotions jeopardize the case so you make it worse for the kids. People say to me, don't you want to take him out back and beat him up with a rubber hose or whatever? Sure, you feel like that sometimes. I've two small kids myself, it really affects me. But often there's other kids in the family, and I think, what's going to happen to them if I let myself go? In the long run it doesn't help. What you've got to remember is that anyone can lose it. I've talked to a lot of parents, especially in cases of physical abuse. They don't wake up in the morning and say, 'Let's kill little Johnny today.'

Our biggest problem is getting families into the programme and making sure they use all the resources the community has. Attorneys can cause problems. If we have to call a dad in before one of us had had a chance to speak to him he's likely to ring his attorney first. Maybe he's an old friend. The attorney says, 'don't say anything to anybody, anywhere, any time.' So we're stuck. A lot of the guys just don't realize that if they agree to go along with the programme they won't get thrown into jail. I'm not going to do it, the district attorney's office here won't do it. But once they refuse to talk I have no choice but to file a criminal charge. I try to get this through to their attorney but often they've not had an incest case for years and they're expecting a really heavy sentence. In fact, I've been here for a year now and I've not yet known anyone at all being sent to jail for incest.

(A rough estimate – an official break-down of figures not being available – put the child abuse cases coming to the unit over the previous ten months at around 600 cases, of which approximately fifty-five were incest cases, out of a population of approximately 150,000. They are aware incest is still only rarely reported.)

The outcome of a court case, even if the father denies it, is probably for the judge to say, 'I believe this did take place and I'm ordering you, Mr Smith, to go for six months to the . . . health centre to find out why you're doing this type of thing.' That's really what we're looking for. And we get it with most of our judges – I've no personal experience of any hard-line judges round here – they're really pretty cooperative.

It all works pretty well. We can't necessarily get through to every policeman what it's all about, but we can to most of them. We have refresher courses for policemen who've been on the streets for ten years. A lot of them, like ordinary people everywhere, have very strong feelings about this – you're not going to change some of these guy's minds, no matter what you do. But we can make sure an incestuous father doesn't have the handcuffs slapped on him and be thrown into the car then into jail.

With the girls, I don't just walk straight into a room and say, I hear your daddy's been screwing you. I don't give my official title and all that; I just say, 'hey, my name's Mike' and then I talk to them – say things like, where do you go to school, what kind of things do you like to do in school, what are your teachers like, that kind of thing. Then I explain I've talked to a lot of girls before, some a lot older, some a lot younger, and that we've talked about personal stuff, intimate stuff. We like to have a social worker, or some woman there, maybe the mother – it's a safeguard for us, apart from anything. If the girl's too embarrassed to talk in front of her mother I ask the mother to wait outside. I do whatever's most comfortable for the girl. The mother understands. I have to know first of all what a kid thinks intercourse is. A lot of childrens' ideas about intercourse isn't intercourse at all.

I have related this detective's experience in such detail because the entire success or failure of future treatment may rest on this initial contact between police and the family. These two detectives were ordinary men chosen with no special previous experience. Perhaps their force was particularly fortunate in their choice, but it seems to me from my own personal meeting with many policemen both in Britain and in America that it is unlikely such understanding and devotion cannot be replicated elsewhere.

My point is that it is not necessary to set up a vast new network in order to cope with an anticipated increase in reporting. Already existing facilities can be expanded or used in fresh imaginative ways. And among the general public there is a wealth of talent waiting to be employed. Deborah Anderson, whose work has been mentioned several times, is now director of the Sexual Assault Services centred at the Hennepin County Attorney's Office, Minneapolis. She began simply as a mother with children doing volunteer work as coordinator for a women's consciousness-raising group which had set up a rape centre. After a couple of years she decided she wanted to work part-time, and applied for a grant from a small foundation. The foundation liked her ideas, rang the county attorney's office to ask if they were interested in having someone from the rape centre work in their offices exploring ideas on coordination between hospitals, police, district attorney, social workers, etc. They agreed, gave her an office and gradually her work developed into a full-time position of authority. She had no legal training – in fact had an arts degree – and inevitably has had her viewpoint changed somewhat by the atmosphere in which she works. Her attitude remains very refreshing and straightforward, and I should imagine both sides must have found the initial experience fascinating, to say the least, but clearly the experiment has been highly successful. Once again, a great deal has been achieved with little extra cost.

The Rape Crisis Centre for London has been less fortunate. It has been trying unsuccessfully since its inception in 1976 to arrange discussions with the Metropolitan Police. They do not seek official collaboration which they fear would spell the end of confidentiality between themselves and their clients, but they are very interested in discussing with the police the question of friendly cooperation. Unfortunately the Metropolitan Police have not responded positively: the London Rape Crisis Centre have made several approaches to them and have also tried working through the Home Office and even the House of Commons with the aid of the indefatigable reformer, Jack Ashley, but with no success. The reply has always been that the police cannot see that any useful purpose would be achieved in arranging the interview requested by the Rape Crisis Centre. I find this attitude disappointing in the light of advances in cooperation between the police and other professionals in the field of physical child abuse. The volunteers at the Rape Crisis Centre, of course, are primarily concerned with rape rather than with incest, but like their sisters in the USA they are finding increasing numbers of incest cases are being reported. In working out statistics they have not separated out family sexual abuse from other kinds of sexual abuse, but figures for April 1978 to April 1979 showed that 2 per cent of the victims were under nine, 20 per cent were between ten and fifteen, and 31 per cent were between sixteen and twenty; i.e. 53 per cent were under twenty. American experience suggests that probably quite a high proportion of these girls had been incestuously assaulted.

Part of the police objection seems to lie in the necessity for confidentiality on the part of the centre; another factor that worried them was that some of the volunteers worked under pseudonyms though the centre's policy now is to show ID cards if requested. Fortunately for London's rape victims there are a number of ordinary constables on the beat who admire the centre's work and who have contacted the centre on their own initiative to find out more about them, but any help to victims via the police has to come through the individual policeman and policewoman's advice rather than from any official directive.

The Rape Crisis Centre in Birmingham, on the other hand, has a more cooperative police force, whose chief constable, I am told, holds the work they are doing in high esteem. The centre's existence is officially acknowledged, and the volunteers are allowed to accompany victims to the police stations and the courts. Victims who are unaware of the existence of the Rape Crisis Centre are often (but not invariably, even here) told about it. So successful has this cooperation been that recently the centre was invited to arrange in-service training with the police on the subject of rape, and have been happy to accept. Other suggestions for cooperation have also been made by the police, but not all are acceptable, partly because of the ever-present concern that if the centre is too widely-linked with the police victims may not approach it out of fear their names will be disclosed and they will have to go through the whole trauma of appearing in court, etc. The centre's policy is to neither discourage nor encourage the victims to report to the police, and the police know and accept this attitude on the part of the Rape Crisis Centre.

This situation is still a long way from what has been achieved in Minneapolis – on the other hand until worthwhile family treatment, some form of diversion and other reforms have been achieved (I am discussing here non-violent incest offenders, not rapists) there can be no question of close collaboration of the kind existing between Deborah Anderson and her district attorney's office.

In other areas in the United States the social services have been the main source of aid, but using resources already available to them. The frequently quoted Sexual Assault Center at the Harborview Medical Center was set up in 1973 with a Law Enforcement Assistance Administration grant as a unit within the Social Services Department of Harborview Medical Center – a university-administrated hospital housing the central emergency room for the Seattle, Washington, area. The SAC staff consists of consultant paediatricians and gynaecologists, social workers and clerical staff, together with the staff of the emergency room who provide a 24-hour service. Again, there is successful cooperation with law enforcement agencies, therapists and other professionals concerned with the family. Although the Sexual Assault Center was not set up with children particularly in mind approximately half of the sexual assault victims seen are under sixteen years of age, and nearly half of these are incest victims.

Finally I would like to mention again Barbara Myers' group at Christopher Street which will be discussed in more detail in the next chapter dealing with treatment. Barbara Myers, herself once a prostitute, has founded a very successful therapy group and travels widely lecturing on her work with incest victims. There are many such women around whose personal experiences have become the foundation of an unexpectedly useful new life; in Britain for example, Pat Stevens, one of the founders of the British Parents Anonymous, used her own difficulties with parenthood to aid other parents. There is an unlimited amount of talent waiting to be used and a vast number of people needing to be helped. The tapping of this talent, combined with a change of heart on the part of those presently unwilling to alter their less than sympathetic attitude towards incest offenders, could dramatically improve the future prospects of many thousands of incest victims.

I will finish this chapter with a quotation from Hank Giarretto that could equally be used to open the next and final chapter. He is discussing the CSATP treatment model, which is based on humanistic principles:

A central notion . . . is the building of social responsibility, the realization that each of us is an important element of society. We must actively participate in the development of social attitudes and laws or be helplessly controlled by them. . . . It is important to mention that the humanistic umbrella includes . . . all the individuals representing the intervening agencies when an incestuous family is reported to the authorities. Particularly sensitive are our relations with law enforcement personnel who are inclined to view the humanistic approach as soft and unrealistic. . . . if [policemen, probation officers, lawyers and judges] are attacked, through arm-waving, righteous indignation, or insidiously by the piety that often contaminates humanism, an adversary situation develops that further victimizes the clients. We try, instead, to convince them by demonstration that a supportive approach is more effective than a punitive one in the treatment of troubled families, and is much less costly to the community (Giarretto 1978).

Chapter 9

Collaboration and treatment

The five primary disciplines that deal with the sexual abuse of children are: medical, legal, law enforcement, social services, and schools. But the way these disciplines work – often they are as crazy if not crazier than the families we deal with. We scapegoat each other, we don't understand each other's roles, often we have much worse communication than the families we are dealing with. We bicker, we fight, each of us thinks *we* are right. In all, we're very much like those families we are supposed to be helping – we're a dysfunctional family of services.

This comment is from a professional who works in an area which is very much more cooperative than most, and yet she still expresses the problems which have to be faced when different disciplines attempt to come together.

Basically we're trying to mesh social services and legal requirements, and they're oil and water, you just can't mix them. They each think differently, have different rules, view life differently. They need hours and hours of talk together to understand each other. Lawyers are very confused on this issue, because they know the law but they've never been trained about children, except for Juvenile Law. And social workers don't really worry about an action being constitutionally sound, which it should be, it needs to be. There's a lot more work to be done before we can really work out this dilemma.'

This basic problem of different attitudes first became clear to me when I was writing *Children in Danger* and came to realize that lack of cooperation was allowing many battered children to fall through the net of public care. In theory, and in some cases in practice, this problem has been solved, but still we repeatedly read in the newspapers of children who have died because something went badly wrong with the coordination of public services. Investigations are made, reports drawn up, and we hear that such a mistake cannot happen again, but sooner or later, sometimes in a frighteningly short time, it does. Progress has certainly been made, but it is a slow process even where intentions are impeccable.

As yet, not even these intentions exist in many areas as far as incest is concerned. The question of cooperation has come up again and again in this book, but I am stressing it here. because this chapter is dealing mainly with treatment, and no treatment can hope to be successful unless it is multi-disciplinary. When members of different disciplines work together it is inevitable that sometimes feelings are going to be hurt, people will consider their views are being ignored or ridden over, frustration and anger will sometimes cloud judgments about the worth of other members of a case conference who are meant to be your allies but who seem determined to be your enemy. But somehow these problems have to be overcome. They are not unique to any one set of social services, any one particular police force. They occur everywhere, no matter how fine the intention. Just as incestuous fathers, battering parents and victims of both are relieved and their burden lightened by the knowledge that others are suffering exactly their pain, their confusion, so the following quotation from a senior clinical psychologist might possibly relieve those professionals who are in despair about ever achieving the quality of cooperation they are seeking and whose plight is not made better by a sneaking suspicion that perhaps they themselves are not a hundred per cent in the clear.

Communication and coordination of activity does not happen naturally or easily between different professional groups or across agency lines. Ongoing efforts are required to bridge the barriers between professional groups. Each group has its own values, goals, language, role expectations, and view of reality. These can and often do become barriers to the understanding and trust necessary for good working relationships. We probably all agree in general that we should communicate and cooperate with one another, but, as we encounter stress and conflicts in our daily efforts with these especially difficult cases, it is easy to retreat into blame, withdrawal and mutual hostility. It is these human responses that the team is designed to counteract (Muldoon 1979).

It is difficult to achieve total coordination without one particular person or agency agreeing to take basic responsibility for seeing that the family receives all the help that is available. And the family's needs are immense: firstly the victim may need medical aid and/or temporary fostering; she or he will probably need psychiatric care and therapy, as will the rest of the family including the offender. If the last is the father and he is removed from the home the family may need practical help such as money, food, housing and, at the very least, emotional support through the trauma of the early days. They will need to be helped to understand the legal processes – what their rights are, what to do if the mother decides to apply for divorce or wants to attempt a reconciliation, whether the child will have to testify against the father and how to prepare her – the list is endless.

Before the case reaches the courts many reports have to be pre-pared – police, medical, and psychological and psychiatric evalu-ations, reports from the victim's school and from health visitors or social workers if a family has already been receiving treatment for other reasons. In court social workers sometimes have difficulty in overcoming the complications of the law and may not always set about the right way of achieving what they want for their clients. In criminal court they may be facing a prosecution whose sole aim is to achieve for the offender as lengthy a jail sentence as possible, regardless of the needs of the family as a whole.

No one service can fully answer all these needs. Everyone's bur-den will be considerably eased if multi-disciplinary case conferences are held very early on, with a genuine desire for coordination of effort on everybody's part. One great advantage of such cooperation is that no single person has to feel overwhelmed by the sense of total responsibility which has been the main cause of many cases of burn-out. Also, individual reactions to any particular case must vary; in dealing with child abuse, sexual or physical, it is almost impossible for any worker to invariably maintain objective judgment at all times. There will be many occasions when the sheer relief of being able to share the burden with colleagues from other disciplines will outweigh any irritations that might arise through the conflict of differing sets of values.

A major problem facing professionals is that involvement with incest families makes unique demands on them. The combination of an-cient taboo, forbidden sex, abused children and offenders who themselves may have been abused sets up a situation so loaded with potential inner conflict for the worker that it is no wonder many close their eyes and pretend not to see what is going on.

Some openly feel disgust or revulsion when investigating a case and see this reaction as morally appropriate. At the same time a kind of fascination with the details of the case may be experienced which heightens the worker's uneasiness and probably results in an increase of disgust directed at the offender and perhaps also at the victim. This type of reaction can have disastrous consequences. Self-knowledge is an essential tool for anyone working with incest cases, self-knowledge of a deeper kind than is needed for any other work, involving feelings about sexuality and buried memories of childhood. Clients are very quick to pick up nuances, and any suspicion on their part that they are being condemned will probably result in a drying-up of confidences and the withdrawal of the family from cooperation. Giarretto, writing about this problem, explained how in the first case he dealt with he found it easy to maintain a warm acceptance of the mother and the child. But then, preparing for working with the father, he read

> the lurid details in the police report of his sexual activities with his daughter which included mutual oral copulation and sodomy at age ten. The compassionate attitude which I now write about so freely completely fell apart and I felt murderous instead. I forced myself to go into deep exploration of my unconscious for my own incestuous impulses. Although I had just begun the endless task of working through the incest-related garbage within me, I felt I could at least face my client. When I actually met with him, my problem was much less difficult than I had anticipated. His despair and confusion needed to be attended to and my hang-ups were set aside for the time being (Giarretto 1978).

For young counsellors working in this field there can be the added difficulty that they may still be working through various sexual conflicts of their own and it may be almost impossible for them to maintain a necessary detachment from the young client. After all, the information that has to be discovered needs to be extremely detailed, while at the same time the questions must be carefully organized so that give-away details come from the victim, not from the investigator. The worker needs to know: did the child have to put her hand on the man's penis, did he touch her breasts, did he insert fingers inside her, what happened to his penis, did it become hard, etc. A child will probably not know the correct terminology, and the 'etc.' so quickly written has to be spelt out graphically using the child's own words, with phrases such as 'what did the juice taste like?' to verify the child is telling the truth and to discover exactly what the perpetrator did. Such intimate questions do not come easily to most of us, especially when they have to be asked of a distressed child. It is vital therefore that the worker is comfortable with his or her own sexuality and can give all of his attention to putting the child at ease and forming a warm relationship in which the victim can confidently talk about what has happened to her.

Incest families have difficulty in trusting other people and expect disapproval and condemnation, so it is important for professionals to be honest about their own reactions – this is particularly so when dealing with possible punishment of the father. If an investigating social worker will have to report any incriminating details revealed to him, he should make this clear. To say that he has come to help the family, then to be responsible for the father's incarceration, is dishonest and will make future work with the family virtually impossible. If these two functions of reporting and of help can be separated out and dealt with by different agencies this is by far the best method. If the initial contact is with a social worker who has no option but to report the case then he or she must be honest with the client, but at the same time the importance of accepting help can be explained, along with the worker's belief that if nothing is done the abuse will probably continue, and that if and when the offender is at last brought to court he will probably have a far heavier sentence than if the whole family cooperated at this earlier stage.

Many parents will still refuse to cooperate, and may put the blame for everything that has happened on to the child, or they may insist that she is 'ruined forever' and they cannot continue to keep her in the same house as their other 'innocent' children. When this happens psychiatric treatment for the entire family sometimes helps, or there may be no choice but to remove the victim and place her in a foster home. It is essential that therapists are familiar with the psychology of incest families and do not expect too much. I was told about one self-reported couple who were seen over a period of a year by two therapists, during which time the father continued to molest his daughter. The two therapists had not reported the original incest nor did they openly tackle the father about his sexual

behaviour, assuming that because the parents had referred themselves to the clinic the incest must have ceased. The family was
deeply relieved when they were reported to the authorities by someone else who had learned of the continuing incest, and that it was
at last being dealt with openly. This is not an uncommon situation
and therapists need to be aware just how compulsive the fathers'
actions are, in spite of their strong desire to change their behaviour.
Geri Hatcher (personal communication), said

> You need special training for this. For neurotic families, for
> instance, you don't use a directive kind of therapy, but for
> these families you need to, you must provide a lot of
> structuring. You really have to parent them, keep at them –
> you cannot let a person break a court order and get away with
> it, for example. Many therapists don't like acting this way, but
> with incest families you have to, or they just get nowhere with
> treatment.

In group therapy it is often customary to select two therapists of
opposite sex. This situation has its own special problems. The
victims, though wanting nurturance from both therapists, will often
play one off against the other in their attempts to come to terms
with what has happened to them. Ruth Kempe at a CIBA meeting
in London in 1981 described how in such a group the girls first
turned to the male therapist for love and attention, ignoring the
female therapist. The male therapist had difficulty with this until
he understood what was happening, then he was able to explain to
the girls what they were doing and to assure them that although he
would willingly give them the love and attention they wanted that
was all they were going to get. After they had reassured themselves
on this they were then able to turn to the female therapist and ask
the same of her. Commonly victims try to sexualize any male/female
situation and it is very important they learn it is possible to have a
warm and close contact with a member of the opposite sex without
sexuality being involved; obviously this is not always easy for a male
when the victim is an attractive adolescent who has become sexually
uninhibited through years of practice. They must also learn something not learned from their mothers, that it is possible to have a
warm nurturant contact with a member of the same sex, that women
can support other women, and that there does not have to be a
rivalry for the attentions of any available male.
Bruce Gottlieb has written an interesting paper on this subject,

together with his co-therapist Janet Dean (1981). Because of the pressure coming from their group of adolescents the two therapists found it necessary to discuss privately at a fairly profound level various issues concerning sex, including any possible sexual attraction between themselves and also their relations with their partners. The girls would make comments about how they imagined the two therapists behaved together when no one was looking, for example, and would ask what the male therapist's wife would think about such a liaison. Because the therapists had discussed all aspects of their own sexuality with each other they were able to be open with the girls, to whom a useful example was given of how two people of opposite sex could work together in a close friendly relationship without it necessarily having to be sexualized. Once this difficulty had been dealt with and trust established the girls then attempted to set off the therapists against each other (as happened in Ruth Kempe's group), working out their own feelings relating to their mothers and their fathers through these new 'family' figures. The importance of the working relationship the two therapists had established outside the group now became even more obvious – although even with the advantage of mutual understanding neither of them found it always easy to remain calm and balanced when pressure was put on them by the group members.

Doctors have their own problems in coping with incest. Unless the patient has been brought in specifically because of sexual abuse, many find it almost inconceivable that the small child in front of them could have been sexually molested and do not consider the possibility when making a medical examination. Many cases of gonorrhea, for example, are overlooked or ascribed to causes that would never be put forward in the cases of adults, such as infection through sleeping on germ-laden sheets. I met at a children's group a pretty little child of five who for a long time had been incorrectly diagnosed. When she was two and a half her father had started having intercourse with her. Being sore around the genital area she often touched herself there, and when it was found she had a badly-torn vagina it was thought that she herself had caused the damage through pushing objects up herself in attempts at masturbation. Some time passed before it was discovered that it was her father who had injured her and that he was still sexually abusing her, even while she was being treated by the doctor.

Genital injuries, persistent irritations and discharge may be caused by sexual abuse, but too often doctors treat these symptoms without looking for a cause (Rosenfeld 1979c). Other symptoms may be unusually frequent masturbation, or an exaggerated interest in sex play with other children. Victims sometimes complain of headaches, stomach-aches and other psychosomatic problems. Muldoon (1979) gives the following list of possible symptoms; a marked distrust on the part of the patient towards the examining physician, with the patient demanding to know what part of the body will be touched; low self-esteem, headaches, hysterical-type symptoms; rebellious or acting-out behaviour; poor work or attendance at school; excessive fear or clinging behaviour; the onset of bedwetting, especially among older girls; marked seductive behaviour and an unusual preoccupation with sex. Early pregnancy may also be due to incestuous activity, though family pressure may cause a child to deny it.

Obviously it is very important that a physical examination is not forced upon a child and is only carried out when her or his cooperation has been fully gained. This can take time and great sensitivity on the part of the doctor. Unfortunately in many cases when the discovery of incest has been made through an outside source the child may be picked up and taken to some place of authority where she may have to sit around in a waiting-room for some time, being looked at with curiosity, before she is finally examined by a doctor who may have had no training in dealing with this sort of case. If she is adolescent and the doctor either suspects her of lying or of having 'asked for it', his examination is likely to be curt and insensitive. If the victim is small the doctor will probably be both angry and embarrassed, and his disturbance may come through to the child as an unkind lack of sympathy, adding further pain to an already traumatic experience.

Having looked at some of the problems facing professionals, it is important to repeat that I was often told that the prognosis for most incest families receiving proper treatment is excellent. This does not include multi-problem families whose needs are so great that a whole battery of help would have to be called in and years of aid given before a lasting difference was made. Nor does it include certain offenders who cannot or will not accept treatment. Giarretto (1976) suggests that some 10 per cent of offenders cannot be reached, at least with present methods. Rosenfeld and Newberger (1977) write of the dangers implicit in the compassionate approach, one of which is that

over-identification with an abusive parent can be paralysing. We have seen injuries and fatalities that are traceable to a physician's, nurse's, social worker's, or judge's inability to act on perceived danger for want of alienating the parents. Fused with utopian notions about the curative power of love and genuine concern, the compassionate model may also demoralize professionals when the treatment relationship proves hopeless.

He is talking here about child abuse in general, but the same remarks apply to child sexual abuse.

The first essential for successful treatment, then, is a willingness by the family, including the offender (though his willingness may need to be reinforced by a court order) to receive treatment over a prescribed period of time. On the part of the offender, at least, this should be for a minimum of a year, and more probably two years. Giarretto and others have reported that a single hour of weekly therapy is unlikely to be sufficient to effect a change, and that too often offenders continue to molest victims even while undergoing this form of treatment.

The next essential is to find the most appropriate type of therapy for the individual concerned. To quote Dr Gene Abel, referring to his studies on deviant arousal in adult males:

Treatment must be individually tailored for each patient to take into account his specific treatment needs. The traditional view of psychiatry and psychology of applying one treatment, such as aversion therapy or psychotherapy, to every type of disorder now seems outdated and is giving way to the development of specific treatments for specific problems. The assessment and treatment of sexual aggressives are no exception to this approach.

While aversion therapy has its proponents, many people have an instinctive dislike of it. There is also a widespread feeling that molesters have already suppressed so much in their lives that to use aversion therapy to make them suppress themselves even further is merely to compound the problem. Those against aversion therapy believe that undesirable behaviour is not eradicated, only temporarily crushed, and that while such therapy may be effective in the short term, in the long run it is a waste of time. I was told there was no proof to the contrary, and certainly I have not yet come across any.

To achieve a permanent improvement it is essential that the

offender's whole attitude be changed, and that while standard psychotherapy of the kind which is only interested in the offender's first few years of life does not seem to work, therapy which allows the offender to explore his entire life, his feelings and compulsions, does. Wenet, for example, said:

> It is not until the offenders (so many of whom have been victims themselves) begin dealing with their own experience of being a victim that they seem to appreciate the impact that *their* behaviour has had on their victims. Sexual offenders tend not to accept responsibility for their behaviour and that's the thrust of our treatment programme, to try and develop a greater sense of responsibility, a greater sense of control (personal communication).

Those who find aversion therapy a useful tool see the inappropriate sexual behaviour as the primary problem, and believe that if this is changed and appropriate behaviour substituted, then the main problem is solved. Doris Stevens, working at the Sexual Assault Center, Seattle, said:

> We've come to this conclusion not through research but through clinical experience. We've done quite a bit of work with offenders who have repented, were sorry for what they had done and got supportive help or some kind of traditional psychotherapy, but whom we found were still continuing to molest their own or other children. We believe pretty much that incest is not a result of dysfunctional problems within a family culminating in incest and other kinds of maladaptive behaviour; we believe that because a member of the family – usually the father – has a sexual deviancy, that that causes other problems in the family. I truly don't believe that just by doing family therapy or supportive groups (which are necessary and helpful), that you can correct the problem of the man. He will still have his sexual attraction and arousal to children. This has to be treated. When we started we didn't think too much about the fathers – it was the victims we were concerned with – but we came to realize that what happened to the father was crucial to the outcome, and that you cannot separate the two problems (personal communication).

Roger Wolfe and his wife, whom we have previously quoted, are psychologists who believe whole-heartedly in their own form of

aversion therapy (covert conditioning) and who treat many of the
men passing through the Seattle Sexual Assault Center. They explained to me how their groups work:

> It's very structured, with a new leader being elected each week.
> They have a lot of homework – they write out their sexual
> feelings, what they did, then read it out to the group. Almost
> invariably the first time it's very sugar-coated, and the group
> knows this and tells them to go back and do it again. They
> have to do a lot of work in group, answering questions, being
> truthful, and after a bit they get full of insight, talk like
> messiahs, and that's really rich for the newcomers. But we
> believe that – like alcoholics – once a sex offender, always a sex
> offender. The potential is always there. So our approach is very
> behavioural. When they're ready they have individual therapy,
> where we do some really straightforward conditioning things.
> We want to wipe out the deviant attractions and enhance the
> appropriate attractions. We use imagery for this. We have him
> replay his outlet pattern while he's deeply relaxed – we use
> drugs, deep muscle relaxation, deep hypnosis – and we try to
> get him to imagine vividly, say, that he's walking up to the
> bedroom door, getting ready to approach the child, we get him
> to really live it. Then we change the script, shift it over to the
> most aversive, terrible imagery we can think about. We spend a
> lot of time working with the men to find out what really shuts
> them down. Say it's spiders – he opens the door and the room
> is filled with spiders and he slips and falls and everywhere there
> are spiders crawling all over his body. We don't use films or
> anything like that – it's much more powerful when it's self-
> created. We put it on a tape and he takes it home and listens to
> it every day.

The Wolfes do not use electric shock treatment or nausea-induc-
ing drugs, but they have found overt conditioning with the use of
bad smells helpful for persistent offenders with really severe compulsions. The individual treatment, which because of the use of
tapes at home is on a daily basis, is continued for three or four
months and makes a considerable impact. The offenders continue
to work with the group for a year or so. The Wolfes cannot recall
a single case of recidivism among those they have treated, though
of course if the offenders had moved to another state it is unlikely
they would have heard about them. I was, however, left with a

worry about future relations between father and daughter if, whenever he thought of touching her, he imagined spiders or whatever. Warm touching is so essential to a child's growth – how, under these circumstances, could this be achieved?

What has become clear to me during my research is that, ultimately, it is less the type of treatment that is given to an offender that counts, than the quality of the treatment received. Giarretto reports over many years of therapy with large numbers of people a recidivism rate of 0.6 per cent. This is a remarkable achievement, especially bearing in mind that Giarretto's programme, like the Wolfes, has treated many sexual cases who had previously received treatment elsewhere which had not worked at all. Wolfe's reply to my comment to him about quality was: 'What all these successful programmes have in common is that they focus specifically on the problem of sexual behaviour. That's what is necessary.' In fact, the majority of professionals seem to consider family dynamics to be at the root of the problem, and that that is where the focus of the treatment should be. But it is certainly true that the successful programmes do not fudge the issue of the responsibility of the offender for his harmful sexual behaviour, and this aspect is dealt with on an individual basis.

Giarretto's methods are perhaps the ones most opposed to any form of aversion therapy. Many of his beliefs have already been mentioned, and probably a general picture of how he and his colleagues work has already been gained, but it will be useful to explain the methods in more detail.

Since the Child Sexual Abuse Treatment Program (CSATP) had its beginnings in Santa Clara County (California) Juvenile Probation Department, cooperation with the legal enforcement agencies has always been a necessary part of their procedures. There could never be any question, as with some social service personnel both in the United States and in Britain, of the law not being informed when new cases are discovered. A great advantage of their cooperative work with other agencies is that CSATP has immediate access to emergency housing, educational and legal services, assistance with employment, and other services. But even CSATP were not able to avoid money problems, which became increasingly severe as its reputation grew and inquiries for information and training came in from all over the United States. State and federal funding now helps with CSATP's ever-increasing responsibilities not only to its own locality but as a centre of training, but as its fame has spread even further afield so have the demands on it.

One interesting aspect of CSATP is that Santa Clara County is primarily a middle-class suburban community with a large professional population, which provides its full share of incest families. This has meant that CSATP's findings have disproved those of earlier workers which gave the erroneous impression that incest was strictly confined to the deprived classes: CSATP has shown that this is not so, and that incest is to be found among every race and class.

In spite of the police being aware of every reported case, over half of the known offenders were not sent to jail. A most important result of this is that by 1978 referrals from people 'heretofore fearful of reporting the problem' had grown to 39 per cent of the total. A survey of 127 cases showed that the men who were incarcerated (20 per cent of the total – litigation was still pending in the case of the others or no further information was available) spent between 1 to 365 days in jail, the mean time being 143.5 days, a considerably shorter period than is usual for sexual abuse cases. A further important statistic is that over half the child victims never left home at all, and of those who did leave but returned home later their absence ranged from 7 to 450 days, with a mean time of 150 days. The conclusion drawn from the available figures was that 92 per cent of the victims receiving counselling through CSATP would eventually be returned to their homes.

This high figure owes much to the foundation, early on in the programme, of groups for the parents and the children, known as Parents United, and Daughters and Sons United. So successful have these been that by 1979 there were twenty chapters of Parents United in California alone, and the number is still growing. Other states have set up their own chapters, but at the time of writing there are none in Britain, although this will probably be set right soon. Parents United are basically self-help groups formed by families who have been through CSATP, but professional counselling is available along with an extraordinary number of specialized groups, ranging from 'couples' groups which help couples learn how to communicate (usually the most serious difficulty between parents), through men's groups, groups for mothers molested as children, orientation groups and a human sexuality class. Daughters and Sons United (to which affected siblings as well as the victims can come) helps children from five to eighteen years of age adapt to what has happened to them, and includes a play therapy group, a pre-adolescent girls' group and a similar one for boys, and other groups for the older children. Although professional help plays an important part the main support is given by members who themselves have been through the trauma of incest and its public discovery and who can convey sympathy, based on personal experience.

The involvement of a newly referred incest family with the whole CSATP set-up is immediate (remember John's story from Chapter 1). The programme coordinator draws together all the other agencies involved and assigns a counsellor to the new family. The parents are contacted by Parents United members who take them under the group's wing, as do members of the children's groups with the victims. Counselling begins straight away for everyone, offender included, which is helpful in evaluating what his sentence should be. He may be sent to the Elmwood Rehabilitation Center, a kind of open prison, from which a man if thought suitable is allowed to go daily to his work (without his employer or friends necessarily knowing what has happened to him – he might be coming from home as far as they know); arrangements are also made for him to attend individual counselling and Parents United meetings. When both are ready father and child meet at family counselling sessions, usually within the first three months.

Because of this sensible approach, by the time the man is freed he is well on the way to rehabilitation, unlike so many prisoners released from normal jails where they have regressed rather than progressed as far as social skills are concerned. Most families receive professional counselling for about eight months, while they continue with Parents United for at least a year. Many stay on longer and help others, while a few, like John, become paid workers in the field. The length of time children are involved in counselling is more variable, depending on individual cases and how far the father takes full responsibility for what he has done, and ranges from three months to a year or so.

The success of CSATP is undoubted. An independent evaluator, after painstakingly working through results, asked rather breathlessly how one was supposed to keep a sense of unbiased distance when examining a programme in which he has seen that

1 in every 2 victims enters therapy showing some nervous symptoms while 9 in 10 leave it without any such symptoms; when he sees that for every county that sends one of its social workers or counsellors to CSATP for a brief two-week

workshop, 68 per cent will ultimately initiate new programmes directly as a result of the idealism and inspiration which derive from this training experience. . .

A further important gain has been that the self-abuse behaviour of victimized children, 'usually amplified after exposure of the incestual situation, has been reduced both in intensity and duration' (Giarretto 1976).

The personal philosophy of Hank Giarretto has played a major part both in the organization and in the success of CSATP. He is not always the simplest of speakers as he likes to elucidate points that seem important to him, and if – as is often the case – it is a philosophical point at issue he may well lose a listener uninterested in following such talk. I have heard people comment after he has spoken that they heard nothing new, that he gave nothing but obvious truths. Giarretto would be the first to agree with them – what he says has been going the rounds for some thousands of years. If people had been acting on these truths all those years there would be no need for Giarretto's work now. An example of how he speaks is:

> You have to recognize they're not *them out there* – they're my
> brothers and sisters. It's an I-thou respect for humanity. We all
> have parts we would rather not have. If you do not respect each
> other as human beings, respect each other's intrinsic value and
> intrinsic viability, then we can't help each other – you see? And
> so our caring is very pragmatic, very practical. Uncaring,
> unbridled competition, adversary relationships are not practical.
> Parents United aims at creating an environment for what I call
> resocialization. In other words, to put it bluntly, it takes a lot
> of people to screw these people up, and it'll take a lot of people
> to set them straight (personal communication).

He writes in his paper, 'Humanistic treatment of father-daughter incest', how he arrived at the 'humanistic orientation which guides CSATP', and refers to work of humanistic psychology, in particular that of Robert Assagioli, Berne, Chaudhuri and Maslow. His approach, he writes, is

> fundamentally different from the medical model which tries to
> identify pathology or mental disturbances in the major role
> players of an incestuous situation. . . . If I face my client busily
> trying to plug him into some pet theory, I defraud both of us of

the rich potential inherent in an I-Thou relationship. . . . The purpose is not to extinguish or modify dysfunctional behaviour by external devices or to cure 'mental disease'. Rather, we try to help each client develop the habit of self-awareness (the foundation for self-esteem) and the ability to direct one's own behaviour and life-style. But it is essential they probe the painful areas connected with the incest. . . I tell them that buried feelings (fear, guilt, shame, anger), if not confronted, will return as ghosts to harass them. If confronted now, they will lose their power to hurt them in the future (Giarretto 1978).

Talking to me about first-time visits by new members to a Parents United group, he said:

They all come, accompanied by older members – the father if he's available and the youngster too – and they see other people who seem to be doing well, whereas previously they'd seen themselves as unique, a derelict family. Immediately they're given hope. And mothers who had resolved to divorce their husbands see other couples doing quite well, and the eventual result is that 90 per cent of the marriages are saved – this in a locality which has a 50 per cent divorce rate! We don't set out to save marriages, but these people begin to talk to each other, perhaps for the first time ever.

For Giarretto, the mother/daughter relationship is sacrosanct, and it is on the establishment of this relationship that efforts are con-centrated. At the same time the self-esteem of the mother is built up.

The therapy programme is often – feministic, if you will – because we say to this woman, do you really want to stay with this man, are you staying because of economic fear, because of loss of status, and we build her up so she can make a decision based on her own needs. Interestingly enough, as the woman gains in stature, becomes more assertive, more independent, so at first the man is frightened a little bit, then he finds he has a richer personality to deal with. It uncovers part of themselves they didn't suspect. And they like it. Though it doesn't work in all cases – we have our failures (personal communication).

The issue of feminism has a bearing on the way various profes-sionals view the importance of the father. As we have seen, many women have become involved in child sexual abuse through participation in women's groups and rape centres, where incest has been seen primarily as a father/daughter offence, with the female as a helpless victim. We have discussed this aspect elsewhere, but it should be borne in mind that feminists have a natural bias towards wanting to see women independent, able to make up their own minds. I refer to this because many workers with feminist convictions consider that too often children who would rather leave home and get entirely away from their fathers are pushed into remaining because of the common social worker conviction that the family is nearly always the best place for a child to grow up in. Among others, Lucy Berliner (Sexual Assault Center, Seattle) expressed this view to me:

> I think that most kids after incest don't in fact feel closeness or affection towards the father, so they are put in a psychological bind which is reinforced by most mental health professionals who believe that all children want to stay with their families and that is better for them. And that if the guy makes any effort at all, even if it is the most minimal effort, the mother and child should forgive him and help him and support him. People do not encourage kids to say, hey, I don't want ever to see you again. Whenever do you see any support for a kid saying that? Here we don't tell kids what to feel. We want them to feel whatever *they* want to feel. And whatever they feel, we say to them – that's normal, if that's what you feel, that's fine. Because dad will have been telling them they're to blame if he's found out, or they get given the impression they're to blame if the family break up. They hardly know what they do feel, and it's up to us to help them find out.

This is certainly a valid argument. On the other hand if the daughter's relationship with the father can be put on a new and healthy basis only good can result. As Joyce Moulton, who has made several films of her sexual abuse workshops, commented:

> Our own fathers are the only real fathers we've got. We might know what we'd like, but we also know what we've got. The natural father is the basic acceptance of ourselves. In children given up for adoption at some level they feel rejected. I'm not going to call it love, but it's a need to belong. As children we identify our 'alrightness' with who cares about us (personal communication).

In talking in glowing terms about treatment such as the CSATP at San José, Santa Clara, it is easy to forget the hard work that lies behind the success stories. Of course it would be marvellous if the father could simply hold out his arms and have the child run into them, in safety and love. But watching damaged children make the first steps towards rehabilitation is a painful experience, and among very young ones in particular the length of the journey to be travelled can be imagined only too vividly. I spent some hours observing a small group of children between the ages of three to six playing in a special nursery – boys as well as girls. Several therapists were with them, almost one to every two children, and the amount of attention the children needed was phenomenal. Sometimes the play was overtly sexual, while home-making (building up 'houses' with boxes and blankets which were often destroyed again, either by the maker or another child) was an obsession with most of them. Their aggression and anger was worked out on the dolls or sometimes on each other, but tenderness too, sometimes heartbreakingly so. Emotive words are difficult to avoid when speaking of damaged children; it is not easy to remain detached when watching, say, a four-year-old girl who has had vaginal surgery because of her father's sexual molestation, express her problems in play form. It is also deeply disturbing when an already tough little boy of five who has been the subject of anal abuse, also by his father, throws a tantrum and becomes abusive – it is only too easy to imagine what emotional and physical chaos he may be causing around him in twenty years time. He might be lucky and manage to work through his problems, but there are few such therapy groups in the world, and there can never be enough devoted people to give every damaged child the warmth and care he or she needs.

New methods of coping with victims need to be worked out so that where intensive individual therapy is not possible some other method can be substituted. Mavis Tsai, at the University of Washington, has been comparing different types of therapy, and in particular the use of video-tapes. At the time of writing her work on this last had not yet been consolidated, but she considers video-tape therapy has a very useful future where help has to be limited for economic or other reasons. Briefly, she and her colleagues made video-tapes of their clients in therapy groups – the women, who had been molested as children, were willing to cooperate in the experiment as they had found the most helpful part of the group treatment was being able to listen to other members talking about their experiences and their problems. A number of new clients, also women who had been molested when young, were shown these tapes (which lasted an hour and a half) individually each week for five weeks (sometimes bringing their spouses). Live contact with staff was deliberately limited to ten minutes or so, and usually undergraduate or other non-professional help was used. Certain skills were taught and homework assignments, similar to those used in individual therapy, were set. Analysis of the data had not been carried out, but when explaining the study to me Tsai commented it had been evident that the women had found the treatment, short as it was, very helpful – not as helpful as actually being present in a live group, but very well worth doing.

Another experiment carried out by Tsai and her colleagues was a one-day workshop for molested women and their partners, which was apparently also a success. In addition to the therapeutic aid given the clients, the workshop provided useful information on the special difficulties such partners face, which is discussed elsewhere in this book.

When time is very limited different techniques to the more usual slow-moving methods have to be used. In Colorado a confrontive method was used for a while, but this was eventually abandoned because of press publicity after complaints from certain victims who had found the experience distressing. Nevertheless, there are inter-esting lessons to be learned from it, for it had many successes. Basically, Pat Wyka, director of the Victim Services Division of the Colorado Springs Police, built up a series of groups to help victims of sexual assault. The division was never intended to provide long-term therapy and Wyka believes that if any worthwhile results were to be obtained in the few weeks available methods would have to be pretty drastic. In many ways the set-up of the groups was similar to those of others I have seen – there were separate groups for young children, adolescents, older victims. Each group had to make a 'contract' among themselves regarding how they would behave. Officially each contract was arrived at freshly, but they were basically all very similar – members had to be honest, supportive of others but were not to give them advice (because change can only come about by direct understanding of oneself and cannot be im-posed by others). Members must not be made to feel put down, or used, or rejected, and other members must not be made use of (by persuading them to give the wrong sort of help). Loud anger could be expressed, but there was to be no violence.

The feeling in the groups was unquestionably warm and very friendly. At first, the younger ones played verbal games which explored their feelings about themselves, while the older ones behaved much as the other therapy groups I had visited. The two therapists who sat in on the groups made a determined effort to be democratic (one therapist, for example, was proving unpopular, and the children freely discussed her shortcomings in front of her), but if any of the children refused to follow the expected path the leaders' control began to show through. And it was when this point was reached that my own personal difficulty in accepting the programme occurred. The most offensive session for me was among a group of adolescents, which at first I had found inspiring in its warmth and mutual honesty. Then a girl of fourteen or so who had been totally silent was asked why she had not joined in the talk. Very reluctantly she said she wanted to go back home and, pressed further, that she loved her father and she knew he had changed, and that he and her whole family needed her. She looked so sad, so careworn and hurt as she spoke that I was appalled at what then happened. She was repeatedly, relentlessly challenged about her father's love and his ability to change, which clearly distressed her more and more. Why, she asked, did the group always look on the worst side, why wouldn't they accept that people could change? Pat Wyka was goading the group on by now, saying that the girl was being dishonest, cheating on the contract, was taking advantage of them and were they going to let her get away with it? Taking her lead, the group intensified their attack. When after some time the girl still insisted she wanted to go home and that she knew her father had changed the group finally decided to 'get her on the floor', which meant quite literally that. Gently, but very firmly, they pulled her down onto the floor and began to submit her to little indignities such as rumpling her hair, poking her mildly with their fingers. The girl made no effort to resist, and at one point actually smiled, the first time she had done so that evening. She sometimes told them to stop it, but feebly, with no conviction in her voice. They began to tell her she was 'easy', that she was a 'pushover', that anyone could do anything they liked with her.

I felt outraged at what was going on and would have left the room had not my obligation as a guest of the group made me remain silent. I fully believed in the girl's protestations that her father had changed, and felt that her expressed love and concern for him was more important than any other aspect of the case. What I did not know then was that in fact it was less than a month previously that her father had last had intercourse with her, that on very many occasions before he had made similar promises and always he had broken them, and that her mother had taken her usual way out of an appalling situation by retreating to hospital. But the group did know this and were determined to get the girl to admit the truth. They also wanted her to learn that she could stand on her own two feet, that she did not have to accept the indignities they were inflicting on her, nor did she have to accept them from anyone else.

The room was small and full of tobacco smoke, and I think we all had headaches. But the girl would not give in, nor would the group relent. Pat and her co-therapist watched carefully, but intervened no more. Soon after the beginning of the 'flooring' a large lad of sixteen or seventeen, who had at first taken up a dominant (and to me objectionable) position kneeling beside her and leaning masterfully over her chest, apparently became aware of the unsuitability of what he was doing and suddenly got up and moved down to her feet which he cradled tenderly in his hand. The other boy, an intelligent careful lad, sat behind her, gently but persistently rumpling her hair, which clearly irritated her considerably. None of the children lost their tempers, all were very careful of what they were doing. Eventually the girl admitted she did feel angry at her father, and later at her mother for opting out. I was unsure how truthful she was being, whether she wasn't saying this in order to be let up. She even managed to say she didn't really believe her father could change, but soon afterwards she took it back again, saying he could, too. It seemed to me that they were making her deny a hope we all have, that in the end everything will work out, that a hopeless situation will not after all turn out be hopeless. It finally ended when she agreed, genuinely I think, that she hadn't been truthful about the situation, and she was let up, promising, voluntarily, that she would come to the next group. Everyone then hugged her with real affection, and we all embraced each other for a while.

The method was similar but much gentler with the younger children, and with an adult group of victimized women more dignity was allowed the woman who had become the primary focus of that particular meeting. She was not 'floored', but instead had one of the therapists sitting on her lap, refusing to budge.

I discussed these meetings and my feelings about them afterwards both with Pat Wyka and with Anne Topper, who was responsible for cases being sent to the group through the department of social services. Wyka appreciated my objections, but said that with such a short time at her disposal there was no other way she could reach through to the victims, and that in many cases they would get no other treatment at all. Anne Topper shared my feelings but said that results had proved very encouraging, and that as the method apparently worked and where there was no alternative she would, for the time being at least, continue to use the victim service's facilities. In the event, adverse publicity about the confrontive methods used in the groups eventually caused them to be closed down. While it is clear that in the wrong hands such methods could be appallingly destructive, I can only restate that, although I disliked the method, the general atmosphere in the groups was loving and warm, and it obviously worked for many of the children.

Therapists to whom I explained the method, however, had doubts about its long-term value. The general feeling was that the victims should be allowed to love their father and their mother unconditionally if they wished to. Any 'buts' had to be discovered by themselves. The problem here, of course, is that too often the anger, the 'buts', are never discovered, and that a lifetime cloud hangs over the once-victim who receives no treatment.

Finally it will be useful to look briefly at another method, that is used at Christopher Street which has already been mentioned several times. This has produced impressive results, and since it is highly structured and the actual course is strictly limited in time its methods could be studied with advantage. Basically, once a client is ready (and this may not be immediately if they are very distressed) they enter a four-week cycle which consists of sessions lasting four hours, three times a week. These sessions include various lectures, social hours when the clients get to know each other, an opening 'orientation' night, times when the members explore their self-destructive behaviours, their shame and their sexuality. They also learn 'survival skills' and 'finding joy'. After this highly-structured month (which includes a lot of homework) there are weekly meetings of four hours each for half a year or more. Clients for whom the first structured month is insufficient may repeat the whole process.

The groups are prepared for any reaction. It is accepted that most members will have learned to suppress their emotions, so during certain periods clients are encouraged to shout, scream, weep, bash at pillows with tennis racquets and let go in a way they never have before. There is always at least one therapist present who guides the meetings or presents material or gives the lecture.

Some members find it very difficult to let go – usually either anger or crying can be achieved but rarely both, and the unblocking of emotions is an immense release for these women, who after their 'letting-down' are hugged and loved by their fellow-members. Finally, at the end of the course, they are encouraged to confront their families. Most women do this and find it, to their surprise, a good, positive experience.

The majority of the clients coming to Christopher Street, although this is now changing as the programme becomes better-known, were on drugs of one kind or another (including alcohol) and many were lesbians. Their needs were particularly strong because of the drug abuse, and many tried to kill themselves directly as well as indirectly. No statistics were available at the time of my visit to them, but it does seem that their structured approach used intensively over a short period has proved a very effective method.

As we have just seen, a lot of work is going on in the field of incest. Many methods of therapy are being explored, penal reforms are being looked at, ways to achieve collaboration between all the agencies concerned are slowly being forged. But there are many aspects we still know practically nothing about: very little work has been done on boy victims, for example, and few professionals seem to be aware even of the possibility of incestuous assaults on young males. It is as though it is bad enough when one victim is discovered – no one wants to consider that other children in the same family might also be suffering abuse, especially if they are male. Also we need to understand more clearly why it is that some victims are affected so badly, while others seem able to move on and make a satisfactory life for themselves. There has been some research on how victims are affected (running-away, promiscuity, marital problems, etc.) but more is needed on a larger scale to convince the doubters. We know so little about normal childhood sexuality that it is difficult to know exactly how incest differs from it without further research on both. Finkelhor (1980b) has worked out a whole list of risk factors concerning the sexual victimization of children, ranging from whole family characteristics (such as finance, state of marriage, family size, social isolation, etc.), father's characteristics (such as education, drink, general attitudes) and mother's (ditto), and suggests that one way to prevent sexual abuse would be to find potential victims before they are victimized. He considers this would be less difficult than trying to track down possible offenders prior to their offence.

However I cannot see such widespread screening taking place in present circumstances, and I am not sure (bearing in mind the long list of personal details that would have to be recorded by some official agency for every single family before such a selection could be arrived at) that I would approve of state intervention on such a scale. However it would certainly be very useful if the various symptoms often associated with incest, which have been elaborated elsewhere, were borne in mind by all people working with children and young adults, so that whenever they arise incest can be seriously considered as a possibility, especially if more than one symptom is presented.

We want to know more about the offenders, what to do with them, how they can best be treated, and how the family can be treated. We need to learn how to judge effectively the chances of any particular family being successfully reunited. Even the most basic figure of all, the incidence of incest, is still an unknown and will remain so at least until the public and professionals have accepted the subject as readily as they now accept child abuse. It is not only the victim as a child about whom we should be concerned. That child victim will grow up. At the very least, as an adult she or he is likely to have difficulties with sexual relationships, both outside and inside marriage. More importantly, victims often marry someone in whom they recognize similar problems, and we know that in a number of cases male victims will themselves victimize their own children, and the female victims as mothers may – consciously or unconsciously – allow their own children to be victimized. In more seriously disturbed families the whole family may be sexually involved with each other, overtly or covertly as the case may be.

The first stage to be reached is for there to be universal recognition that incest occurs in every class, among every race, and that it is comparatively common. It causes a great deal of misery. But the hopeful side is that in most cases where proper treatment is given to the entire family, including the offender, therapists consider the prognosis to be excellent. There is no excuse for not taking every action we can to make the best possible treatment available to all of whose who need it, thus ensuring that old-fashioned punitive attitudes no longer keep child sexual abuse hidden from public gaze. It is the children, and their children, we are punishing when we refuse to look at reality. It is more wholesome to open up and clean out a dank cellar than to seal it up and let its contents rot.

Appendix

The El Paso County Department of Social Services, Colorado Springs, USA has combined with the various law enforcement agencies to produce an 'Incest Diversion Program'. This allows the non-violent, first offender the opportunity of avoiding a prison sentence providing he is willing to follow and complete the course of treatment prescribed for him. The document setting out this programme is included here in full so that it can be studied by other police and social service departments. The advantages and disadvantages of the programme are discussed in Chapter 8, pp. 172–6.

Incest diversion exclusions

A Persons excluded from consideration by District Attorney's Office:

1 Persons charged with Sexual Assault crimes on victims not related to the suspect by blood, marriage or on victims with whom the suspect has resided for 12 months or less.

2 Persons who use physical violence, overt threats or intimidation which imply or state threats of bodily harm to the victim during or subsequent to the Sexual Assault crime.

3 Persons who have been previously convicted of any Sexual Assault crime, or who are currently charged with any Sexual Assault crime or who have been granted Deferred Sentencing or Deferred Prosecution on any Sexual Assault crime.

4 Persons who have committed Sexual Assault crimes over an extended period of time on multiple victims who the suspect is related by blood, marriage or adoption or multiple victims with whom the suspect has resided for more than 12 months, or a combination of such victims.

5 Persons previously accepted into and/or discharged from the Incest Diversion Program.

B Persons excluded from consideration by the Department of Social Services:

1 Persons who do not desire to participate in the Incest Diversion Program.

2 Persons who are insane as defined in 16–8–101 C.R.S., 1973, as amended or who are certifiable under 27–10–105 or 27–10–106 C.R.S., 1973 as amended.

Incest diversion program

The District Attorney's Office and the El Paso County Department of Social Services have developed and started an adult diversion program for the supervision and treatment of incest offenders.

Background
Incestuous activity is not only a criminal offense, but more specifically a symptom of serious family problems. It causes fear and humiliation for the victims. It creates secrecy and shame in the family. A child has fear and guilt that "telling" may cause a parent to go to prison. A wife fears exposure will destroy a marriage and leave her family without support. These factors strongly hinder discovery and correction of the problem.

And, if the criminal conduct is prosecuted through the judicial system, those same emotional responses are devastating to a child who must testify in court to incestuous acts with a parent.

For these reasons, the Incest Diversion Program was created.

Purpose
The Incest Diversion Program offers the non-violent, first offender an opportunity to be diverted from the judicial process if he is willing to undergo treatment of his problems and to follow through on the programs set up by professional counselors. If admitted into the program, an individual must adhere to the treatment and family counseling programs planned for them for up to two years. Failure to complete the program or dismissal for failure to cooperate can lead to the filing of criminal charges by the District Attorney. If the program is successfully completed, no criminal charges will be filed. All proceedings will be handled in a confidential manner.

Knowledge of the existence of this program will overcome the reluctance to report incestuous activity and treatment can help to rebuild a healthy family unit.

Eligibility
The Incest Diversion Program was established to provide a non-judicial alternative to non-violent incest offenders with a recent history of incestuous conduct. Individuals who use threats of violence against victims or who have a long-standing history of incestuous conduct will be handled through the criminal justice system. Only individuals who are willing to acknowledge their problems and voluntarily submit to the program will be accepted.

This program was modelled after the District Attorney's Juvenile Diversion Program with input from members of the following groups:

1 District Attorney's Office
2 Department of Social Services
3 Colorado Springs Police Department
4 El Paso County Sheriff's Department
5 Public Defender's Office
6 Children's Legal Advocate

Reporting
Incest is a form of child abuse which must be reported and which is subject to criminal penalty for failure to report.

Report incest/child abuse to the following agencies:

Department of Social Services   471–5951 (office hours)
     or 475–9593 (after hours)
Victim Services   471–6616 (office hours)
     or 471–6611 (after hours)
Any law enforcement agency   911   (24 hours)

Adult diversion agreement

Name .... DOB ....

Address .... Phone ....

Employment .... Address ....

SSN or Military ID (no.) ....

I, ... have been advised of my right to speedy prosecution and to have a speedy trial and I hereby waive those rights for a period of two months until the date of .... for consideration by the Adult Diversion Program. Upon acceptance into the program I will give an unconditional waiver of those rights.

I, ... admit responsibility for the situation which brought this matter before the Adult Diversion Program, and I understand that such admission will not be used against me in any criminal prosecution, including impeachment but this will not extend to any new offenses admitted to.

I, ... agree to give a release to the Adult Diversion Program for medical or psycho social information from any physicians and counselors whose services are secured as a requirement of this program.

I, ... agree to participate in any counseling or therapy that is recommended as a requirement of my Adult Diversion Program or any counseling or therapy approved by the Adult Diversion Program and I agree to pay any costs incurred by these requirements.

I, ... understand that if I fail to co-operate or comply with any requirements or conditions placed upon me by the Adult Diversion Program that I may be removed from the Program and criminal prosecution may be instituted against me.

I, ... understand that in any pro-ceeding to remove me from the Adult Diversion Program, I will be informed of the recommendation for removal from the Program. I will be notified of the date on which the Child Protection Team will review the recommendation and I may be present to hear the reasons for removal from the Program and I may respond to the Child Protection Team on those reasons.

I, ... understand that the duration of this Agreement is to be no more than 24 months and that upon successful completion of the Program, that the District Attorney agrees not to prosecute me upon the incident which brought me into the Adult Diversion Program.

I, ... understand that the date of the signature of the District Attorney's Office will be the effective date of my acceptance into the Program.

I, ... understand that I will inform the Adult Diversion Program of any change in address or employment.

I, ... have read this Agreement and understand the statements and requirements it contains and agree to abide by those statements and requirements.

....
Date   Dept. of Social Services

....
Date   Participant

....
Date   Deputy District Attorney

Bibliography

Abel, G., Becker, J., Murphy, W. D. and Flanagan, B. (1979), paper presented at 11th Banff International Conference on Behaviour Modification, 21 March.

Abel, G., Becker, J. and Skinner, L., (1980), 'Aggressive behaviour and sex', *Psychiatric Clinics of North America*, vol. 3, no. 1, April.

Adams, M. and Neel, J. (1967), 'Children of incest', *Pediatrics*, vol. 40, no. 1, July.

American Humane Association (1972), National Symposium on Child Abuse, American Humane Association, Children's Division, Denver.

Anderson, D. (1979), 'Touching: When is it caring and nurturing or when is it exploitative and damaging?' in *Children and Neglect: International Congress Proceedings*, A. W. Franklin (ed.), Oxford, Pergamon Press.

Beezley Mrażek, P. (1980), 'Sexual abuse of children', *Journal of Child Psychiatry*, vol. 21, pp. 91–5.

Beezley Mrazek, P., Lynch, M. and Bentovim, A. (1981), 'Recognition of Child Sexual Abuse in the United Kingdom', in *Sexually Abused Children and their Families*, Oxford, Pergamon Press.

Berliner, L. and Stevens, D. (1979), 'Special technique for child witnesses', in Leroy G. Schultz, (ed.) *The Sexual Victimology of Youth*, Springfield, Illinois, Charles C. Thomas.

Bonaparte, M., Freud, A. and Kris, E. (eds) (1954), *The Origins of Psycho-analysis, Letters to Wilhelm Fliess, Drafts and Notes: 1887–1902* New York, Basic Books.

British Medical Journal (1981), Leading article, vol. 282, 24 January, p. 250.

Browning, D. and Boatman, B. (1977), 'Incest: children at risk', *American Journal of Psychiatry*, vol. 134, pp. 69–72.

Carter, C. (1967), 'Risk to offspring of incest', The *Lancet*, vol. 1, p. 436.

Cavallin, H. (1965), 'Incestuous fathers: A clinical report', paper read at the 121st annual meeting of the American Psychiatric Association, New York, 3–7 May.

De Francis, V. (1969), 'Protecting the child victim of sex crimes committed by adults', American Humane Association, Denver, Colorado.

Enablers, Inc. (1978), *The Link*, 1–9 August.

Finkelhor, D. (1978a), 'Psychological, cultural and structural factors in incest and family sexual abuse', *Journal of Marriage and Family Counseling*, vol. 4, pp. 45–50.

Finkelhor, D. (1978b), 'Sexual victimization of children in a normal population', paper presented to the 2nd International Congress on Child Abuse and Neglect, September, London.

Finkelhor, D. (1979a), 'What's wrong with sex between adults and children – ethics and the problems of sexual abuse', *American Journal of Orthopsychiatry*, vol. 49, no. 4, pp. 692–7.

Finkelhor, D. (1979b), 'Social forces in the formulation of the problem of sexual abuse', early version of Ch. 1 in *Sexually Victimized Children*, New York Free Press.

Finkelhor, D. (1980a), 'Sex among siblings: A survey report on its prevalence, variety and effects', *Archives of Sexual Behaviour*, vol. 9, pp. 171–94.

Finkelhor, D. (1980b), 'Risk factors in the sexual victimization of children', *International Journal of Child Abuse and Neglect*, vol. 4, no. 4, pp. 265–73.

Fox, J. R. (1962), 'Sibling incest', *British Journal of Sociology*, vol. 13, pp. 128–50.

Freud, S., (1953), 'The aetiology of hysteria', *Collected Papers*, vol. 1, London, Hogarth Press.

Freud, S. (1966), *The Complete Introductory Lectures of Psycho-Analysis*, New York, W. W. Norton.

Gagnon, J. (1965), 'Female child victims of sex offences', *Social Problems*, vol. 13, pp. 176–92.

Giarretto H. (1976), 'The treatment of father-daughter incest: A psycho-social approach', *Children Today*, vol. 5, no. 4, July/August.

Giarretto, H. (1977), 'Treating sexual abuse – working together', from the Proceedings of Missouri Statewide Conference on Child Abuse and Neglect, 30 March.

Giarretto, H. (1978), 'Humanistic treatment of father-daughter incest', *Journal of Humanistic Psychology*, vol. 18, no. 4, Fall.

Gottlieb, B. (1980), 'Incest: Therapeutic intervention in a unique form of sexual abuse', *Rape and Sexual Assault, Management and Intervention*, Ch. 9, London, Aspen Publications.

Gottlieb, B. and Dean, J. (1981), 'The co-therapy relationship in group treatment of sexually abused adolescent girls', *Sexually Abused Children and their Families*, Oxford, Pergamon Press.

Harborview Medical Center (no date), 'Child sexual assault – Sexual Assault Center', Harborview Medical Center, Seattle, Washington.

Henderson, D. (1972), 'Incest: A synthesis of data', *Canadian Psychiatric Association Journal*, vol. 17, pp. 299–313.

Johnston, M. Krentz (1979), 'The sexually mistreated child: diagnostic evaluation', *Child Abuse and Neglect*, vol 3., pp. 943–51.

Julian, V. and Mohr, C. (1979), 'Father daughter incest: profile of the offender', *Victimology: An International Journal* vol. 4. no. 4.

Justice, B. and R. (1979), *The Broken Taboo: Sex in the Family*, New York, Human Science Press.

Kempe, H. (1978), 'Sexual abuse, another hidden pediatric problem: the 1977 C. Anderson Aldrich lecture', *Pediatrics*, vol. 62, no. 3, pp. 382–9.

Kent, C. '1979), *Child Sexual Abuse Prevention Project – an educational program for children*, Hennepin County Sexual Assault Services, Minnesota.

Lukianowicz, N. (1972), 'Incest', *British Journal of Psychiatry*, vol. 120, pp. 301–13.

Maisch, H. (1973), *Incest*, London, André Deutsch.

Mead, M. (1950), *Sex and Temperament in Three Primitive Societies*, New York, Mentor Books.

Meiselman, K. C. (1979), *Incest: A Psychological Study of Causes and Effects*, San Francisco, Jossey-Bass.

Muldoon, L. (ed) (1979), *Incest – Confronting the silent crime*, the Minnesota Program for Victims of Sexual Assault, Minnesota.

Myers, B. (1979), *Incest*, Christopher Street Inc., 2344 Nicollet Avenue South, Minneapolis, Minnesota.

Potter, A. and Mohr, C. (1977), 'A factor analysis of reporting categories used by the national study of child neglect and abuse reporting', paper presented at 8th National Symposium on Protecting the Abused, Neglected and Sexually Exploited Child, Honolulu, 22, October.

Rosenfeld, A., (1979a), 'Incidence of a history of incest among eighteen female psychiatric patients', *American Journal of Psychiatry*, vol. 136, no. 6, pp. 791–5.

Rosenfeld, A. (1979b), 'Endogamic incest and the victim-perpetrator model', *American Journal of Diseases of Children*, April, vol. 133, pp. 406–10.

Rosenfeld, A. (1979c), 'The clinical management of incest and sexual abuse of children', *Journal of the American Medical Association*, 19 October, vol. 242, pp. 1761–4.

Rosenfeld, A., and Newberger, E. (1977), 'Compassion vs control, conceptual and practical pitfalls in the broadened definition of child abuse', *Journal of the American Medical Association*, 9 May, vol. 237, pp. 2086–8.

Rosenfeld, A., Nadelson, C. and Krieger, M. (1979), 'Fantasy and reality in patients reports of incest', *Journal of Clinical Psychiatry*, vol. 40, no. 4, April.

Rush, F. (1977), 'The Freudian cover-up', *Chrysallis*, no. 1, pp. 31–45.

Sgroi, S. (1975), 'Sexual molestation of children: the last frontier of child abuse', *Children Today*, May-June, vol. 44, pp. 18–21.

Shengold, L. (1963), 'The parent as sphinx', *Journal of American Psychoanalyst Association*, vol. 11, pp. 725–51.

Summit, R. and Kryso, J. (1978), 'Sexual abuse of children: A clinical spectrum', *American Journal of Orthopsychiatry*, vol. 48, no. 2, pp. 237–251.

Tsai, M. and Wagner, N. (1978), 'Therapy groups for women sexually molested as children', *Archives of Sexual Behaviour*, vol. 7, no. 5, pp. 417–27.

Tsai, M. and Wagner, N. (1979), 'Incest and molestation: problems of childhood sexuality', *Resident and Staff Physician*, March, pp. 129–36.

Tsai, M., Feldman-Summers, S. and Edgar, M. (1979), 'Childhood molestation: variables related to differential impacts on psychosexual functioning in adult women', *Journal of Abnormal Psychology*, August, pp. 407–17.

Weber, E. (1977), 'Sexual incest at home', *Ms Magazine*, April.

Weinberg, S. K. (1955), *Incest Behaviour*, New York, Citadel.

Wells, N. (1958), 'Sexual offences as seen by a woman police surgeon', *British Medical Journal*, vol. ii, pp. 1404–8.

Index